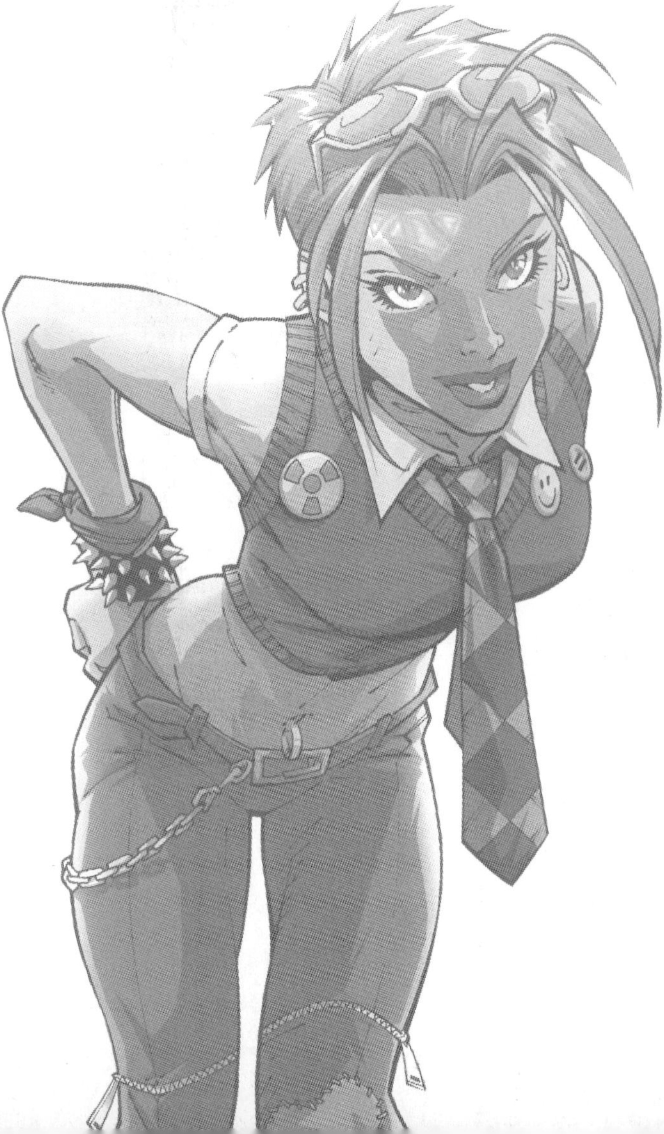

misplaced

Creator/Writer/Artist
JOSH BLAYLOCK

Inkers
CLAYTON BROWN
JOSH BLAYLOCK
PAT BROWER

Grey Tones
ANGELO TSANG
ZID
BEN HUNZEKER

Background Artist
CLINT HILINSKI

Letterer
DREAMER DESIGN
MARSHALL DILLON with **SEAN DOVE**

Cover Illustration by Randy Green
Original Series Covers by Mark Brooks,
Chynna Clugston-Major, Michael Avon Oeming, & Zid

Book Design by Mike Norton

SOMWHERE UNDER THE RAINBOW

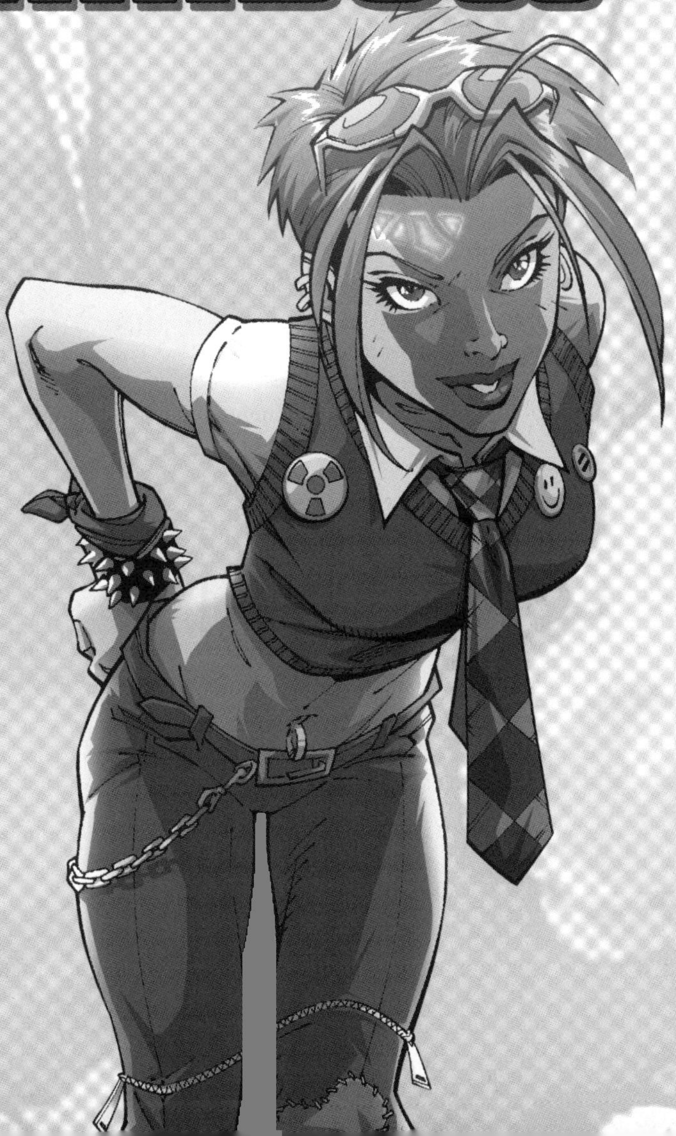

Published By

DIGEST

Josh Blaylock:
President

Mark Powers: Senior
Editor

Mike Norton: Art
Director

Chris Crank: Web
Developer

Tim Seeley: Staff
Illustrator

Sean Dove: Graphic
Designer

Marshall Dillon:
Project Manager

Susan Bishop: Office
Manager

Sam Wells: Office
Assistance

A division of
DEVIL'S DUE PUBLISHING, Inc.

4619 N. Ravenswood Ave. #204
Chicago, IL 60640

www.devilsdue.net

First Edition: December 2004
ISBN 1-932796-04-5
PRINTED IN CANADA

This book is dedicated for once,
not to those who told me it COULD be done,
but those who told me it COULDN'T.

-Josh

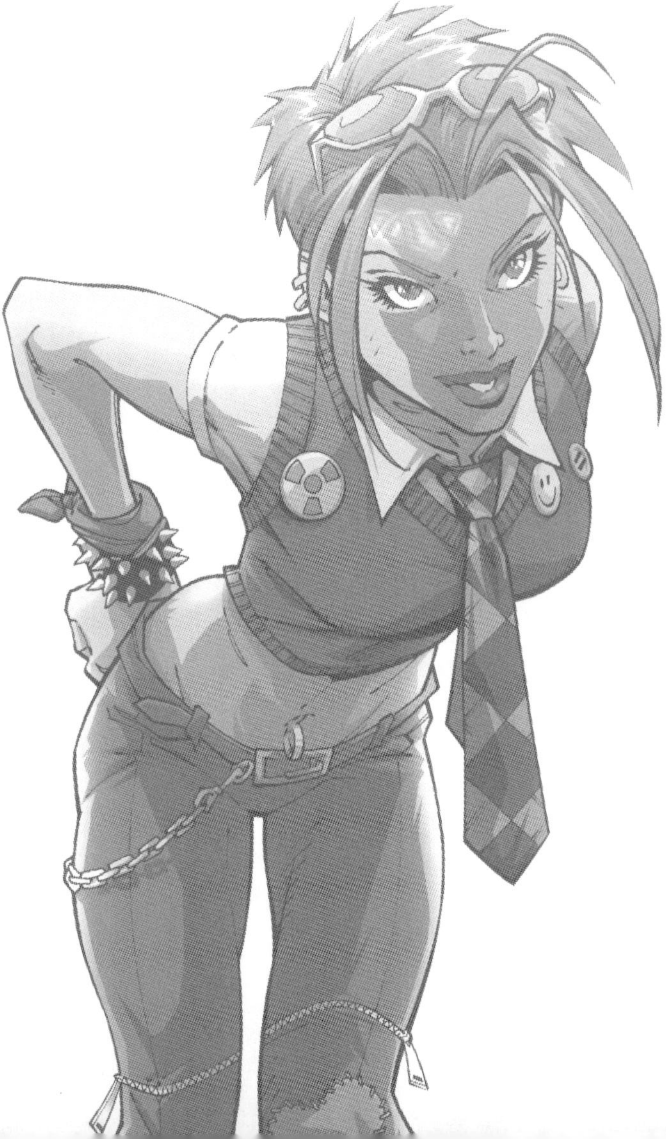

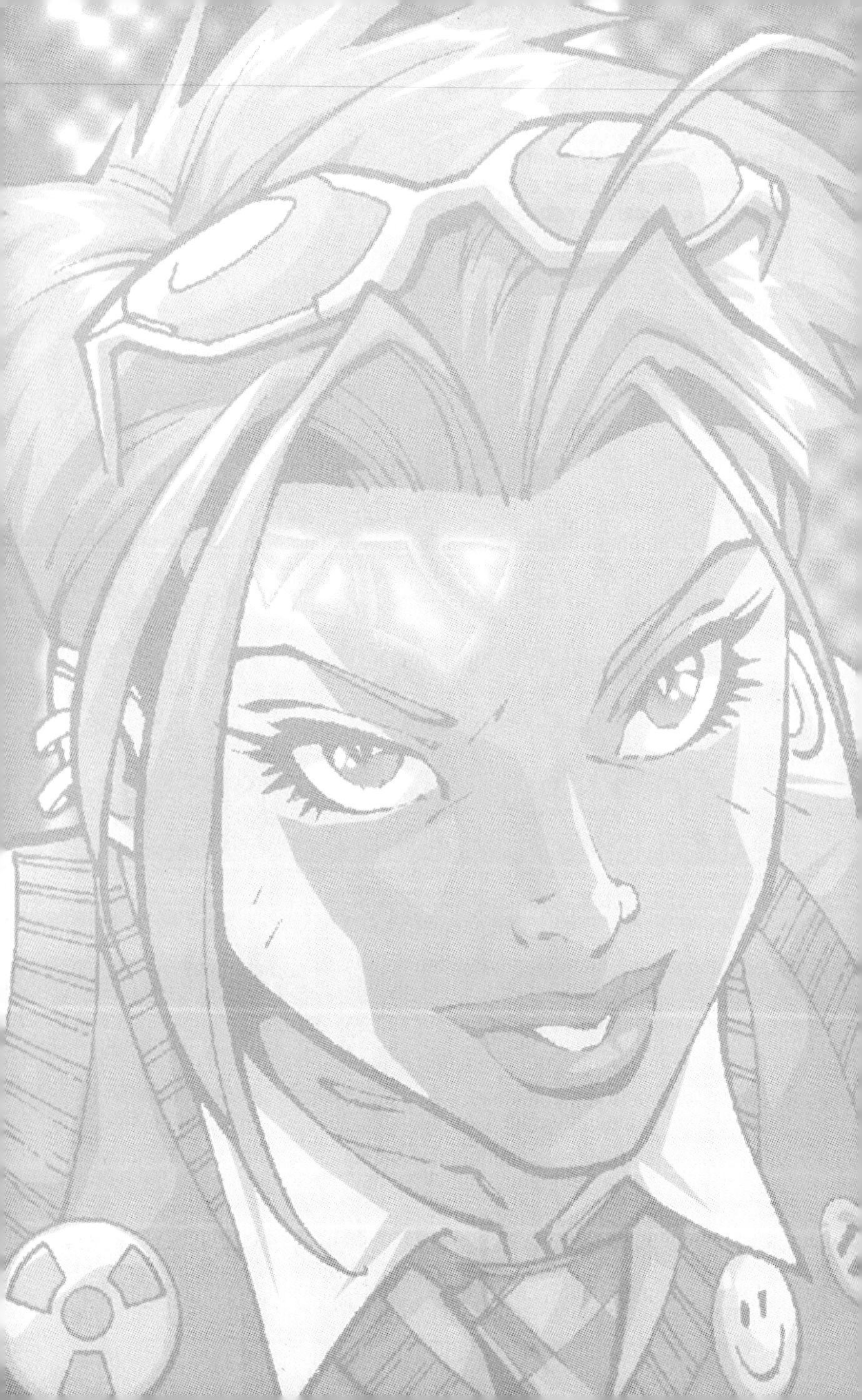

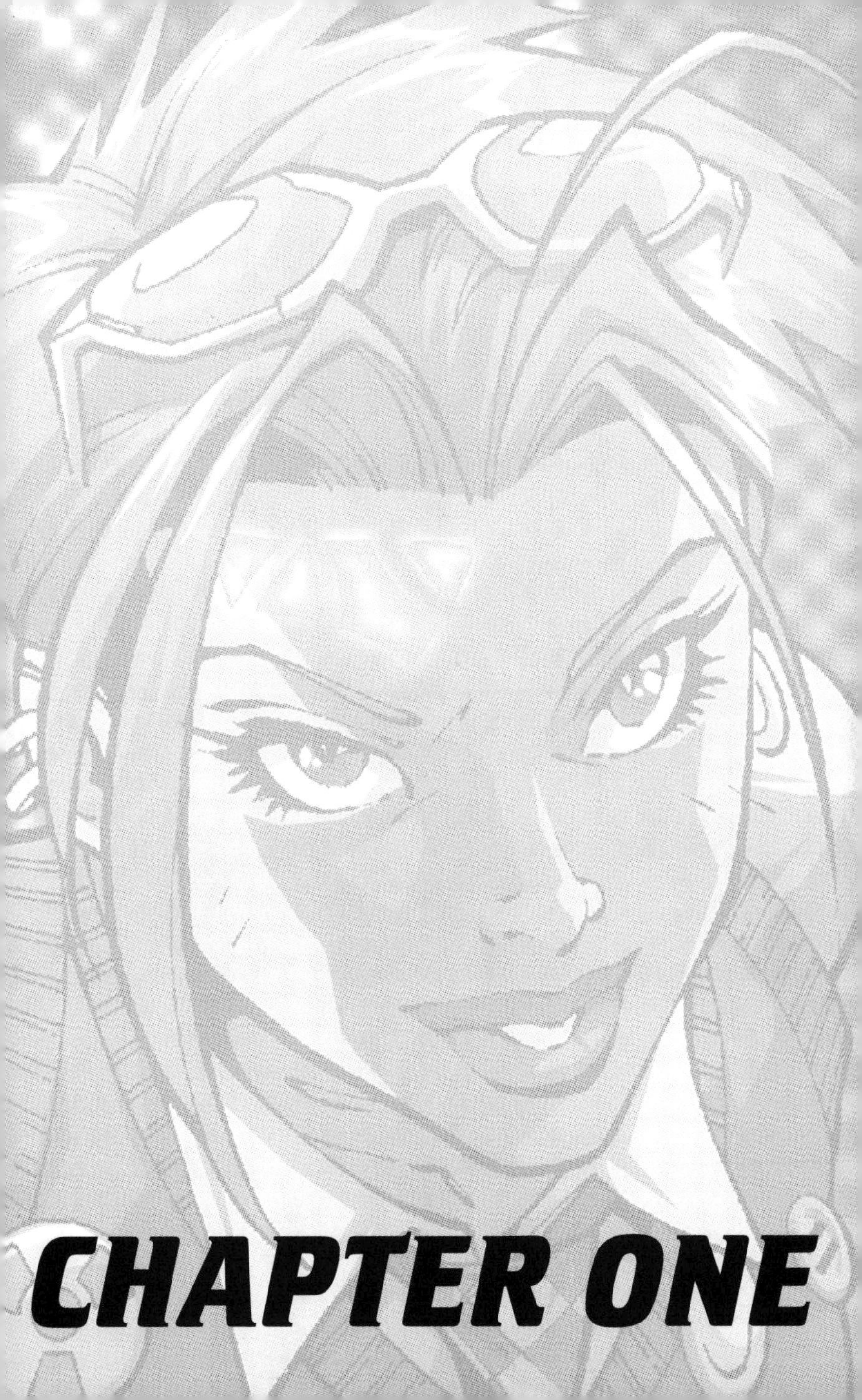

CHAPTER ONE

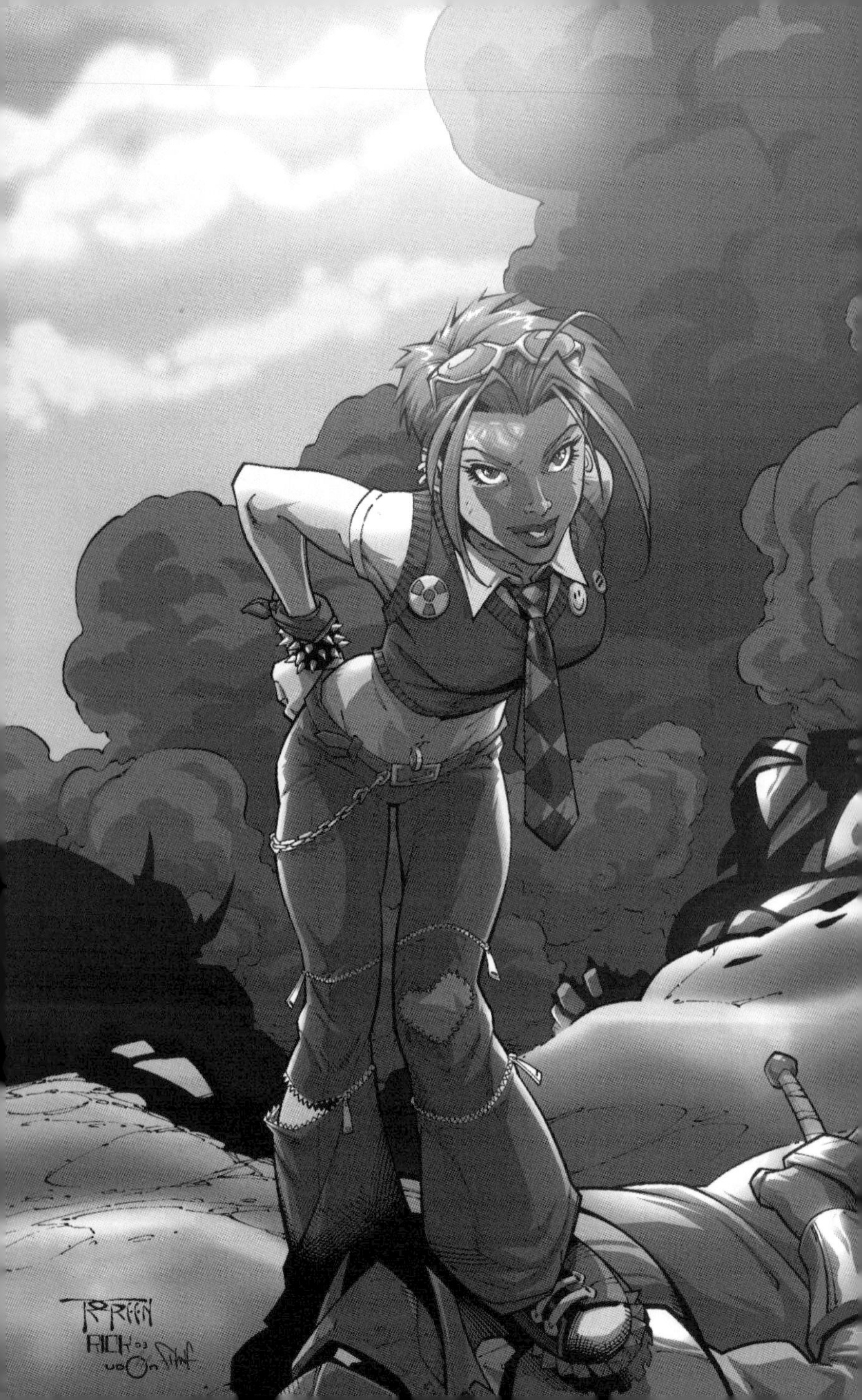

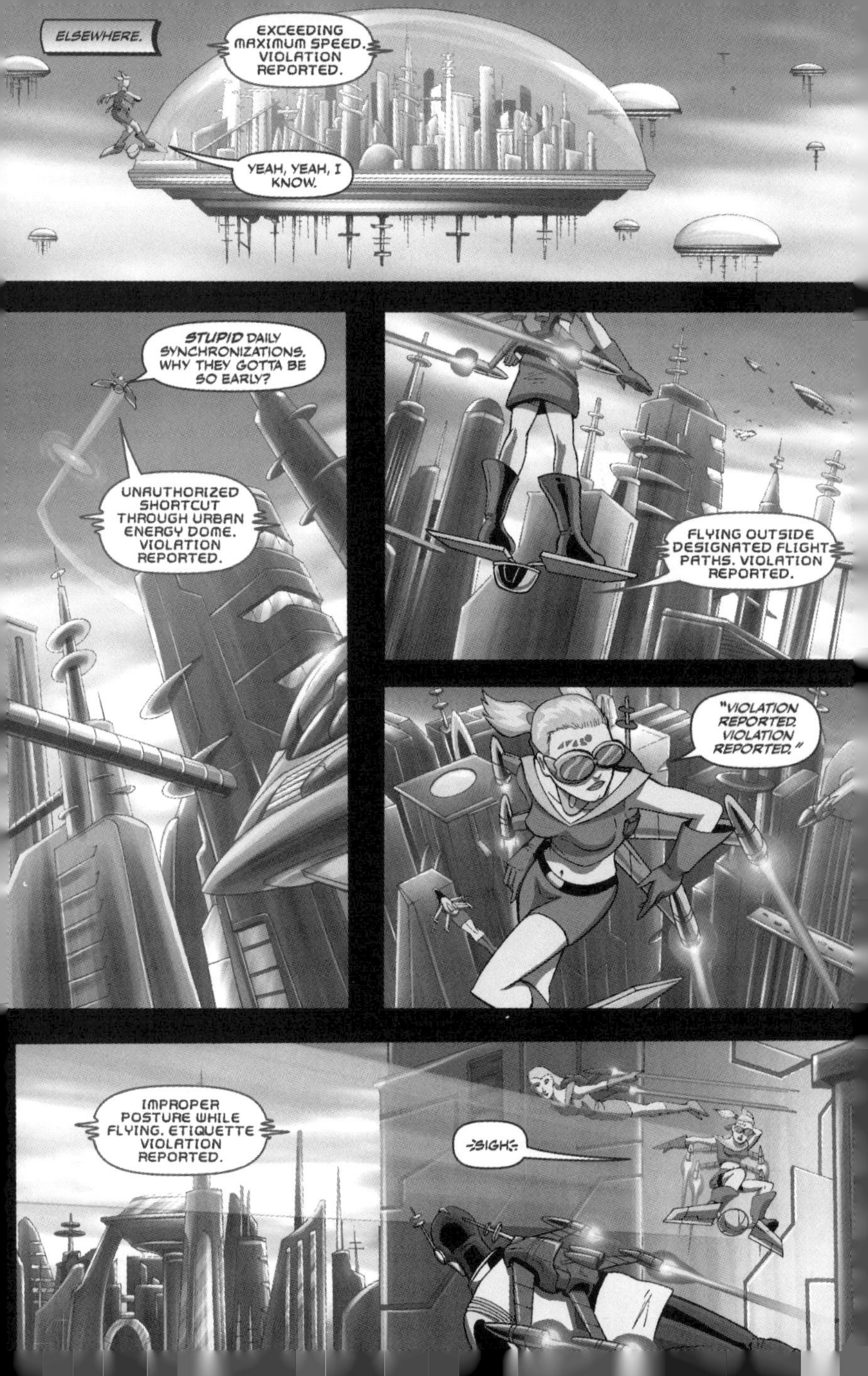
ELSEWHERE.
EXCEEDING MAXIMUM SPEED. VIOLATION REPORTED.
YEAH, YEAH, I KNOW.
STUPID DAILY SYNCHRONIZATIONS. WHY THEY GOTTA BE SO EARLY?
UNAUTHORIZED SHORTCUT THROUGH URBAN ENERGY DOME. VIOLATION REPORTED.
FLYING OUTSIDE DESIGNATED FLIGHT PATHS. VIOLATION REPORTED.
"VIOLATION REPORTED. VIOLATION REPORTED."
IMPROPER POSTURE WHILE FLYING. ETIQUETTE VIOLATION REPORTED.
SIGH

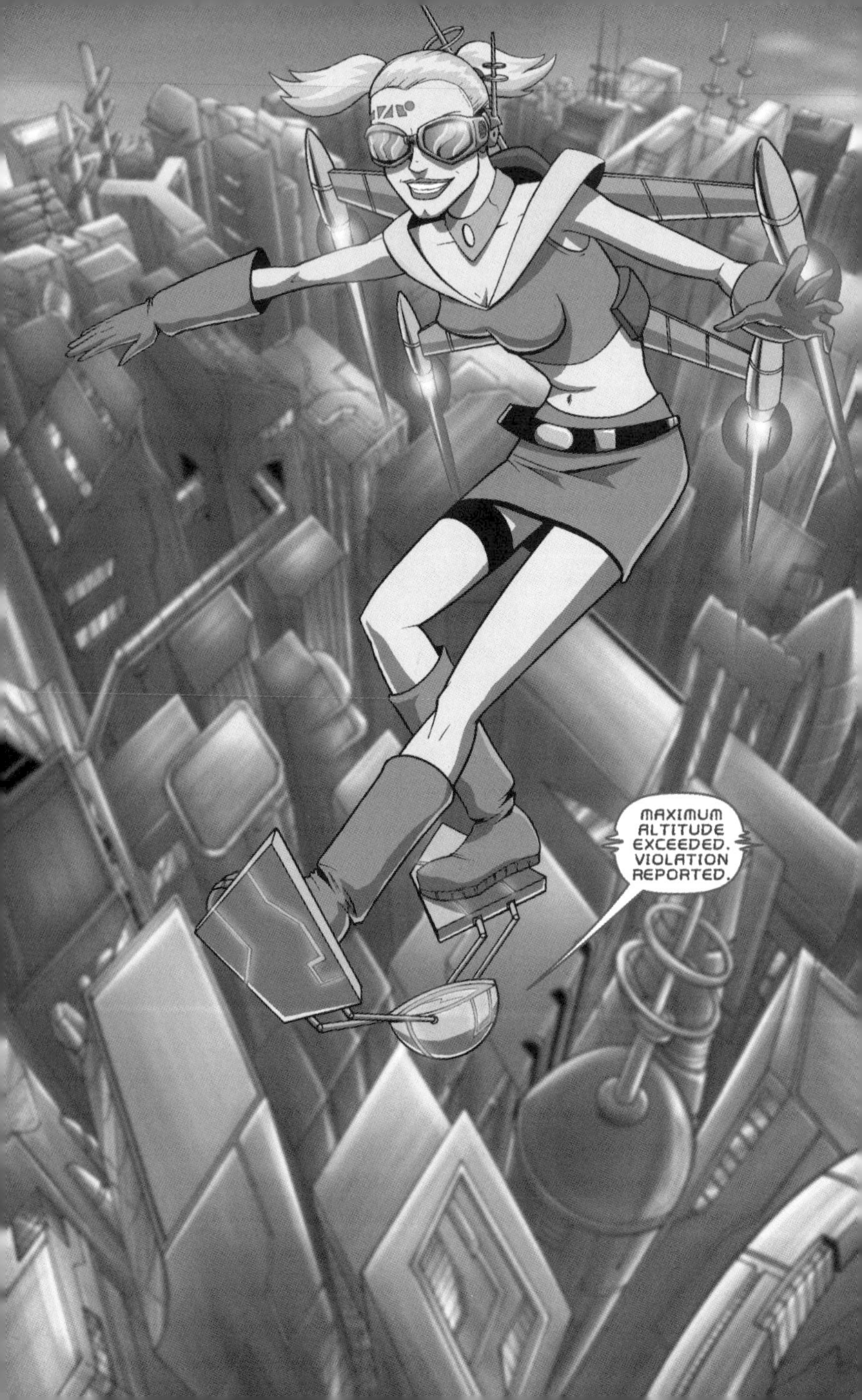
MAXIMUM ALTITUDE EXCEEDED. VIOLATION REPORTED.

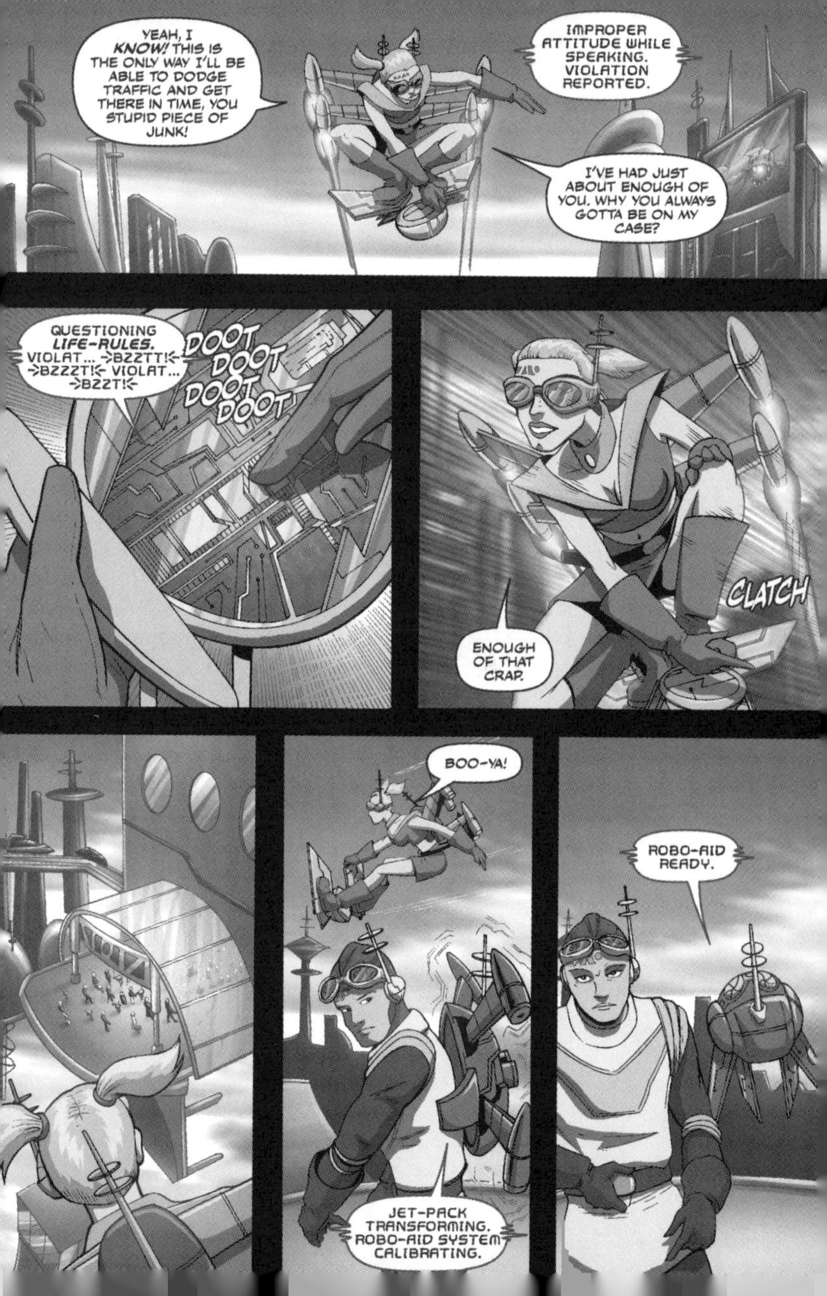
YEAH, I *KNOW!* THIS IS THE ONLY WAY I'LL BE ABLE TO DODGE TRAFFIC AND GET THERE IN TIME, YOU STUPID PIECE OF JUNK!
IMPROPER ATTITUDE WHILE SPEAKING. VIOLATION REPORTED.
I'VE HAD JUST ABOUT ENOUGH OF YOU. WHY YOU ALWAYS GOTTA BE ON MY CASE?
QUESTIONING *LIFE-RULES.* VIOLAT... >BZZTT!< >BZZZT!< VIOLAT... >BZZT!<
DOOT DOOT DOOT DOOT
ENOUGH OF THAT CRAP.
CLATCH
BOO-YA!
JET-PACK TRANSFORMING. ROBO-AID SYSTEM CALIBRATING.
ROBO-AID READY.

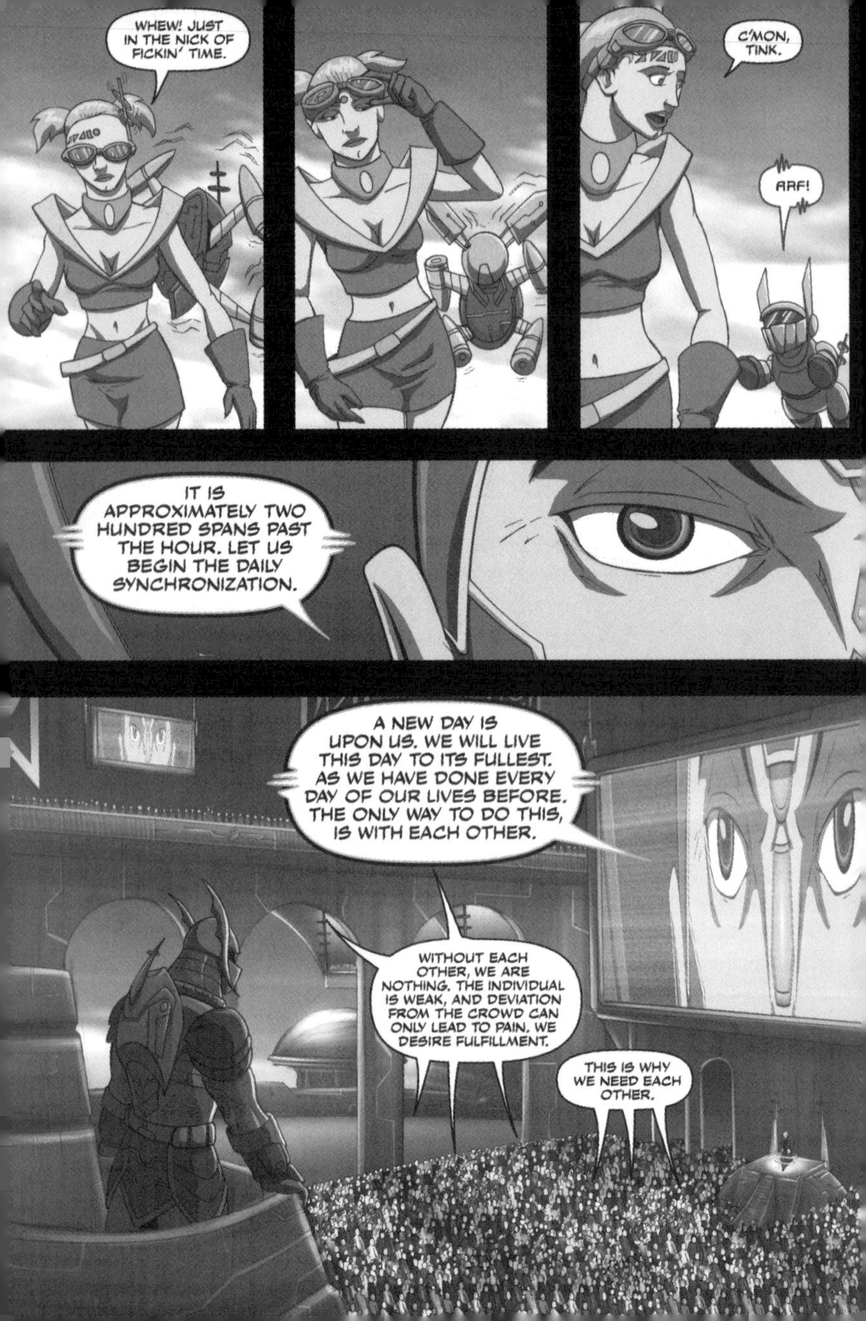
WHEW! JUST IN THE NICK OF FICKIN' TIME.
C'MON, TINK.
ARF!
IT IS APPROXIMATELY TWO HUNDRED SPANS PAST THE HOUR. LET US BEGIN THE DAILY SYNCHRONIZATION.
A NEW DAY IS UPON US. WE WILL LIVE THIS DAY TO ITS FULLEST. AS WE HAVE DONE EVERY DAY OF OUR LIVES BEFORE. THE ONLY WAY TO DO THIS, IS WITH EACH OTHER.
WITHOUT EACH OTHER, WE ARE NOTHING. THE INDIVIDUAL IS WEAK, AND DEVIATION FROM THE CROWD CAN ONLY LEAD TO PAIN. WE DESIRE FULFILLMENT.
THIS IS WHY WE NEED EACH OTHER.

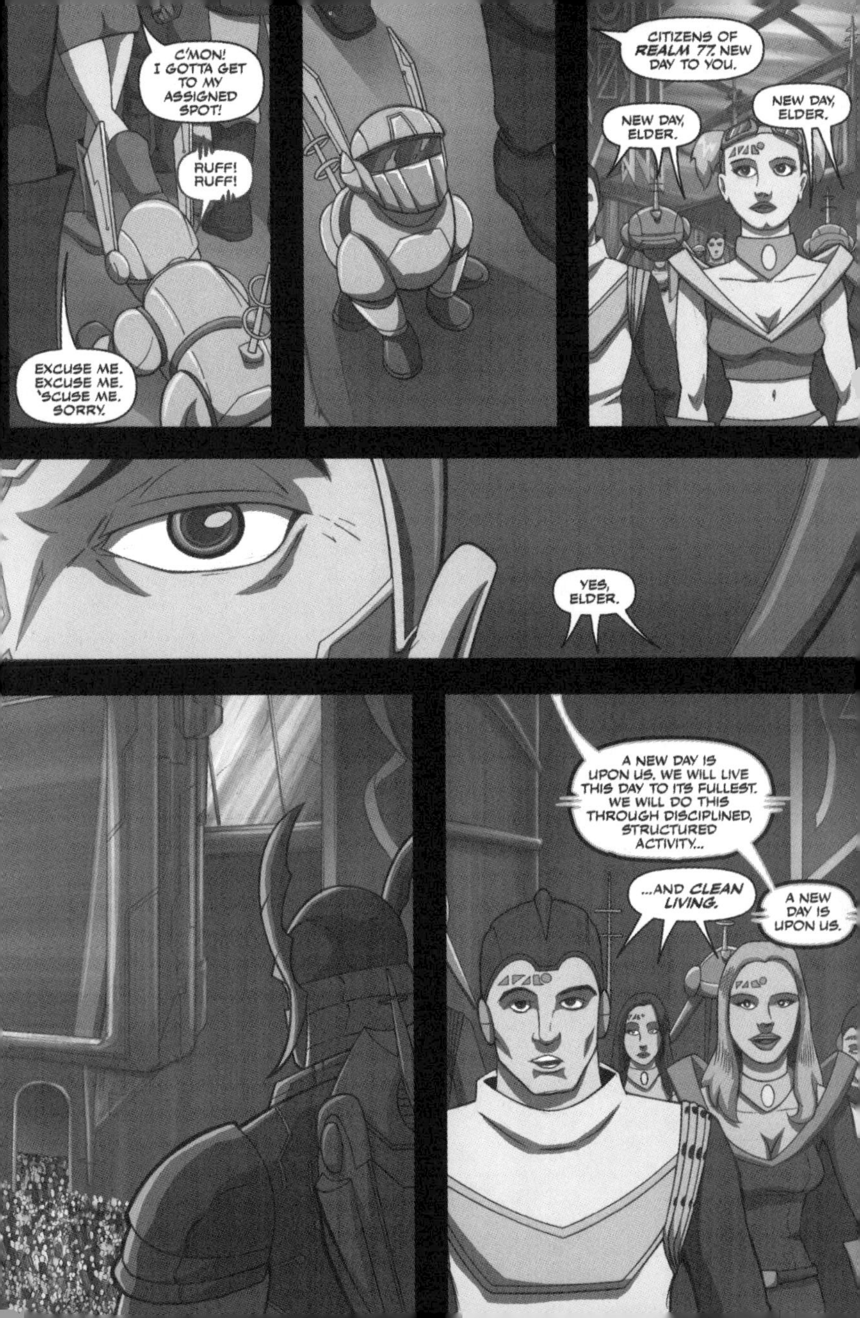
C'MON! I GOTTA GET TO MY ASSIGNED SPOT!
RUFF! RUFF!
EXCUSE ME. EXCUSE ME. 'SCUSE ME. SORRY.
CITIZENS OF *REALM 77*. NEW DAY TO YOU.
NEW DAY, ELDER.
NEW DAY, ELDER.
YES, ELDER.
A NEW DAY IS UPON US. WE WILL LIVE THIS DAY TO ITS FULLEST. WE WILL DO THIS THROUGH DISCIPLINED, STRUCTURED ACTIVITY...
...AND *CLEAN LIVING.*
A NEW DAY IS UPON US.

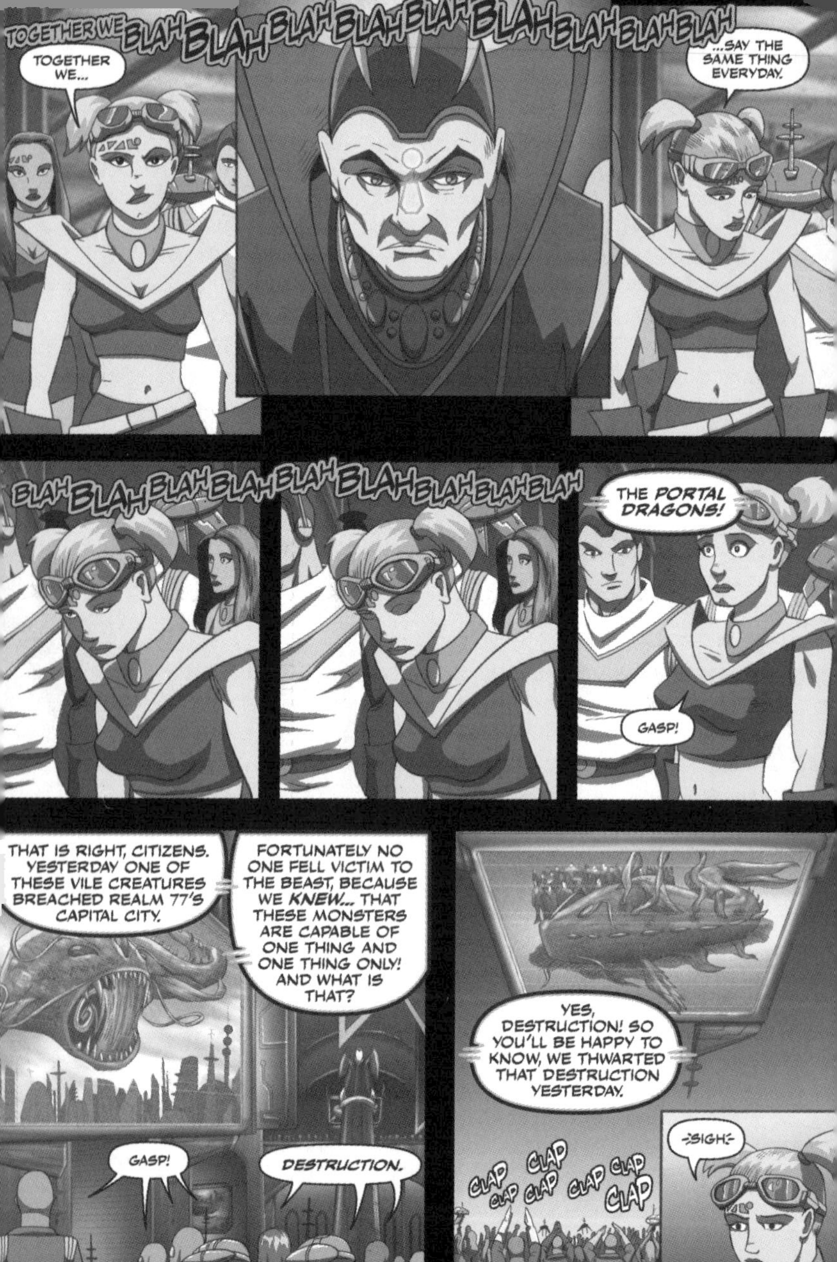
TOGETHER WE BLAH BLAH BLAH BLAH BLAH BLAH BLAH BLAH BLAH
TOGETHER WE...
...SAY THE SAME THING EVERYDAY.
BLAH BLAH BLAH BLAH BLAH BLAH BLAH BLAH BLAH
THE PORTAL DRAGONS!
GASP!
THAT IS RIGHT, CITIZENS. YESTERDAY ONE OF THESE VILE CREATURES BREACHED REALM 77'S CAPITAL CITY.
FORTUNATELY NO ONE FELL VICTIM TO THE BEAST, BECAUSE WE KNEW... THAT THESE MONSTERS ARE CAPABLE OF ONE THING AND ONE THING ONLY! AND WHAT IS THAT?
GASP!
DESTRUCTION.
YES, DESTRUCTION! SO YOU'LL BE HAPPY TO KNOW, WE THWARTED THAT DESTRUCTION YESTERDAY.
CLAP CLAP CLAP CLAP CLAP CLAP CLAP
-SIGH-

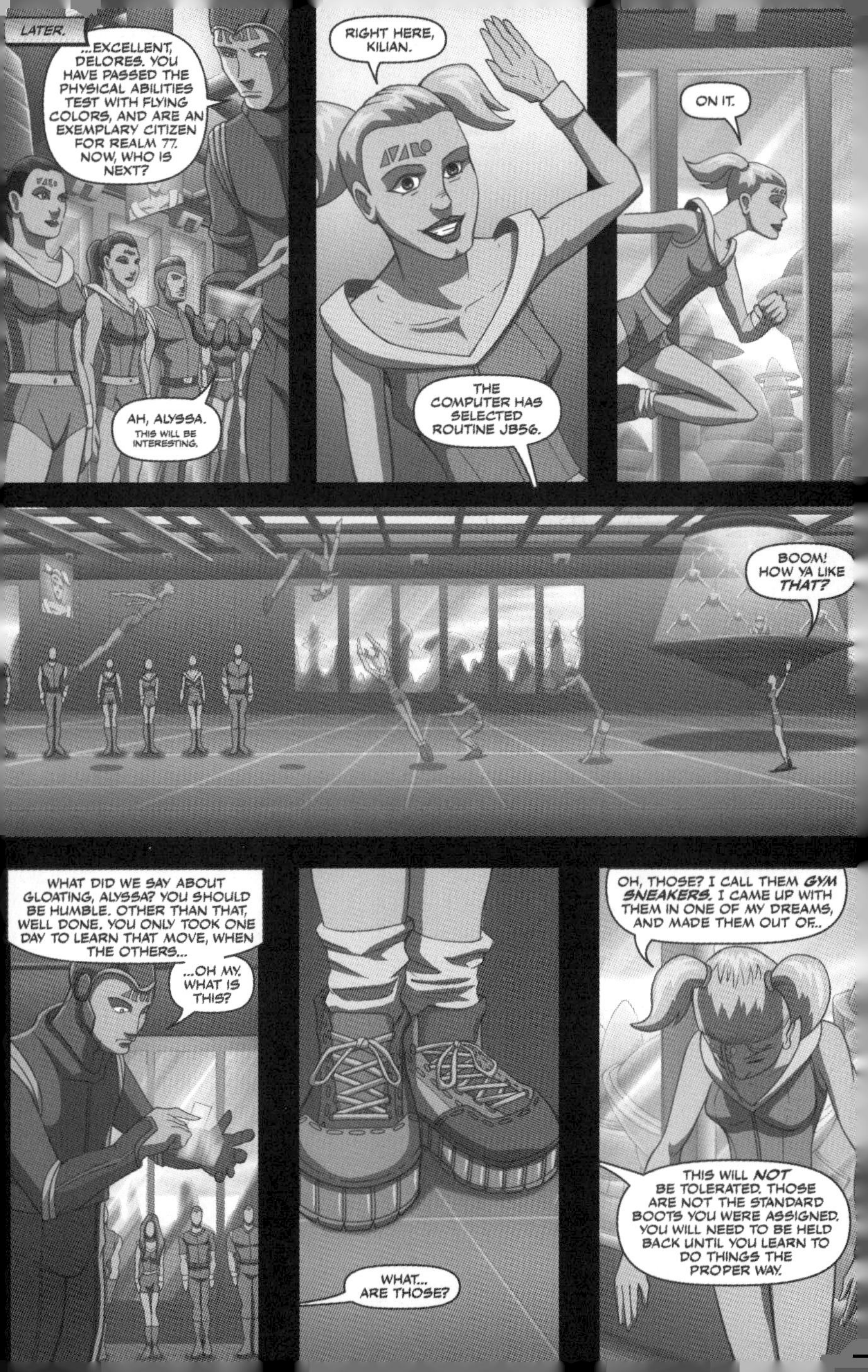
LATER.
...EXCELLENT, DELORES. YOU HAVE PASSED THE PHYSICAL ABILITIES TEST WITH FLYING COLORS, AND ARE AN EXEMPLARY CITIZEN FOR REALM 77. NOW, WHO IS NEXT?
AH, ALYSSA. THIS WILL BE INTERESTING.
RIGHT HERE, KILIAN.
THE COMPUTER HAS SELECTED ROUTINE JB56.
ON IT.
BOOM! HOW YA LIKE *THAT?*
WHAT DID WE SAY ABOUT GLOATING, ALYSSA? YOU SHOULD BE HUMBLE. OTHER THAN THAT, WELL DONE. YOU ONLY TOOK ONE DAY TO LEARN THAT MOVE, WHEN THE OTHERS...
...OH MY. WHAT IS THIS?
WHAT... ARE THOSE?
OH, THOSE? I CALL THEM *GYM SNEAKERS.* I CAME UP WITH THEM IN ONE OF MY DREAMS, AND MADE THEM OUT OF..
THIS WILL *NOT* BE TOLERATED. THOSE ARE NOT THE STANDARD BOOTS YOU WERE ASSIGNED. YOU WILL NEED TO BE HELD BACK UNTIL YOU LEARN TO DO THINGS THE PROPER WAY.

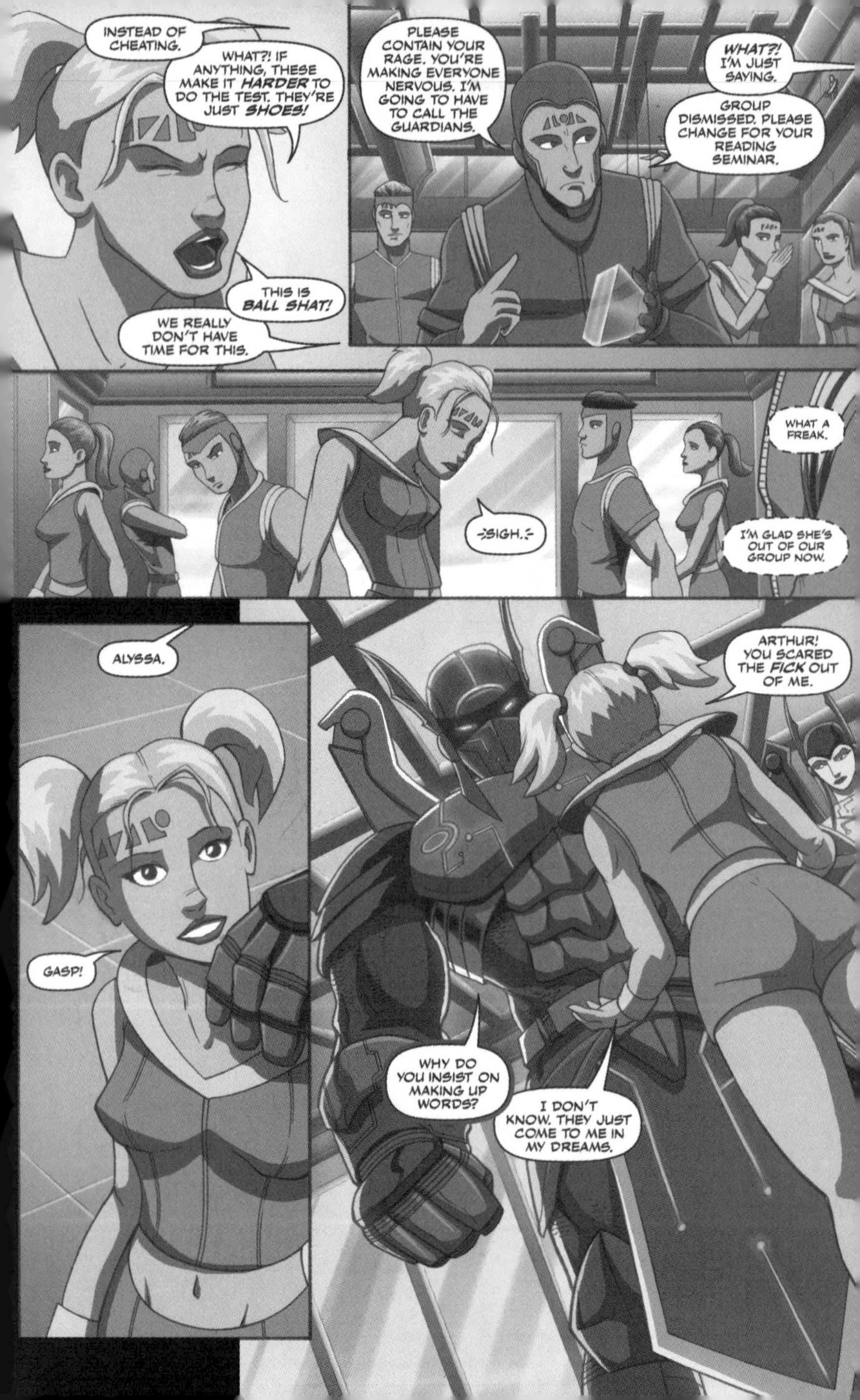
INSTEAD OF CHEATING.
WHAT?! IF ANYTHING, THESE MAKE IT HARDER TO DO THE TEST. THEY'RE JUST SHOES!
THIS IS BALL SHAT!
WE REALLY DON'T HAVE TIME FOR THIS.
PLEASE CONTAIN YOUR RAGE. YOU'RE MAKING EVERYONE NERVOUS. I'M GOING TO HAVE TO CALL THE GUARDIANS.
WHAT?! I'M JUST SAYING.
GROUP DISMISSED. PLEASE CHANGE FOR YOUR READING SEMINAR.
-SIGH.-
WHAT A FREAK.
I'M GLAD SHE'S OUT OF OUR GROUP NOW.
ALYSSA.
GASP!
ARTHUR! YOU SCARED THE FICK OUT OF ME.
WHY DO YOU INSIST ON MAKING UP WORDS?
I DON'T KNOW. THEY JUST COME TO ME IN MY DREAMS.

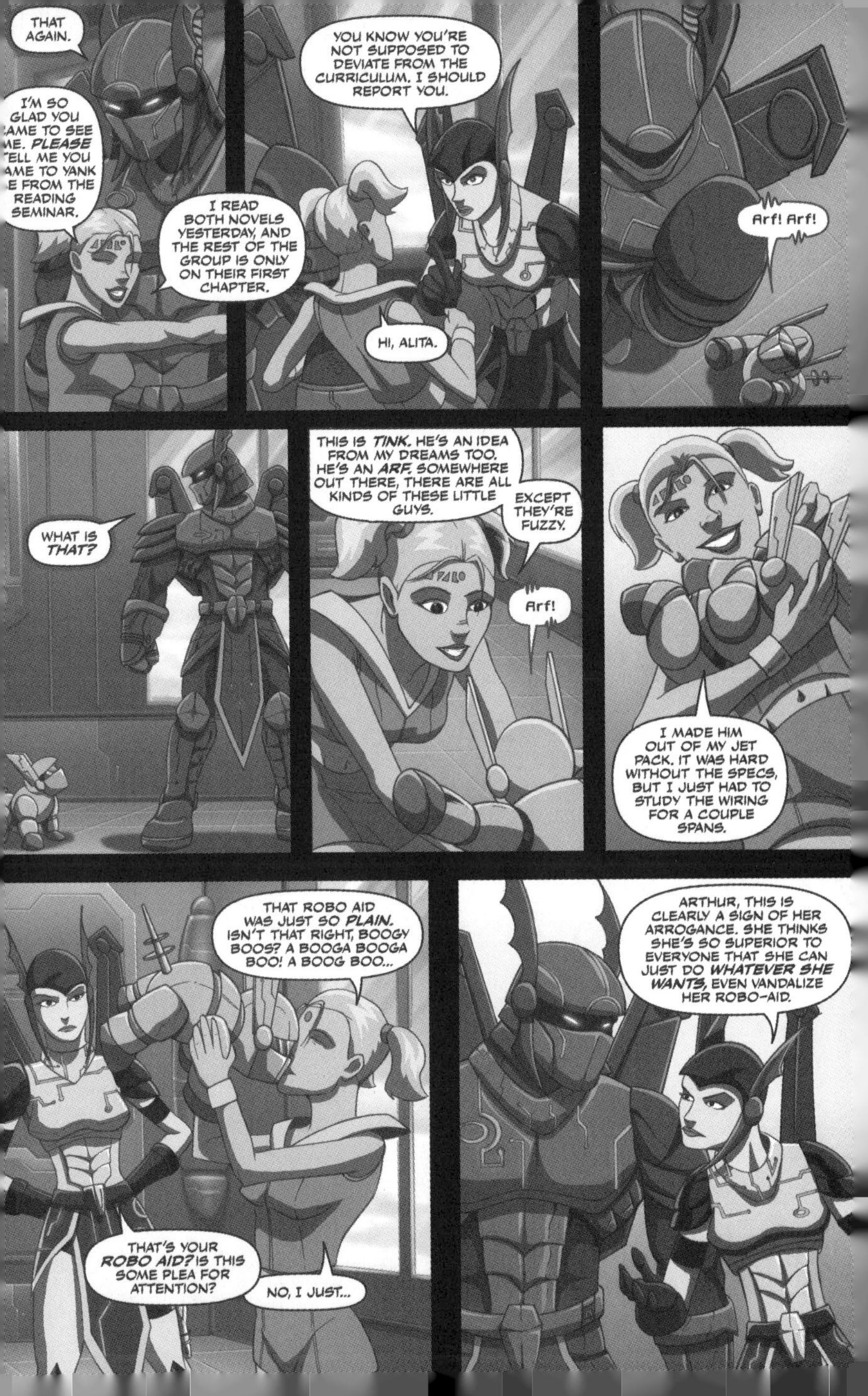

THAT AGAIN.
I'M SO GLAD YOU CAME TO SEE ME. PLEASE TELL ME YOU CAME TO YANK ME FROM THE READING SEMINAR.
I READ BOTH NOVELS YESTERDAY, AND THE REST OF THE GROUP IS ONLY ON THEIR FIRST CHAPTER.
YOU KNOW YOU'RE NOT SUPPOSED TO DEVIATE FROM THE CURRICULUM. I SHOULD REPORT YOU.
HI, ALITA.
Arf! Arf!
WHAT IS THAT?
THIS IS TINK. HE'S AN IDEA FROM MY DREAMS TOO. HE'S AN ARF. SOMEWHERE OUT THERE, THERE ARE ALL KINDS OF THESE LITTLE GUYS.
EXCEPT THEY'RE FUZZY.
Arf!
I MADE HIM OUT OF MY JET PACK. IT WAS HARD WITHOUT THE SPECS, BUT I JUST HAD TO STUDY THE WIRING FOR A COUPLE SPANS.
THAT ROBO AID WAS JUST SO PLAIN. ISN'T THAT RIGHT, BOOGY BOOS? A BOOGA BOOGA BOO! A BOOG BOO...
THAT'S YOUR ROBO AID? IS THIS SOME PLEA FOR ATTENTION?
NO, I JUST...
ARTHUR, THIS IS CLEARLY A SIGN OF HER ARROGANCE. SHE THINKS SHE'S SO SUPERIOR TO EVERYONE THAT SHE CAN JUST DO WHATEVER SHE WANTS, EVEN VANDALIZE HER ROBO-AID.

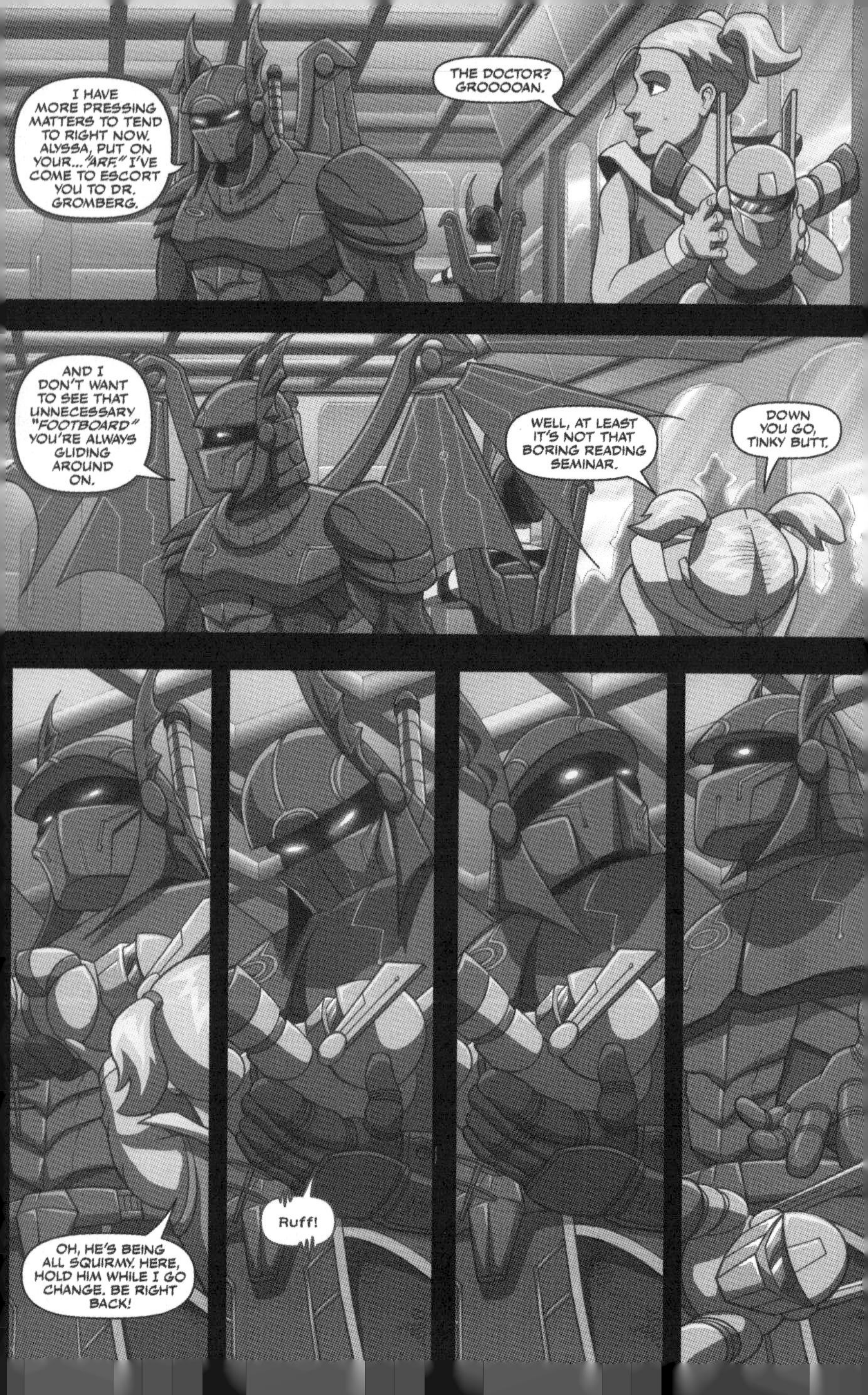
I HAVE MORE PRESSING MATTERS TO TEND TO RIGHT NOW. ALYSSA, PUT ON YOUR... "ARF." I'VE COME TO ESCORT YOU TO DR. GROMBERG.
THE DOCTOR? GROOOOAN.
AND I DON'T WANT TO SEE THAT UNNECESSARY "FOOTBOARD" YOU'RE ALWAYS GLIDING AROUND ON.
WELL, AT LEAST IT'S NOT THAT BORING READING SEMINAR.
DOWN YOU GO, TINKY BUTT.
OH, HE'S BEING ALL SQUIRMY. HERE, HOLD HIM WHILE I GO CHANGE. BE RIGHT BACK!
Ruff!

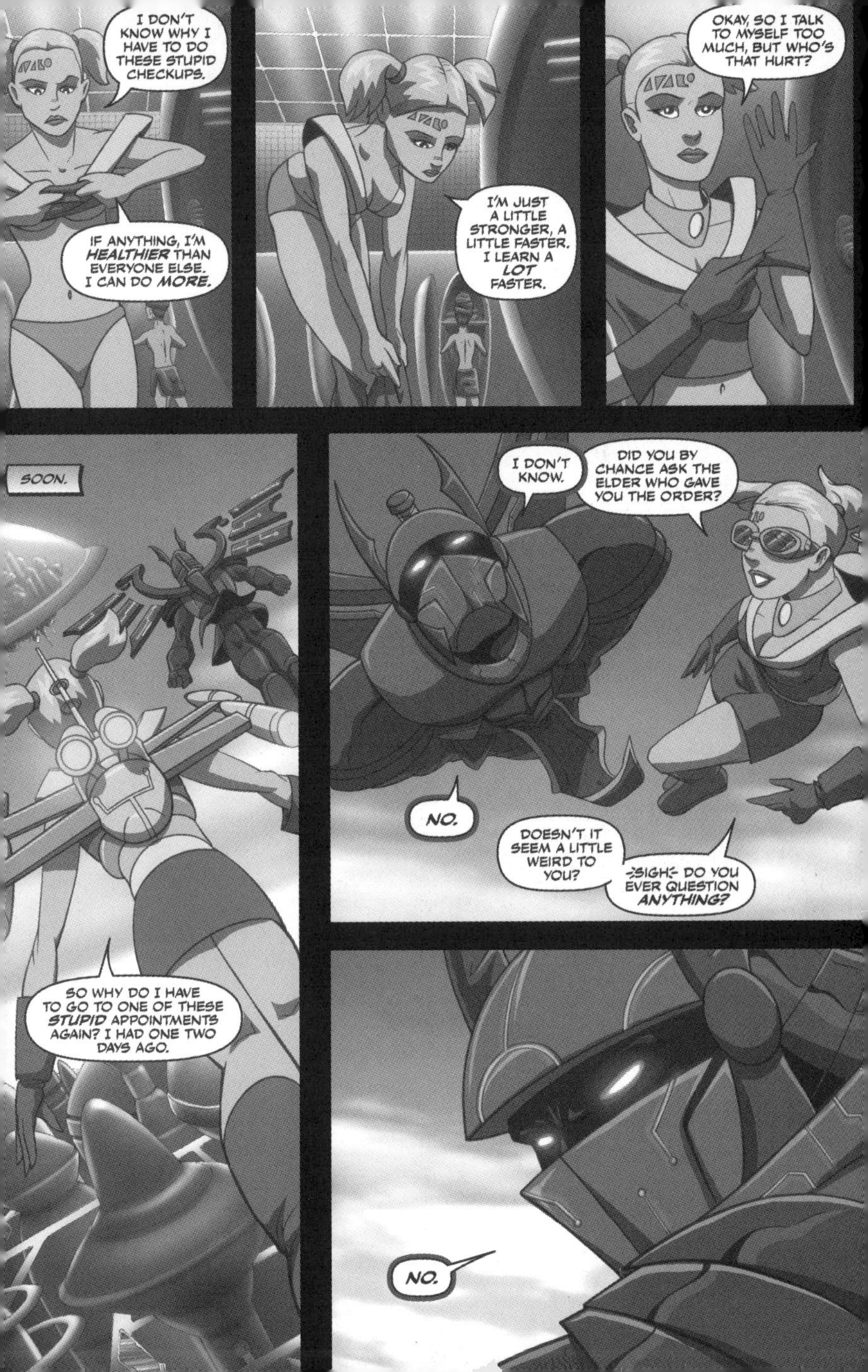
I DON'T KNOW WHY I HAVE TO DO THESE STUPID CHECKUPS.
IF ANYTHING, I'M *HEALTHIER* THAN EVERYONE ELSE. I CAN DO *MORE.*
I'M JUST A LITTLE STRONGER, A LITTLE FASTER. I LEARN A *LOT* FASTER.
OKAY, SO I TALK TO MYSELF TOO MUCH, BUT WHO'S THAT HURT?
SOON.
SO WHY DO I HAVE TO GO TO ONE OF THESE *STUPID* APPOINTMENTS AGAIN? I HAD ONE TWO DAYS AGO.
I DON'T KNOW.
DID YOU BY CHANCE ASK THE ELDER WHO GAVE YOU THE ORDER?
NO.
DOESN'T IT SEEM A LITTLE WEIRD TO YOU?
-SIGH- DO YOU EVER QUESTION *ANYTHING?*
NO.

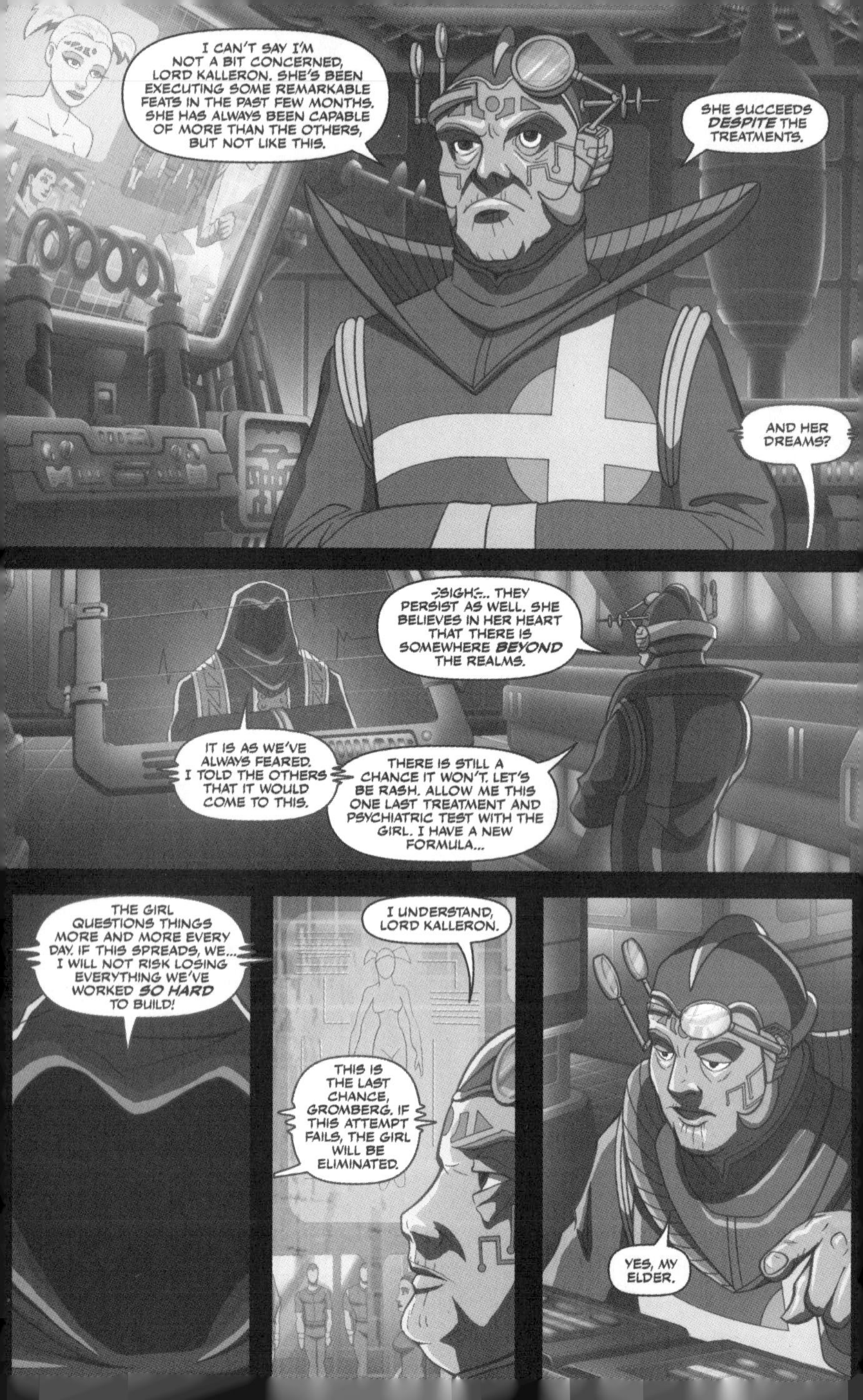
I CAN'T SAY I'M NOT A BIT CONCERNED, LORD KALLERON. SHE'S BEEN EXECUTING SOME REMARKABLE FEATS IN THE PAST FEW MONTHS. SHE HAS ALWAYS BEEN CAPABLE OF MORE THAN THE OTHERS, BUT NOT LIKE THIS.
SHE SUCCEEDS *DESPITE* THE TREATMENTS.
AND HER DREAMS?
SIGH... THEY PERSIST AS WELL. SHE BELIEVES IN HER HEART THAT THERE IS SOMEWHERE *BEYOND* THE REALMS.
IT IS AS WE'VE ALWAYS FEARED. I TOLD THE OTHERS THAT IT WOULD COME TO THIS.
THERE IS STILL A CHANCE IT WON'T. LET'S BE RASH. ALLOW ME THIS ONE LAST TREATMENT AND PSYCHIATRIC TEST WITH THE GIRL. I HAVE A NEW FORMULA...
THE GIRL QUESTIONS THINGS MORE AND MORE EVERY DAY. IF THIS SPREADS, WE... I WILL NOT RISK LOSING EVERYTHING WE'VE WORKED *SO HARD* TO BUILD!
I UNDERSTAND, LORD KALLERON.
THIS IS THE LAST CHANCE, GROMBERG. IF THIS ATTEMPT FAILS, THE GIRL WILL BE ELIMINATED.
YES, MY ELDER.

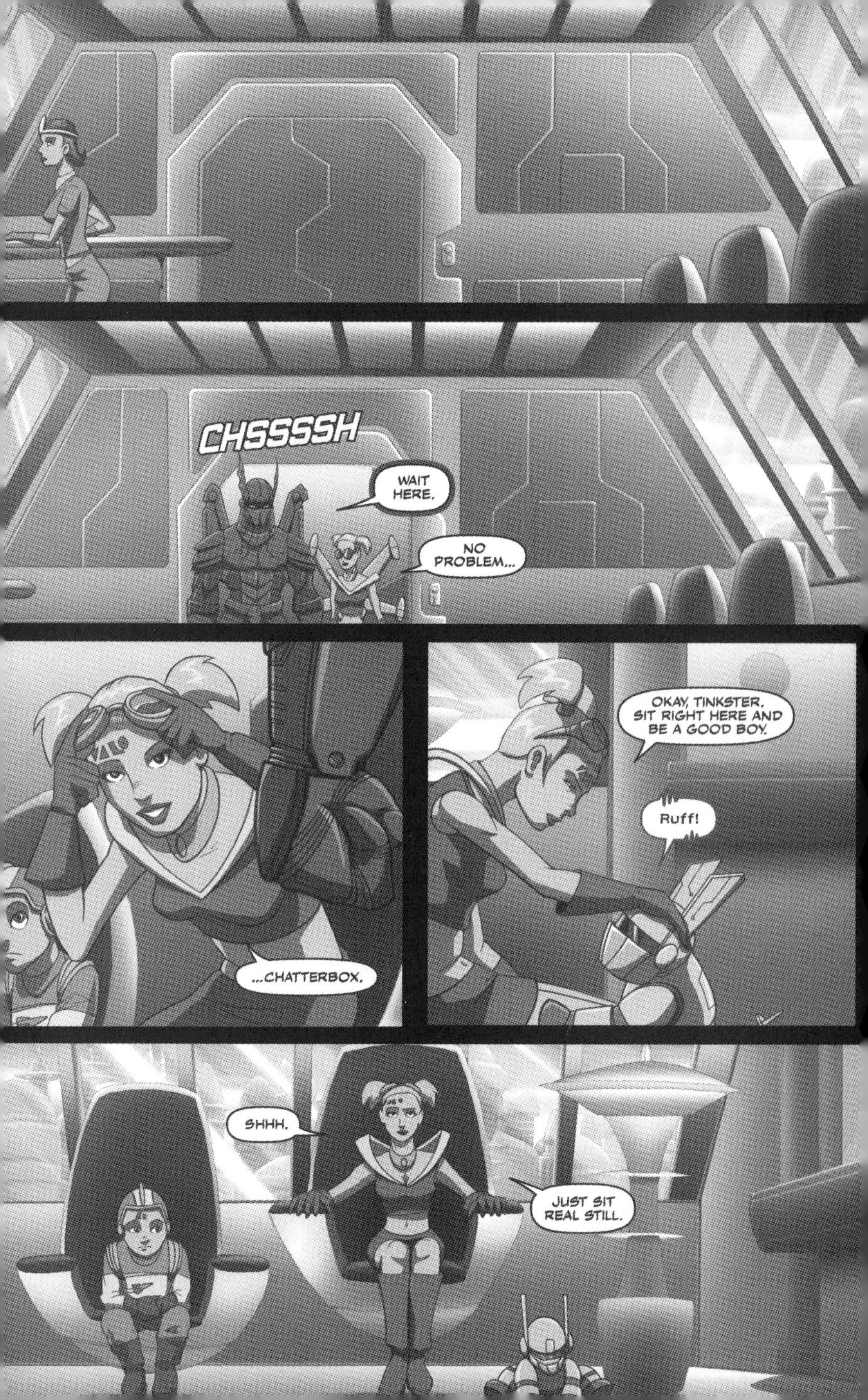
CHSSSSH
WAIT HERE.
NO PROBLEM...
...CHATTERBOX.
OKAY, TINKSTER. SIT RIGHT HERE AND BE A GOOD BOY.
Ruff!
SHHH.
JUST SIT REAL STILL.

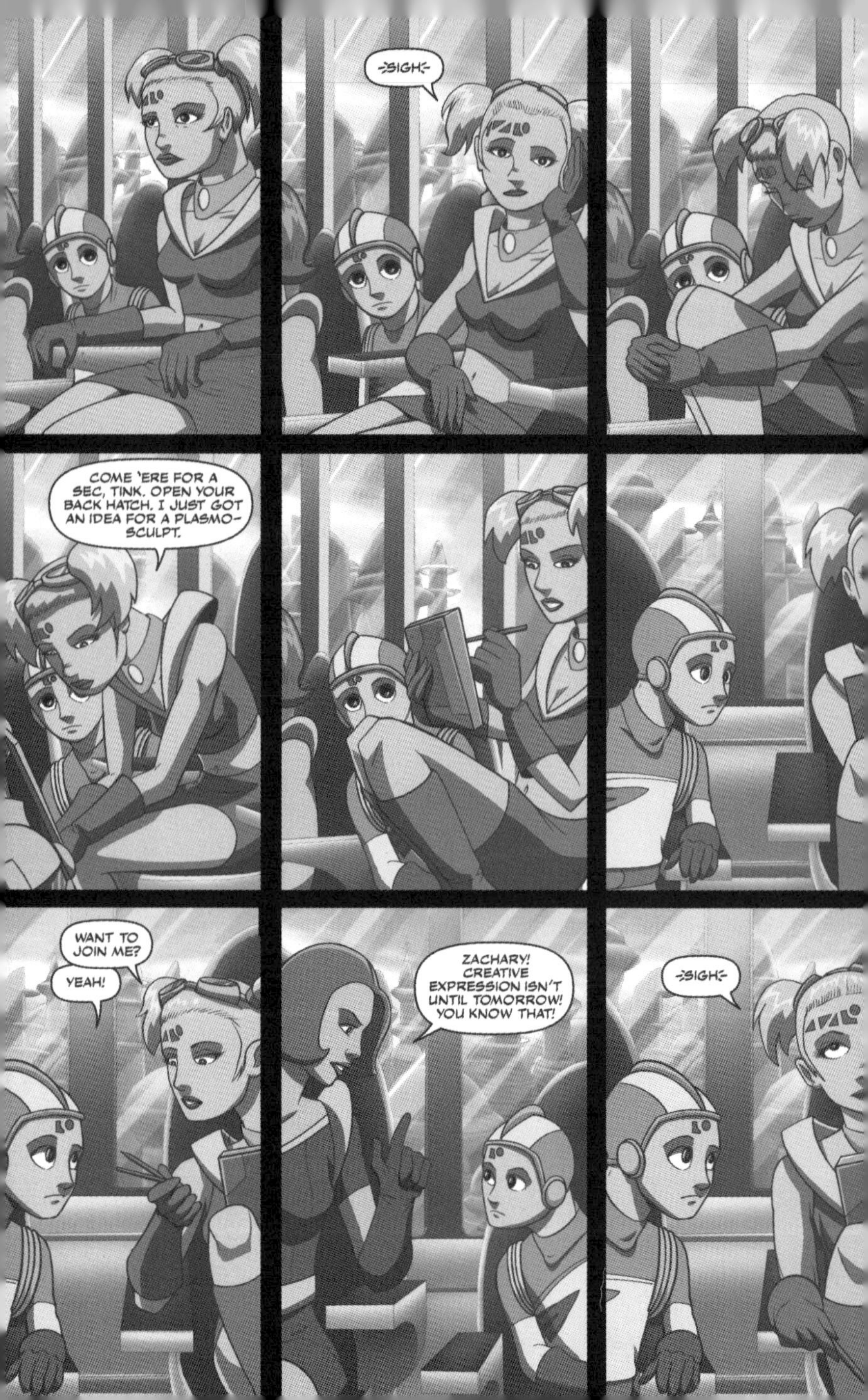
-SIGH-
COME 'ERE FOR A SEC, TINK. OPEN YOUR BACK HATCH. I JUST GOT AN IDEA FOR A PLASMO-SCULPT.
WANT TO JOIN ME?
YEAH!
ZACHARY! CREATIVE EXPRESSION ISN'T UNTIL TOMORROW! YOU KNOW THAT!
-SIGH-

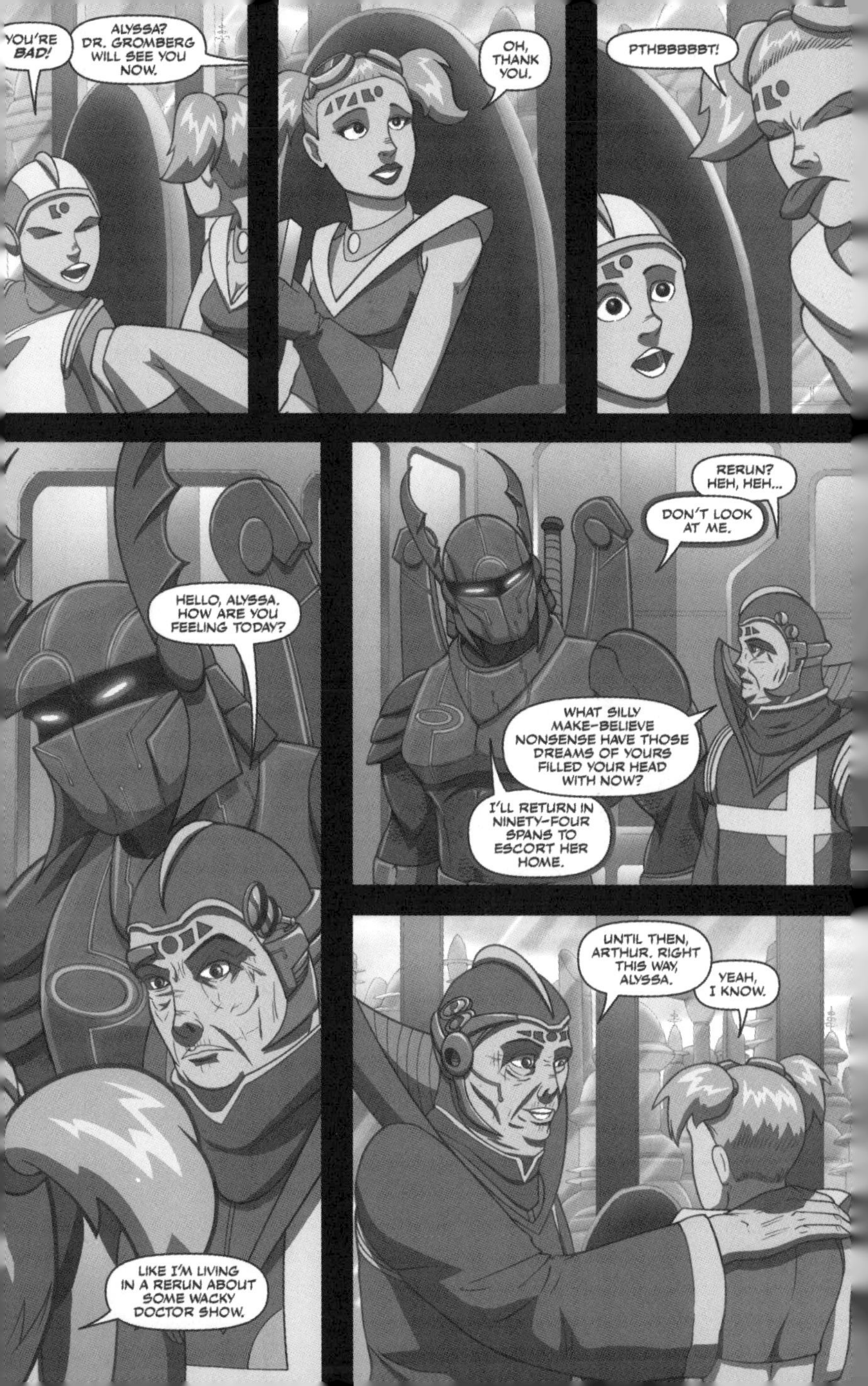
YOU'RE *BAD!*
ALYSSA? DR. GROMBERG WILL SEE YOU NOW.
OH, THANK YOU.
PTHBBBBBT!
HELLO, ALYSSA. HOW ARE YOU FEELING TODAY?
WHAT SILLY MAKE-BELIEVE NONSENSE HAVE THOSE DREAMS OF YOURS FILLED YOUR HEAD WITH NOW?
LIKE I'M LIVING IN A RERUN ABOUT SOME WACKY DOCTOR SHOW.
RERUN? HEH, HEH...
DON'T LOOK AT ME.
I'LL RETURN IN NINETY-FOUR SPANS TO ESCORT HER HOME.
UNTIL THEN, ARTHUR. RIGHT THIS WAY, ALYSSA.
YEAH, I KNOW.

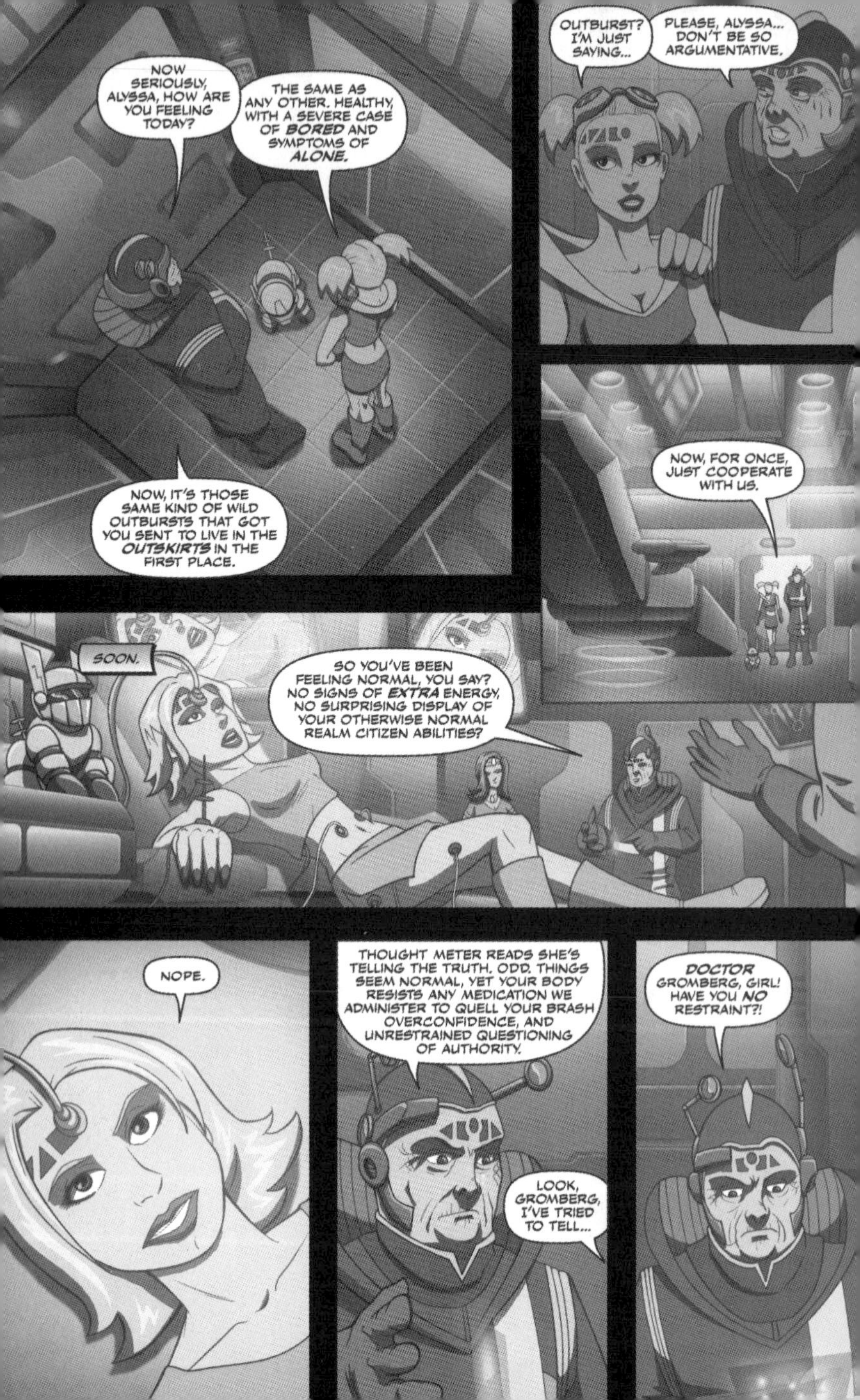
NOW SERIOUSLY, ALYSSA, HOW ARE YOU FEELING TODAY?
THE SAME AS ANY OTHER. HEALTHY, WITH A SEVERE CASE OF *BORED* AND SYMPTOMS OF *ALONE.*
NOW, IT'S THOSE SAME KIND OF WILD OUTBURSTS THAT GOT YOU SENT TO LIVE IN THE *OUTSKIRTS* IN THE FIRST PLACE.
OUTBURST? I'M JUST SAYING...
PLEASE, ALYSSA... DON'T BE SO ARGUMENTATIVE.
NOW, FOR ONCE, JUST COOPERATE WITH US.
SOON.
SO YOU'VE BEEN FEELING NORMAL, YOU SAY? NO SIGNS OF *EXTRA* ENERGY, NO SURPRISING DISPLAY OF YOUR OTHERWISE NORMAL REALM CITIZEN ABILITIES?
NOPE.
THOUGHT METER READS SHE'S TELLING THE TRUTH. ODD. THINGS SEEM NORMAL, YET YOUR BODY RESISTS ANY MEDICATION WE ADMINISTER TO QUELL YOUR BRASH OVERCONFIDENCE, AND UNRESTRAINED QUESTIONING OF AUTHORITY.
LOOK, GROMBERG, I'VE TRIED TO TELL...
DOCTOR GROMBERG, GIRL! HAVE YOU *NO* RESTRAINT?!

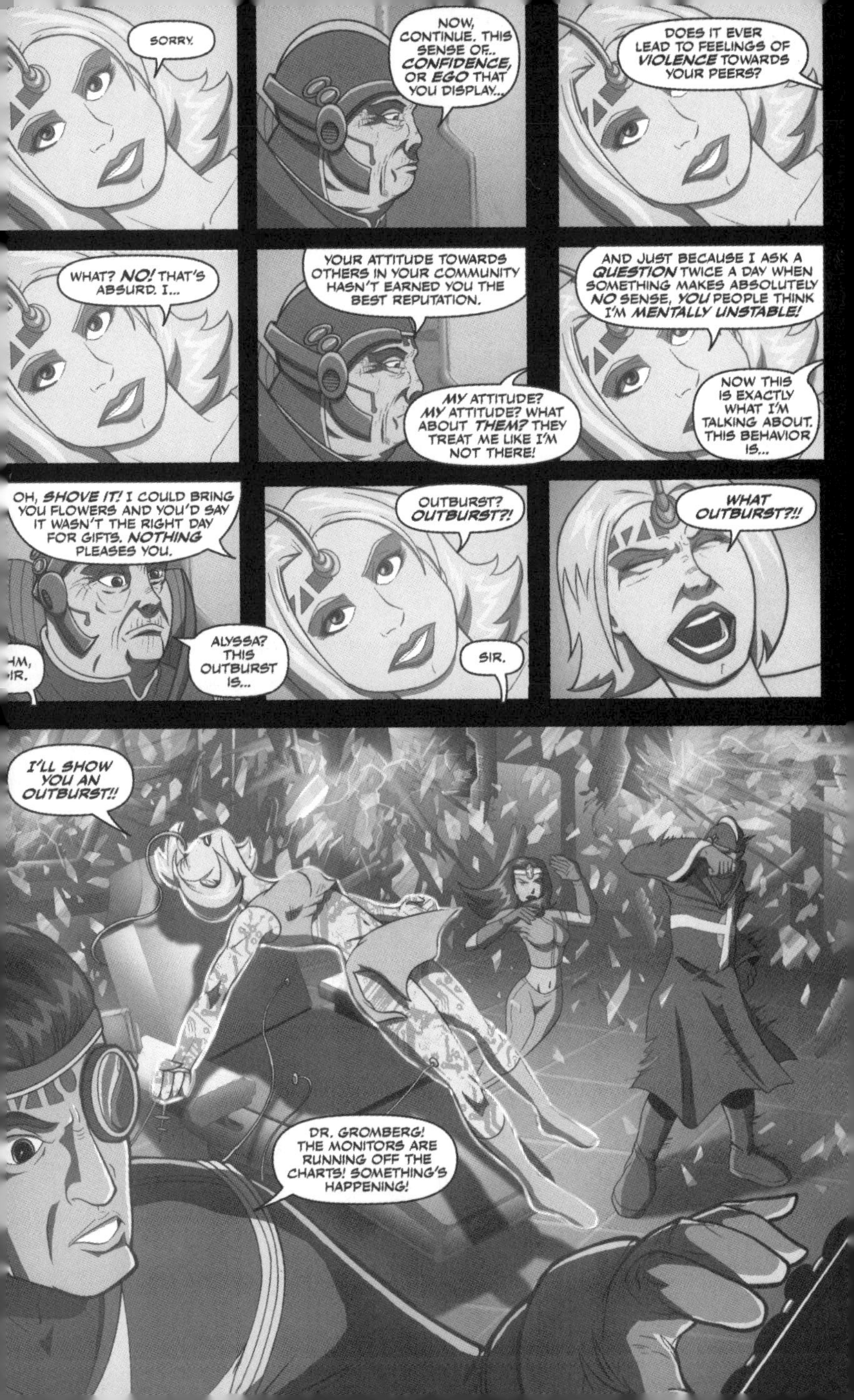
SORRY.
NOW, CONTINUE. THIS SENSE OF.. CONFIDENCE, OR EGO THAT YOU DISPLAY...
DOES IT EVER LEAD TO FEELINGS OF VIOLENCE TOWARDS YOUR PEERS?
WHAT? NO! THAT'S ABSURD. I...
YOUR ATTITUDE TOWARDS OTHERS IN YOUR COMMUNITY HASN'T EARNED YOU THE BEST REPUTATION.
MY ATTITUDE? MY ATTITUDE? WHAT ABOUT THEM? THEY TREAT ME LIKE I'M NOT THERE!
AND JUST BECAUSE I ASK A QUESTION TWICE A DAY WHEN SOMETHING MAKES ABSOLUTELY NO SENSE, YOU PEOPLE THINK I'M MENTALLY UNSTABLE!
NOW THIS IS EXACTLY WHAT I'M TALKING ABOUT. THIS BEHAVIOR IS...
OH, SHOVE IT! I COULD BRING YOU FLOWERS AND YOU'D SAY IT WASN'T THE RIGHT DAY FOR GIFTS. NOTHING PLEASES YOU.
HM, IR.
ALYSSA? THIS OUTBURST IS...
OUTBURST? OUTBURST?!
SIR.
WHAT OUTBURST?!!
I'LL SHOW YOU AN OUTBURST!!
DR. GROMBERG! THE MONITORS ARE RUNNING OFF THE CHARTS! SOMETHING'S HAPPENING!

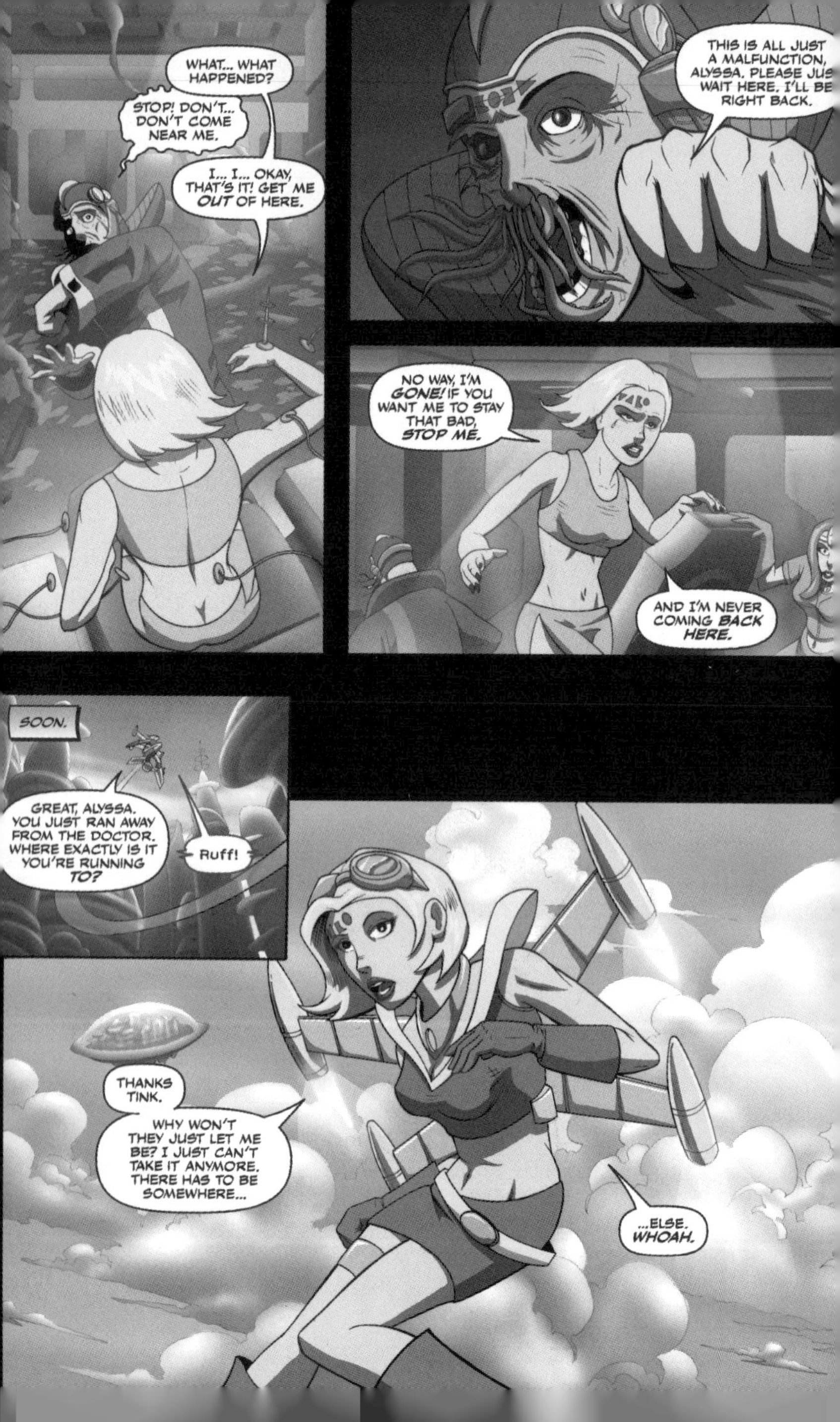
WHAT... WHAT HAPPENED?
STOP! DON'T... DON'T COME NEAR ME.
I... I... OKAY, THAT'S IT! GET ME OUT OF HERE.
THIS IS ALL JUST A MALFUNCTION, ALYSSA. PLEASE JUS WAIT HERE. I'LL BE RIGHT BACK.
NO WAY, I'M GONE! IF YOU WANT ME TO STAY THAT BAD, STOP ME.
AND I'M NEVER COMING BACK HERE.
SOON.
GREAT, ALYSSA. YOU JUST RAN AWAY FROM THE DOCTOR. WHERE EXACTLY IS IT YOU'RE RUNNING TO?
Ruff!
THANKS TINK.
WHY WON'T THEY JUST LET ME BE? I JUST CAN'T TAKE IT ANYMORE. THERE HAS TO BE SOMEWHERE...
...ELSE. WHOAH.

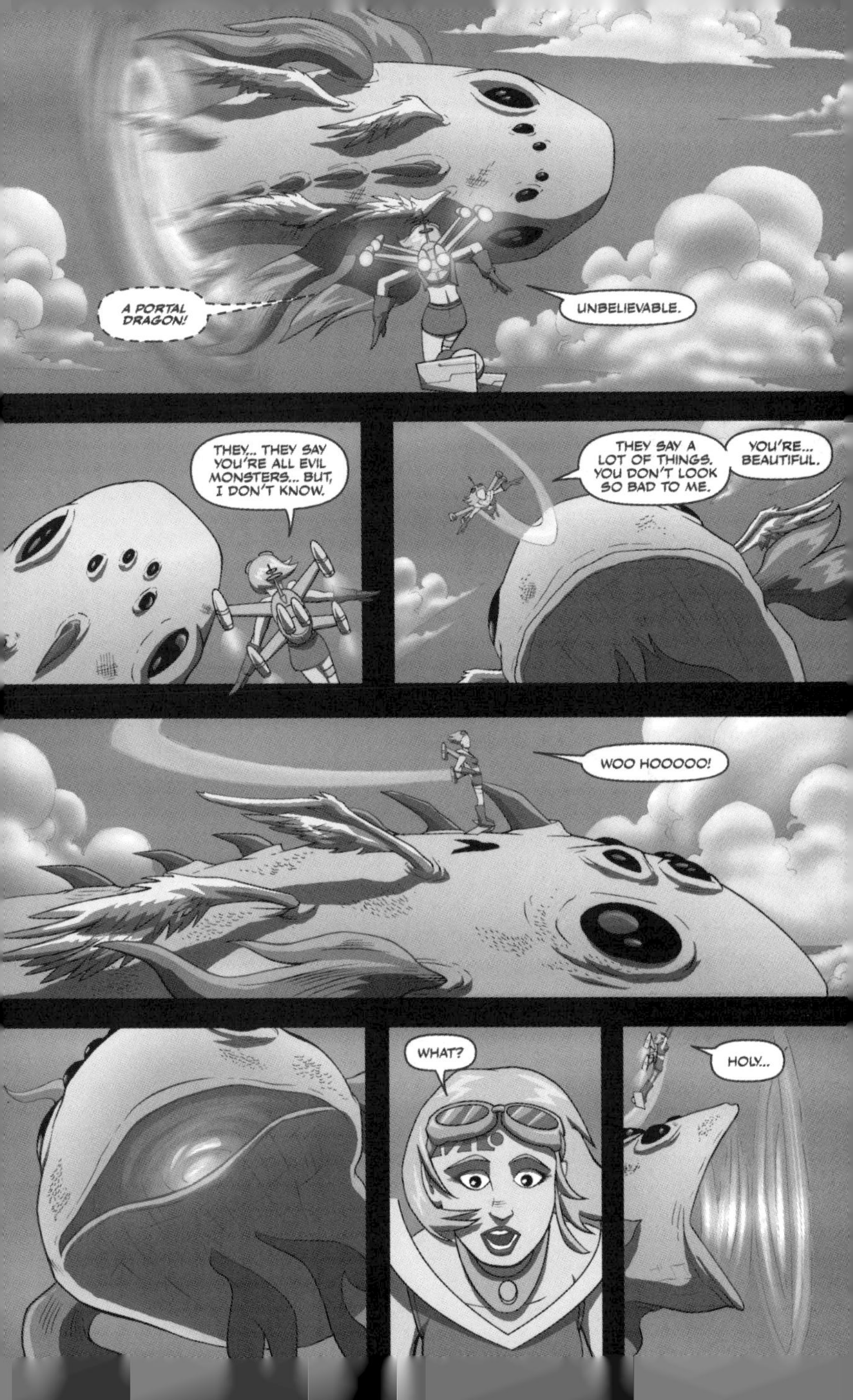
A PORTAL DRAGON!
UNBELIEVABLE.
THEY... THEY SAY YOU'RE ALL EVIL MONSTERS... BUT, I DON'T KNOW.
THEY SAY A LOT OF THINGS. YOU DON'T LOOK SO BAD TO ME.
YOU'RE... BEAUTIFUL.
WOO HOOOOO!
WHAT?
HOLY...

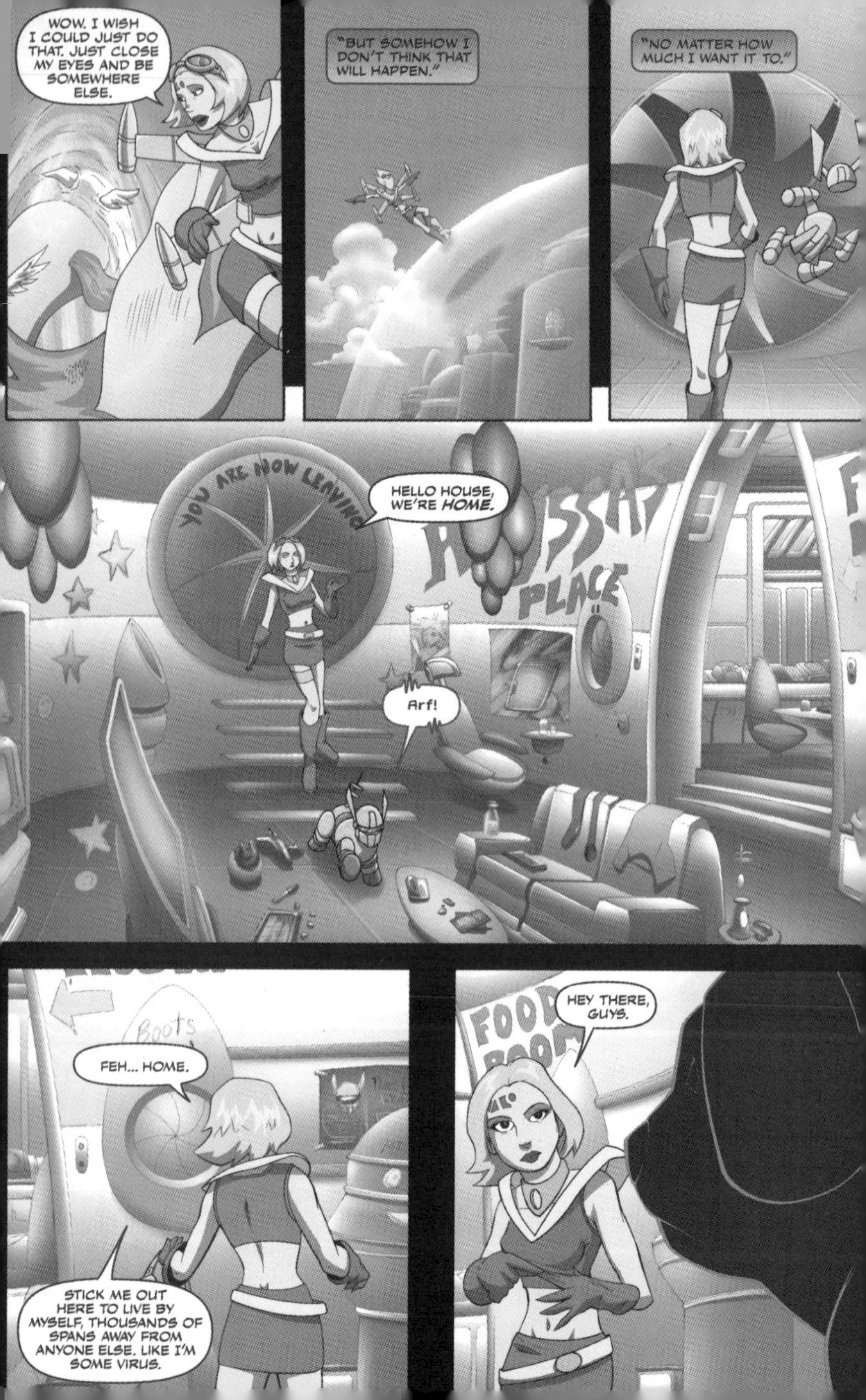
WOW. I WISH I COULD JUST DO THAT. JUST CLOSE MY EYES AND BE SOMEWHERE ELSE.
"BUT SOMEHOW I DON'T THINK THAT WILL HAPPEN."
"NO MATTER HOW MUCH I WANT IT TO."
YOU ARE NOW LEAVING
HELLO HOUSE, WE'RE *HOME.*
PLACE
Arf!
Boots
FEH... HOME.
STICK ME OUT HERE TO LIVE BY MYSELF, THOUSANDS OF SPANS AWAY FROM ANYONE ELSE. LIKE I'M SOME VIRUS.
FOOD
HEY THERE, GUYS.

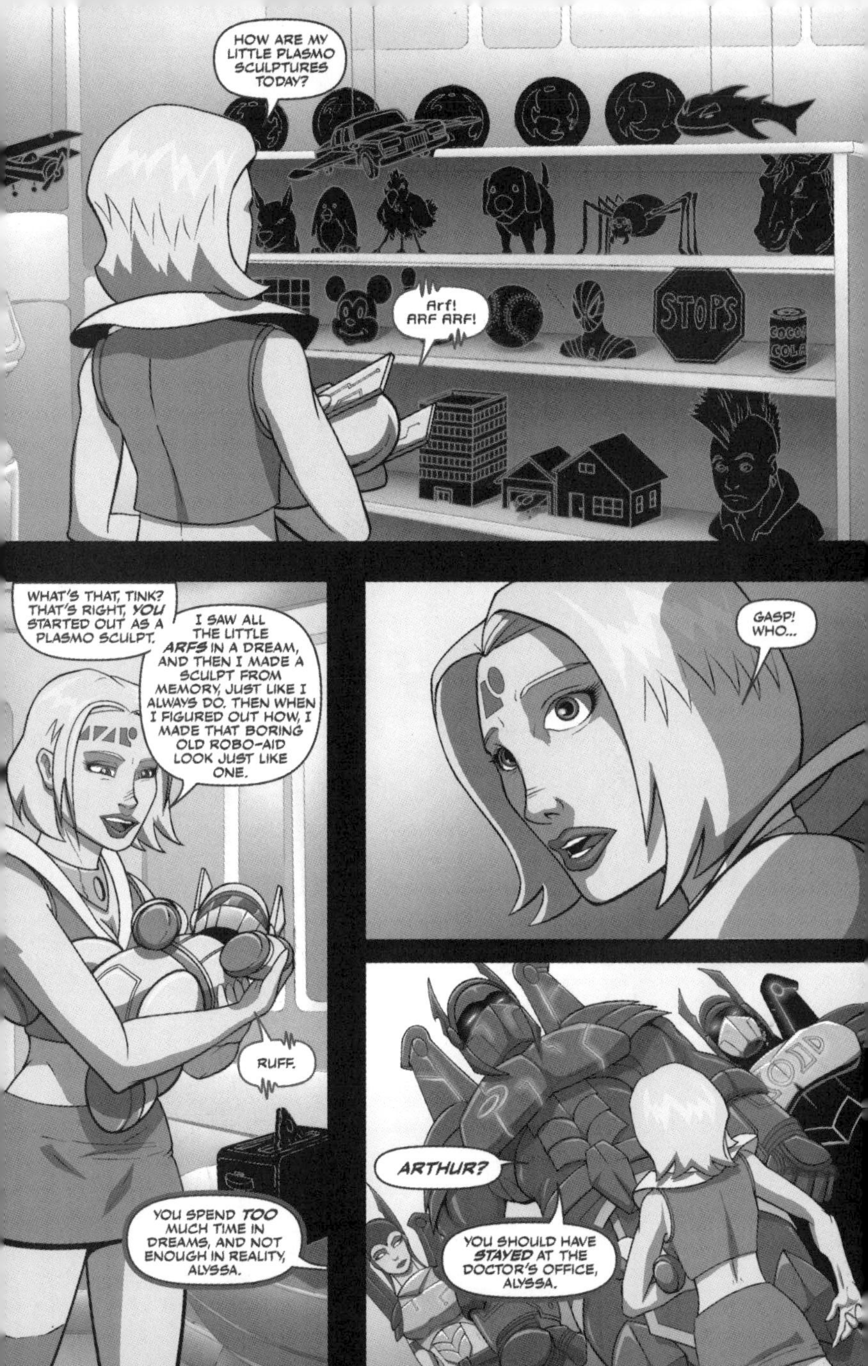
HOW ARE MY LITTLE PLASMO SCULPTURES TODAY?
Arf! ARF ARF!
STOPS
COCO COLA
WHAT'S THAT, TINK? THAT'S RIGHT, *YOU* STARTED OUT AS A PLASMO SCULPT.
I SAW ALL THE LITTLE *ARFS* IN A DREAM, AND THEN I MADE A SCULPT FROM MEMORY, JUST LIKE I ALWAYS DO. THEN WHEN I FIGURED OUT HOW, I MADE THAT BORING OLD ROBO-AID LOOK JUST LIKE ONE.
RUFF.
YOU SPEND *TOO* MUCH TIME IN DREAMS, AND NOT ENOUGH IN REALITY, ALYSSA.
GASP! WHO...
ARTHUR?
YOU SHOULD HAVE *STAYED* AT THE DOCTOR'S OFFICE, ALYSSA.

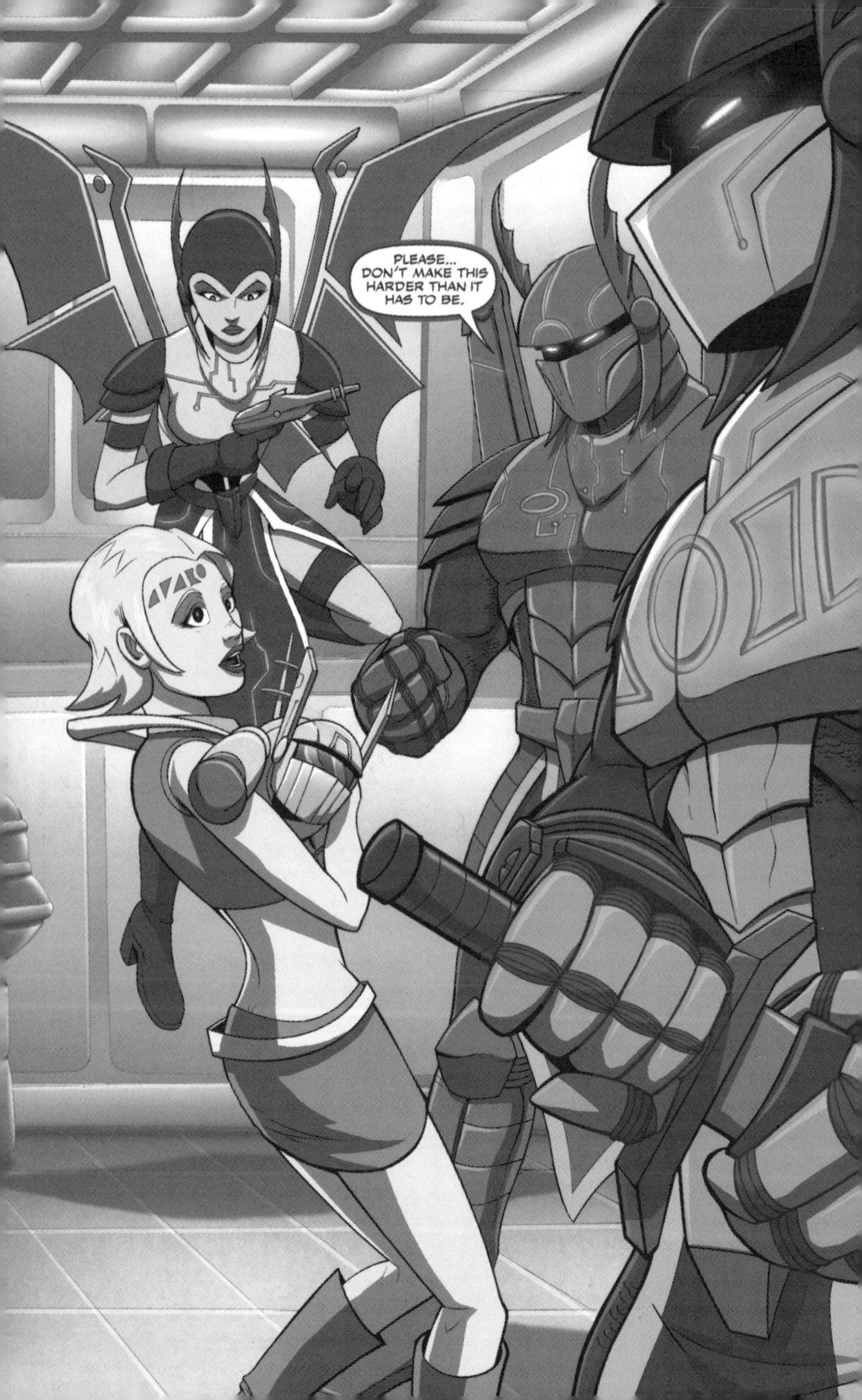
PLEASE... DON'T MAKE THIS HARDER THAN IT HAS TO BE.

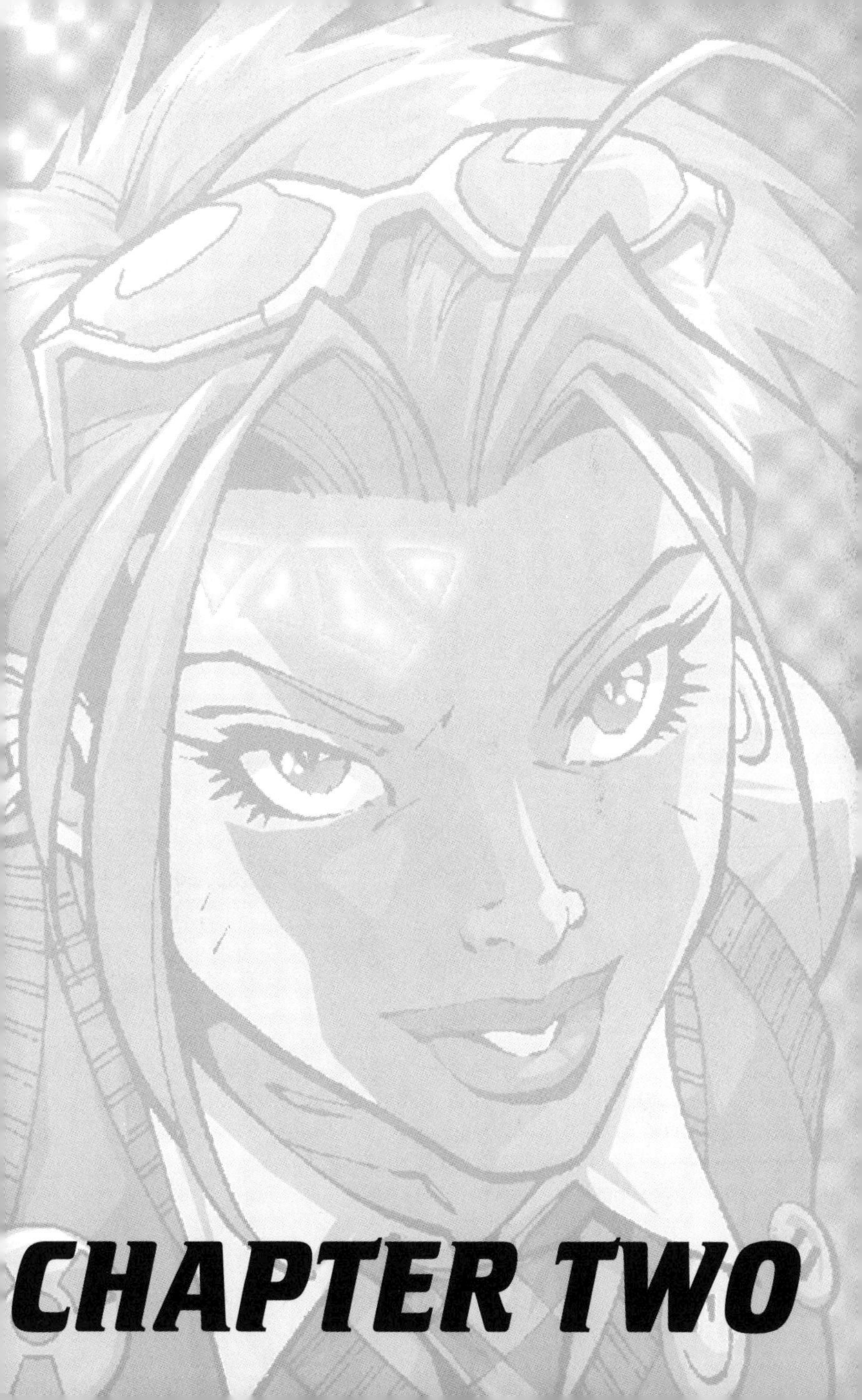

CHAPTER TWO

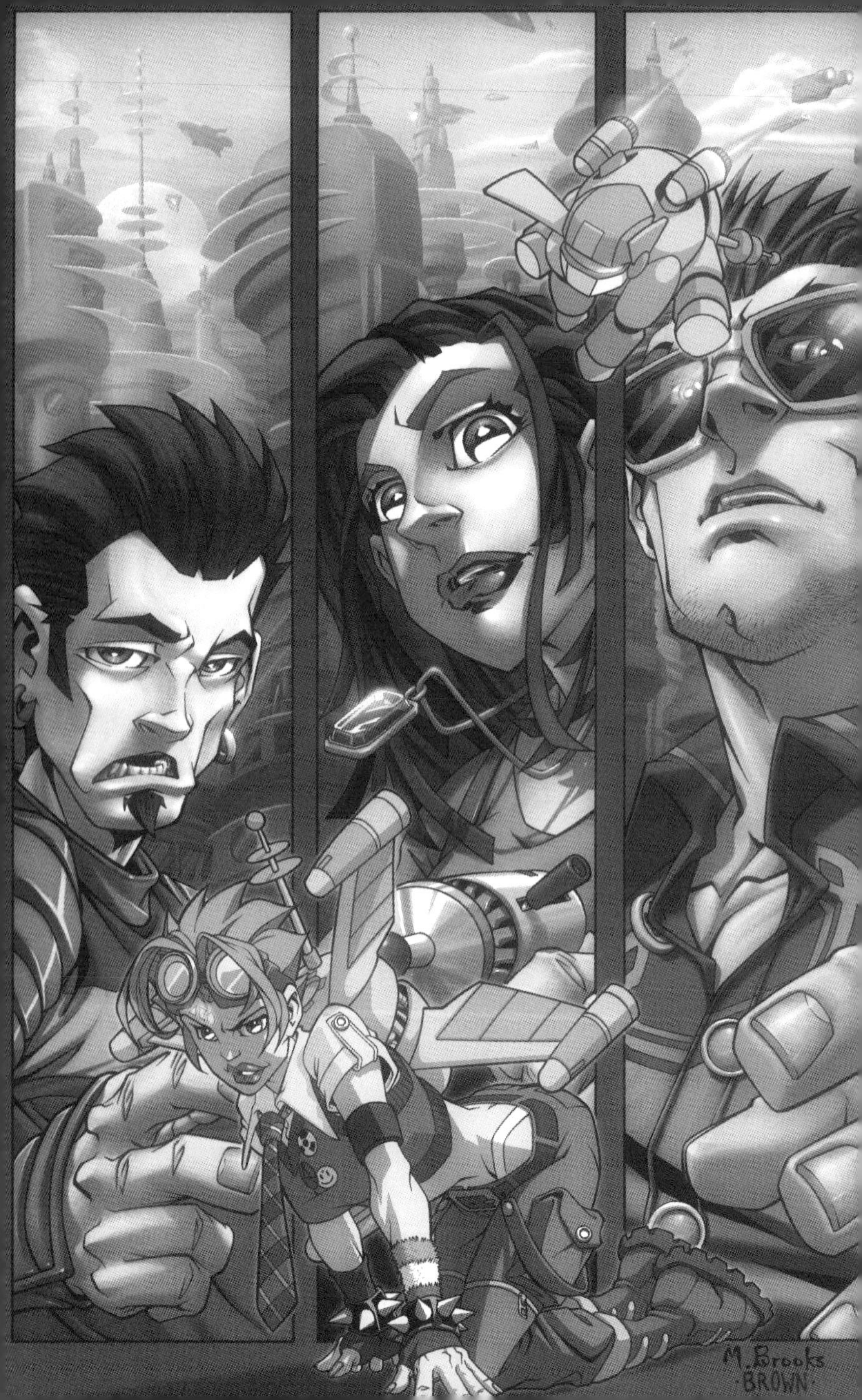
M. Brooks
·BROWN·

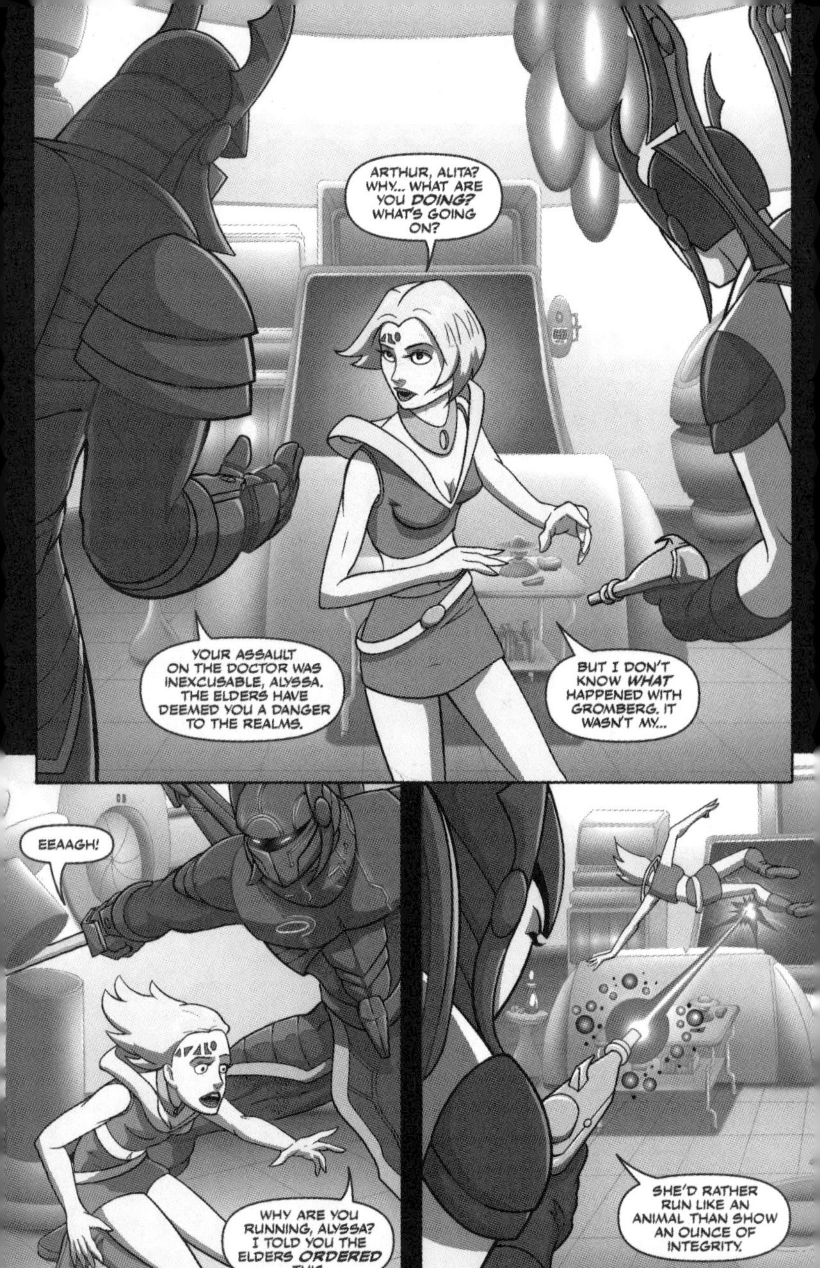
ARTHUR, ALITA? WHY... WHAT ARE YOU *DOING?* WHAT'S GOING ON?
YOUR ASSAULT ON THE DOCTOR WAS INEXCUSABLE, ALYSSA. THE ELDERS HAVE DEEMED YOU A DANGER TO THE REALMS.
BUT I DON'T KNOW *WHAT* HAPPENED WITH GROMBERG. IT WASN'T MY...
EEAAGH!
WHY ARE YOU RUNNING, ALYSSA? I TOLD YOU THE ELDERS *ORDERED* THIS.
SHE'D RATHER RUN LIKE AN ANIMAL THAN SHOW AN OUNCE OF INTEGRITY.

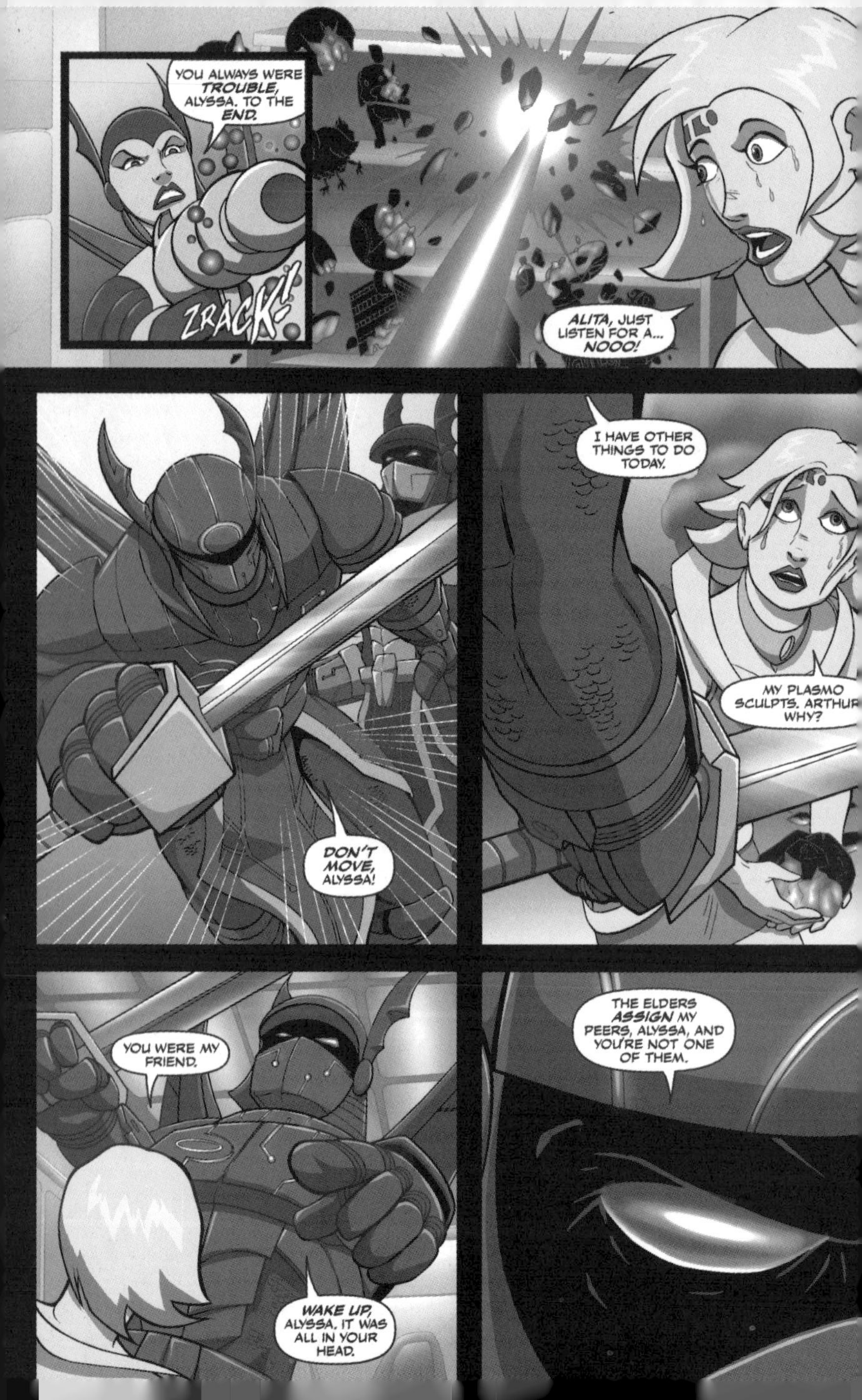
YOU ALWAYS WERE TROUBLE, ALYSSA. TO THE END.
ZRACK!
ALITA, JUST LISTEN FOR A... NOOO!
DON'T MOVE, ALYSSA!
I HAVE OTHER THINGS TO DO TODAY.
MY PLASMO SCULPTS. ARTHUR WHY?
YOU WERE MY FRIEND.
WAKE UP, ALYSSA. IT WAS ALL IN YOUR HEAD.
THE ELDERS ASSIGN MY PEERS, ALYSSA, AND YOU'RE NOT ONE OF THEM.

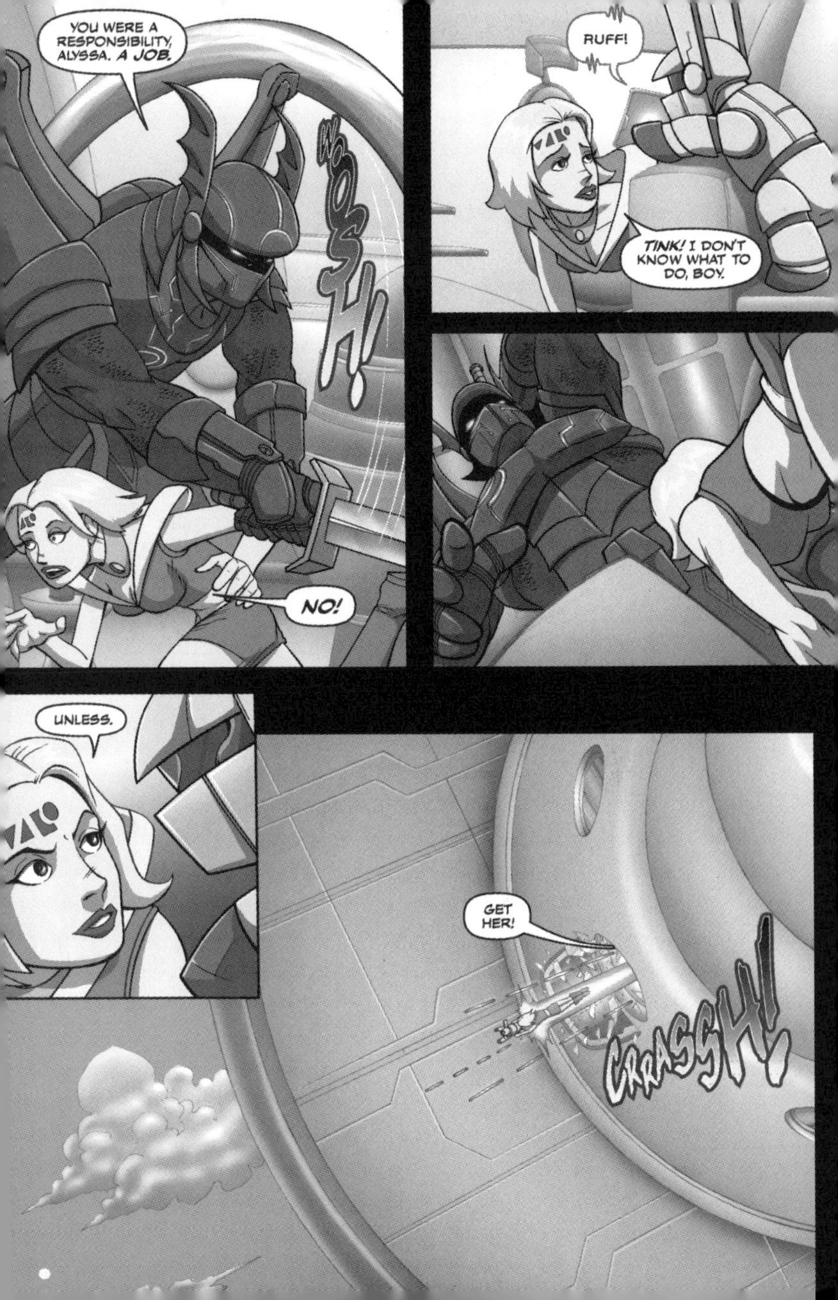

YOU WERE A RESPONSIBILITY, ALYSSA. A *JOB.*
WHOOSH!
NO!
RUFF!
TINK! I DON'T KNOW WHAT TO DO, BOY.
UNLESS.
GET HER!
CRRASSH!

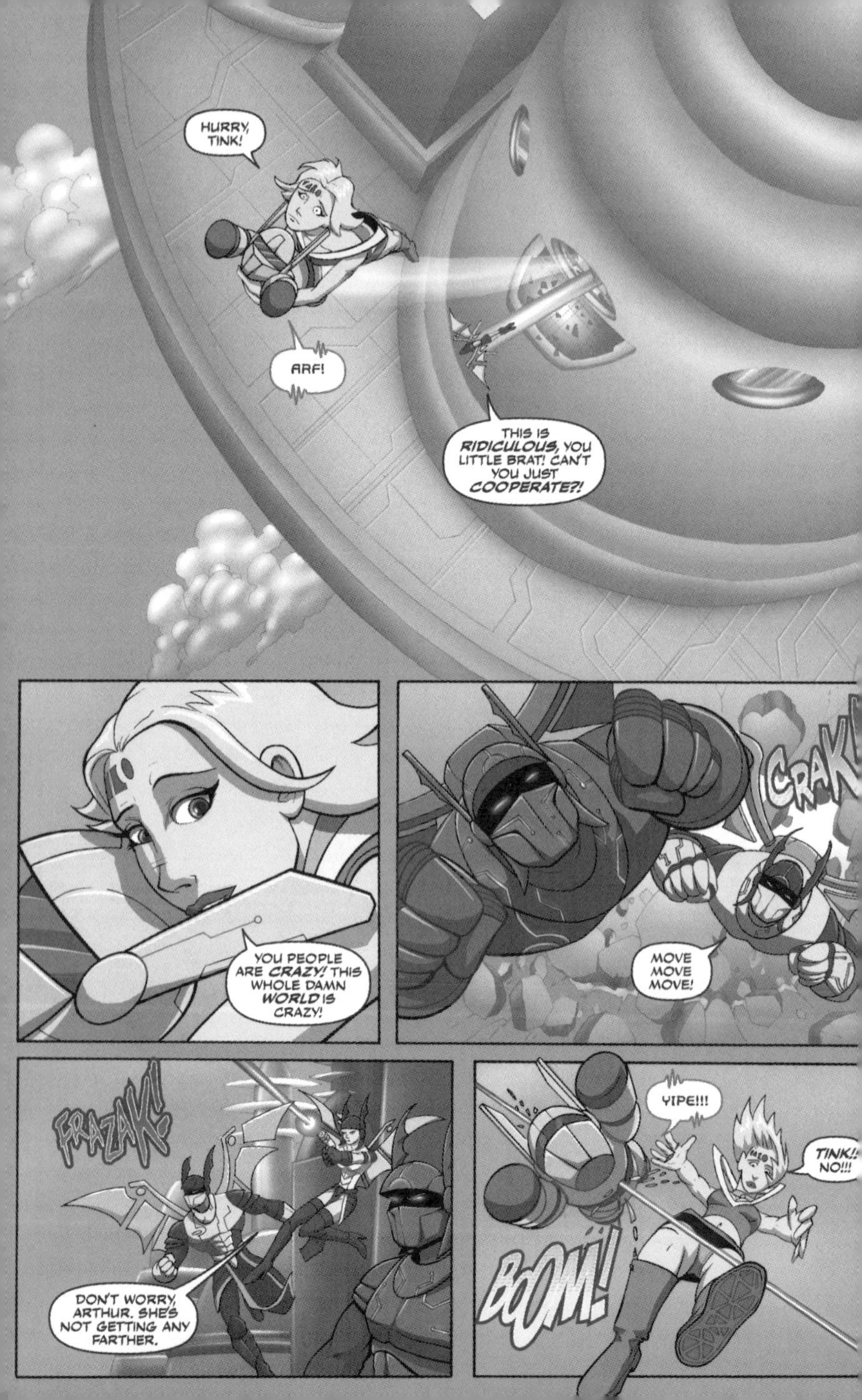
HURRY, TINK!
ARF!
THIS IS RIDICULOUS, YOU LITTLE BRAT! CAN'T YOU JUST COOPERATE?!
YOU PEOPLE ARE CRAZY! THIS WHOLE DAMN WORLD IS CRAZY!
CRAK
MOVE MOVE MOVE!
FRAZAK!
DON'T WORRY, ARTHUR. SHE'S NOT GETTING ANY FARTHER.
YIPE!!!
TINK!! NO!!!
BOOM!

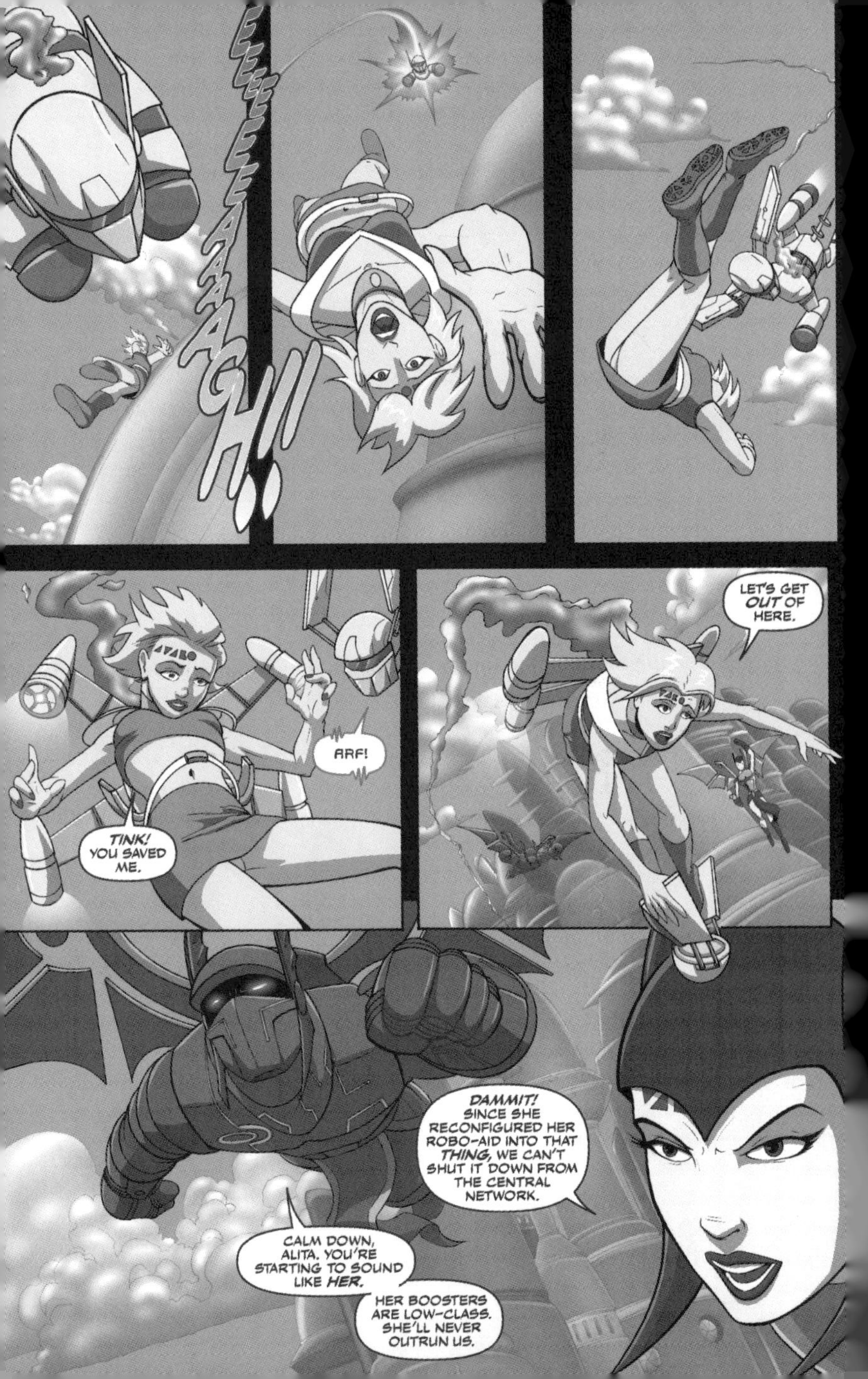
EEEEEEEAAAAAGH!!
TINK! YOU SAVED ME.
ARF!
LET'S GET OUT OF HERE.
DAMMIT! SINCE SHE RECONFIGURED HER ROBO-AID INTO THAT THING, WE CAN'T SHUT IT DOWN FROM THE CENTRAL NETWORK.
CALM DOWN, ALITA. YOU'RE STARTING TO SOUND LIKE HER.
HER BOOSTERS ARE LOW-CLASS. SHE'LL NEVER OUTRUN US.

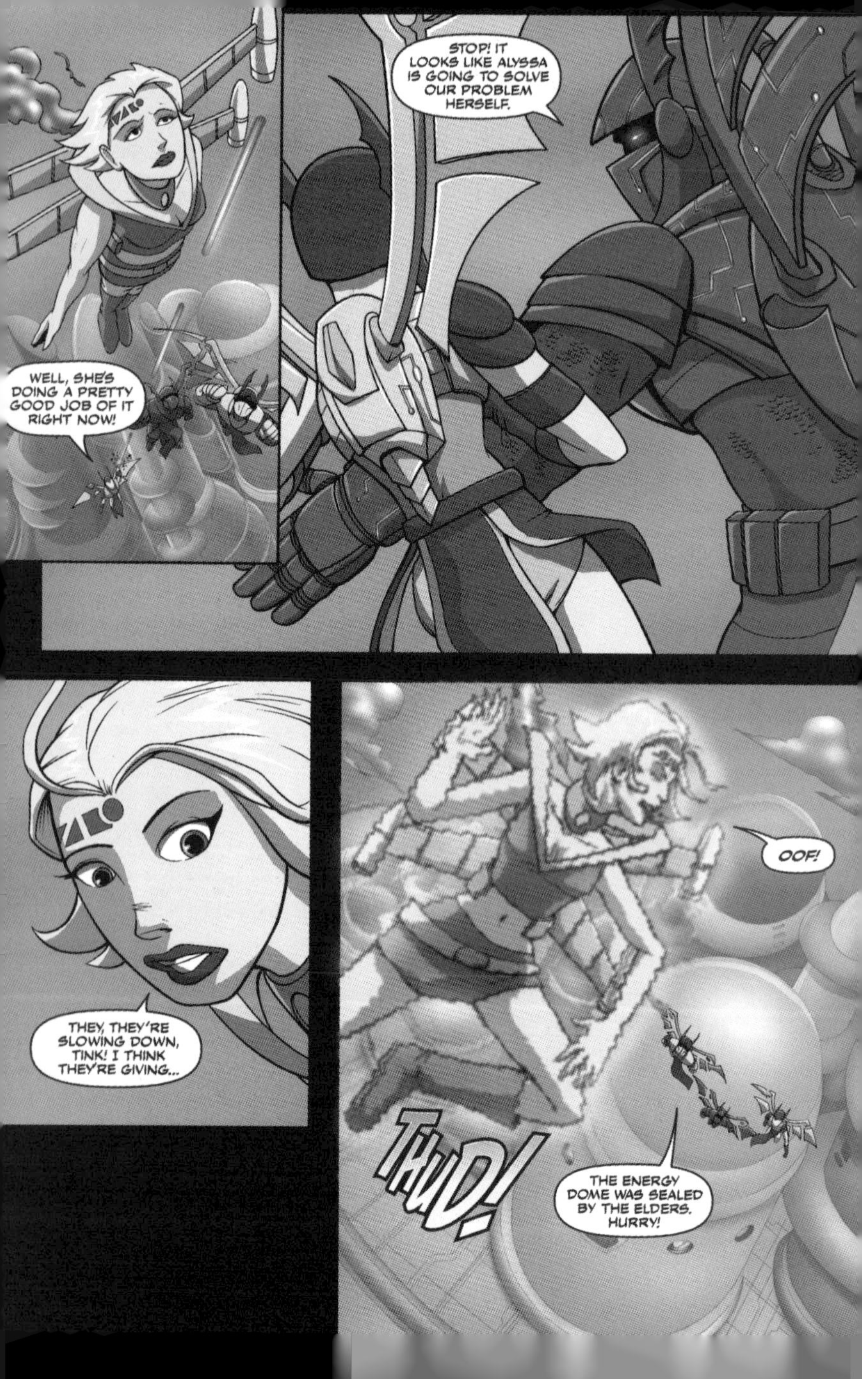
STOP! IT LOOKS LIKE ALYSSA IS GOING TO SOLVE OUR PROBLEM HERSELF.
WELL, SHE'S DOING A PRETTY GOOD JOB OF IT RIGHT NOW!
THEY, THEY'RE SLOWING DOWN, TINK! I THINK THEY'RE GIVING...
OOF!
THUD!
THE ENERGY DOME WAS SEALED BY THE ELDERS. HURRY!

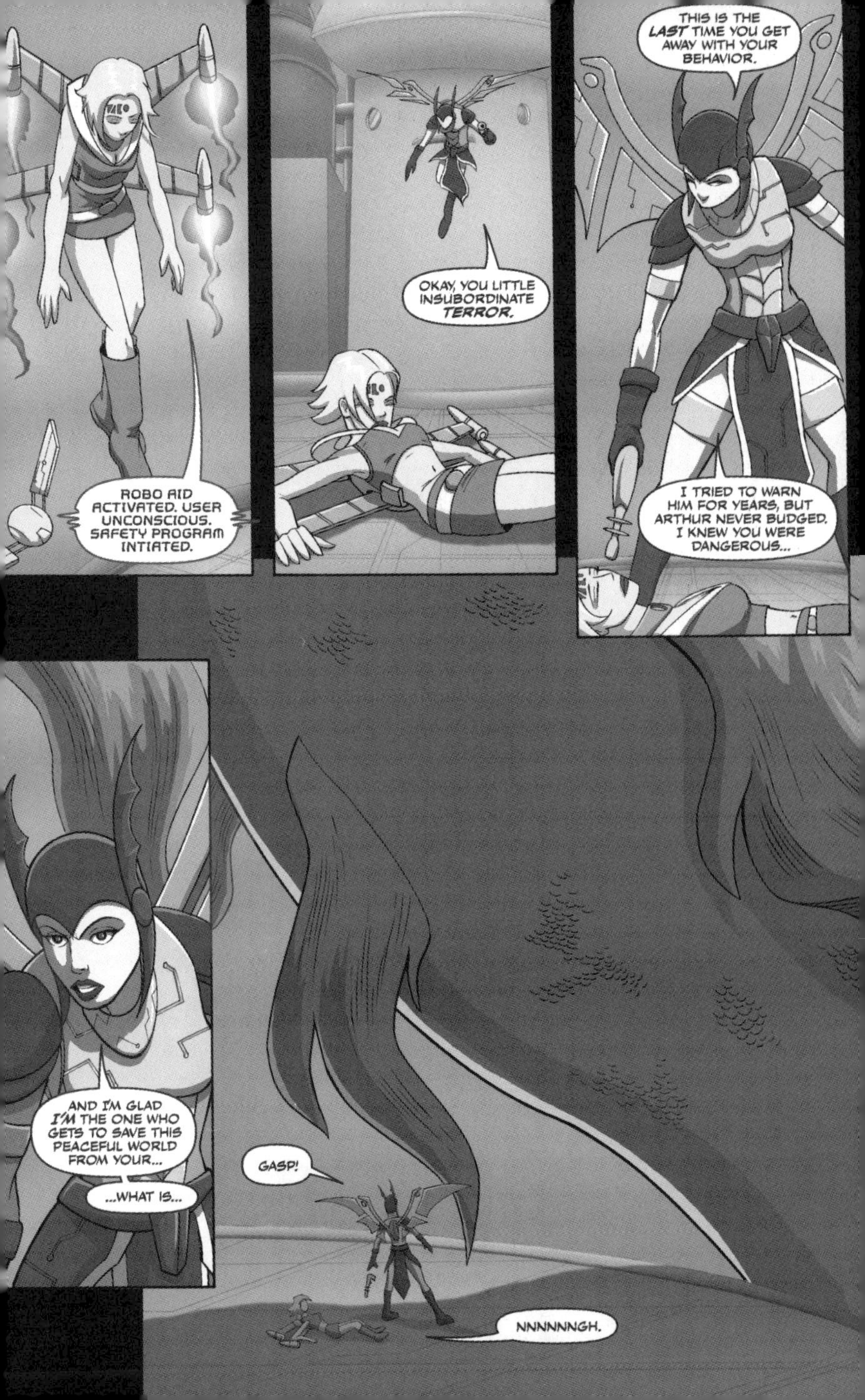
ROBO AID ACTIVATED. USER UNCONSCIOUS. SAFETY PROGRAM INTIATED.
OKAY, YOU LITTLE INSUBORDINATE *TERROR.*
THIS IS THE *LAST* TIME YOU GET AWAY WITH YOUR BEHAVIOR.
I TRIED TO WARN HIM FOR YEARS, BUT ARTHUR NEVER BUDGED. I KNEW YOU WERE DANGEROUS...
AND I'M GLAD *I'M* THE ONE WHO GETS TO SAVE THIS PEACEFUL WORLD FROM YOUR...
...WHAT IS...
GASP!
NNNNNNGH.

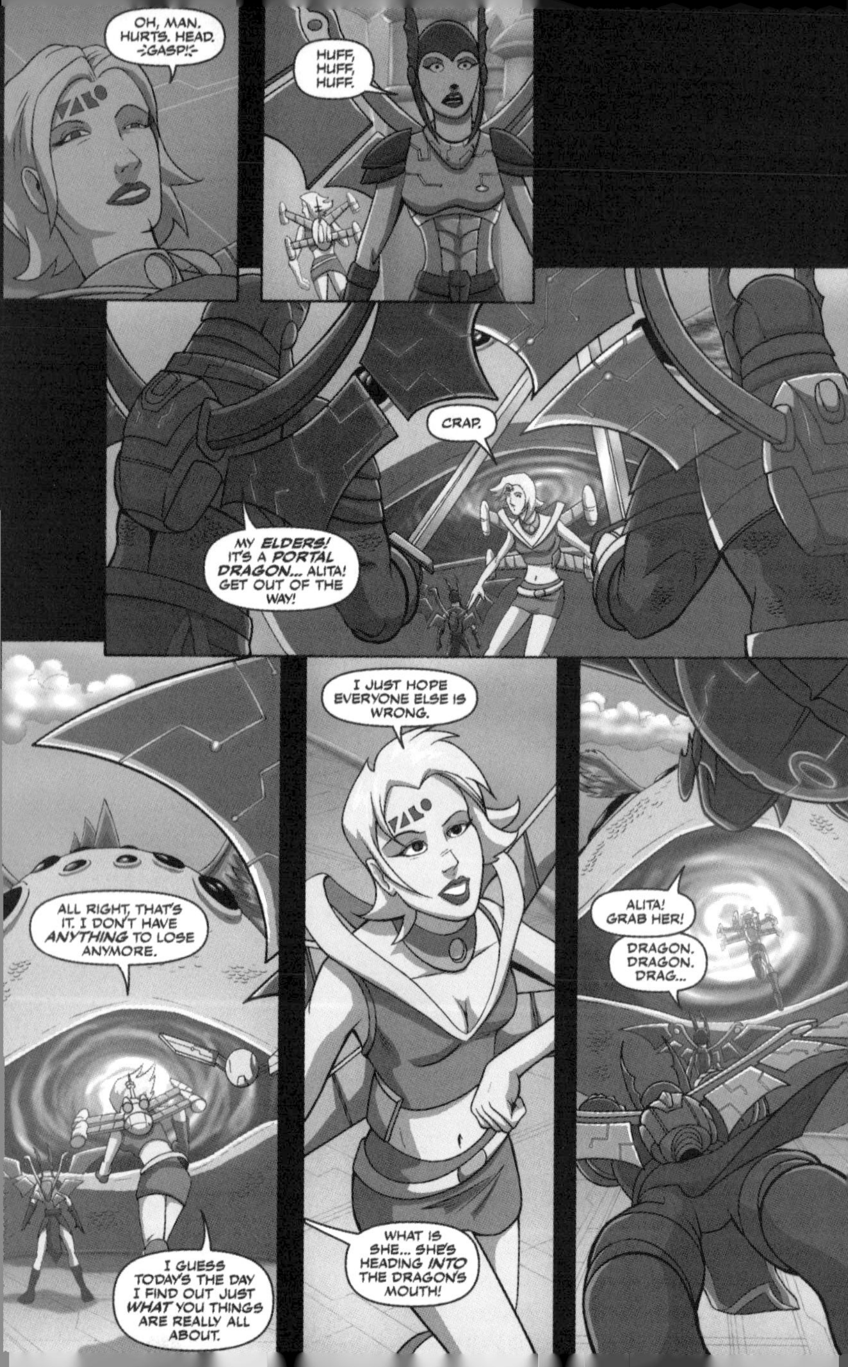
OH, MAN. HURTS. HEAD. -GASP!-
HUFF, HUFF, HUFF.
CRAP.
MY ELDERS! IT'S A PORTAL DRAGON... ALITA! GET OUT OF THE WAY!
ALL RIGHT, THAT'S IT. I DON'T HAVE ANYTHING TO LOSE ANYMORE.
I GUESS TODAY'S THE DAY I FIND OUT JUST WHAT YOU THINGS ARE REALLY ALL ABOUT.
I JUST HOPE EVERYONE ELSE IS WRONG.
WHAT IS SHE... SHE'S HEADING INTO THE DRAGON'S MOUTH!
ALITA! GRAB HER!
DRAGON. DRAGON. DRAG...

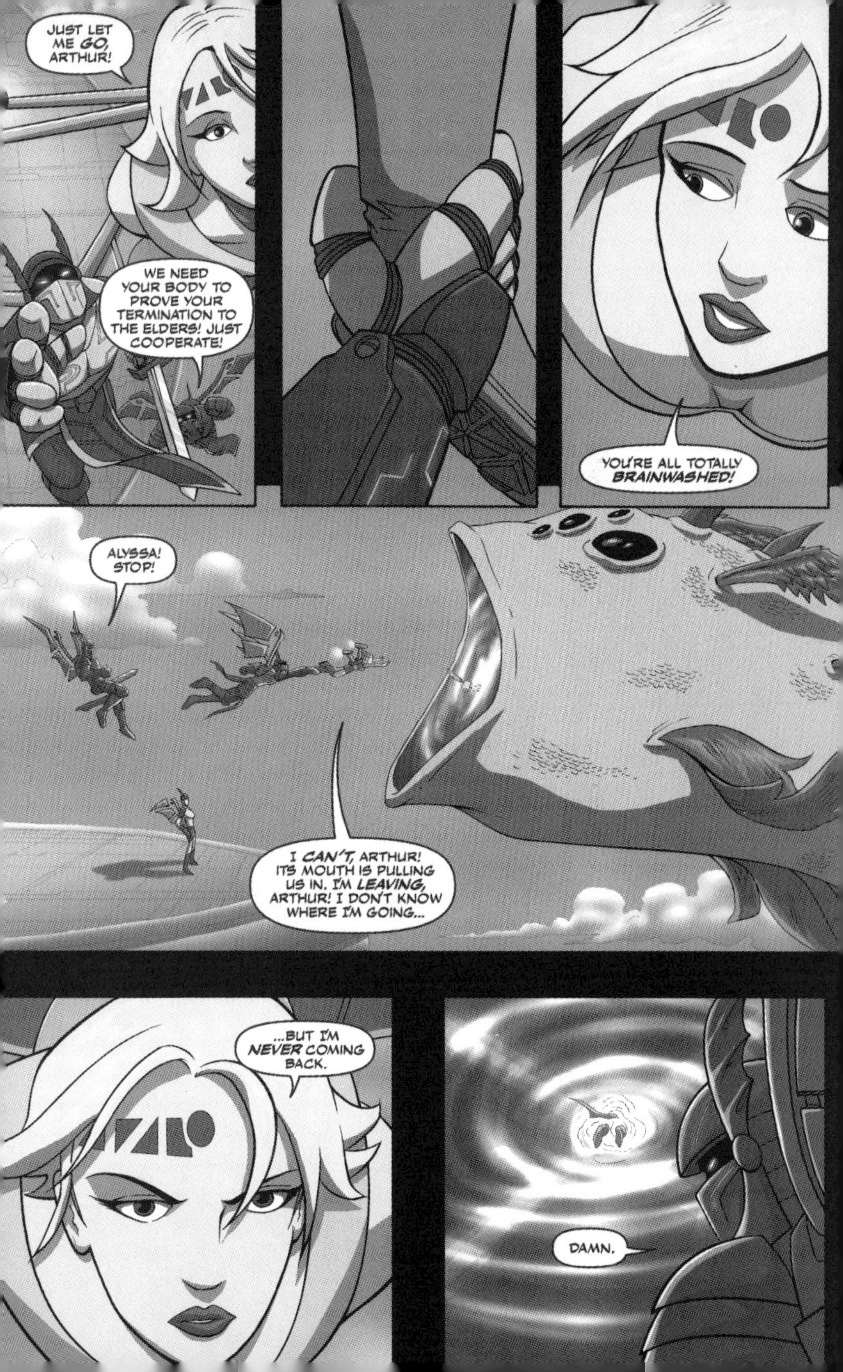
JUST LET ME GO, ARTHUR!
WE NEED YOUR BODY TO PROVE YOUR TERMINATION TO THE ELDERS! JUST COOPERATE!
YOU'RE ALL TOTALLY BRAINWASHED!
ALYSSA! STOP!
I CAN'T, ARTHUR! ITS MOUTH IS PULLING US IN. I'M LEAVING, ARTHUR! I DON'T KNOW WHERE I'M GOING...
...BUT I'M NEVER COMING BACK.
DAMN.

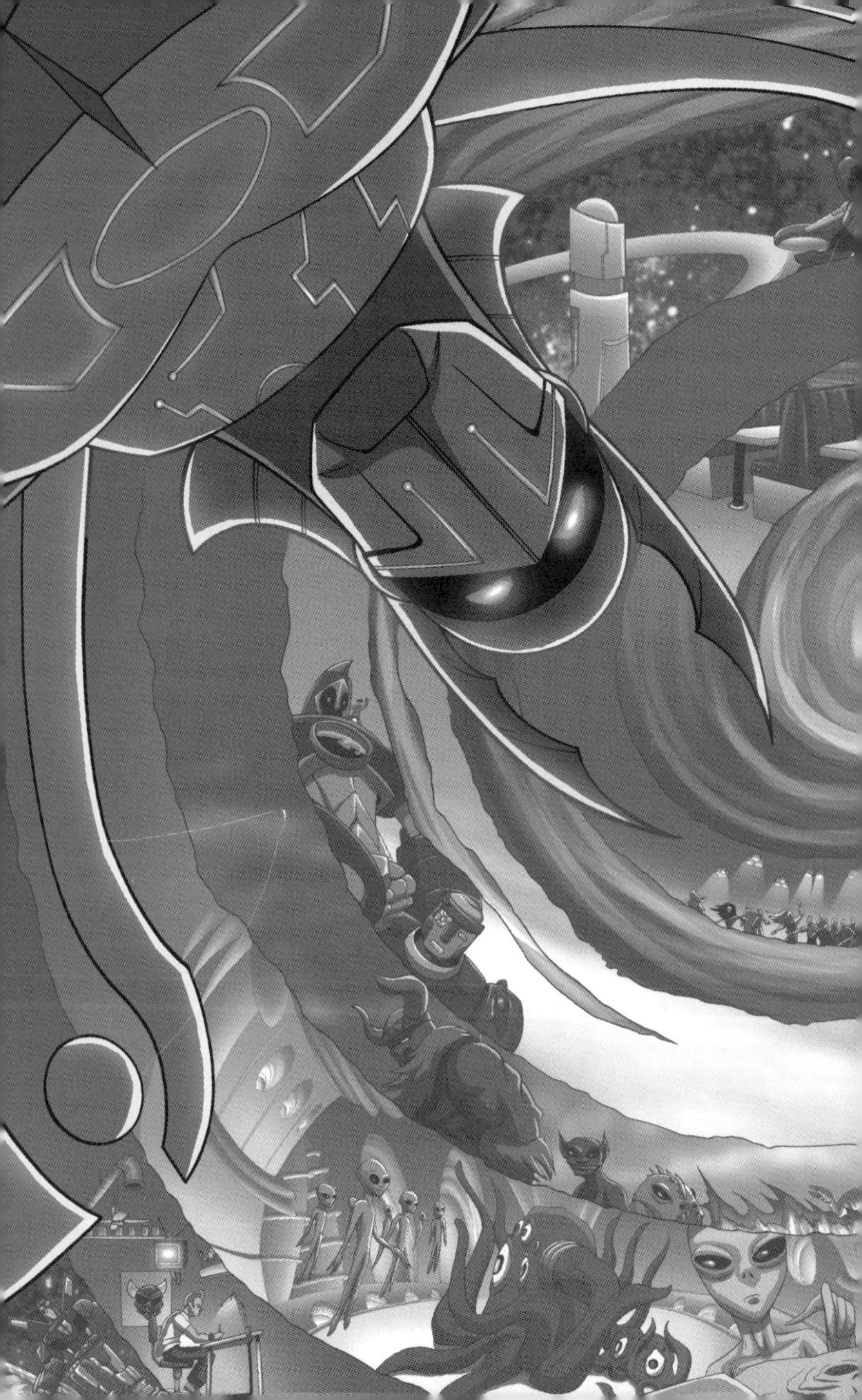

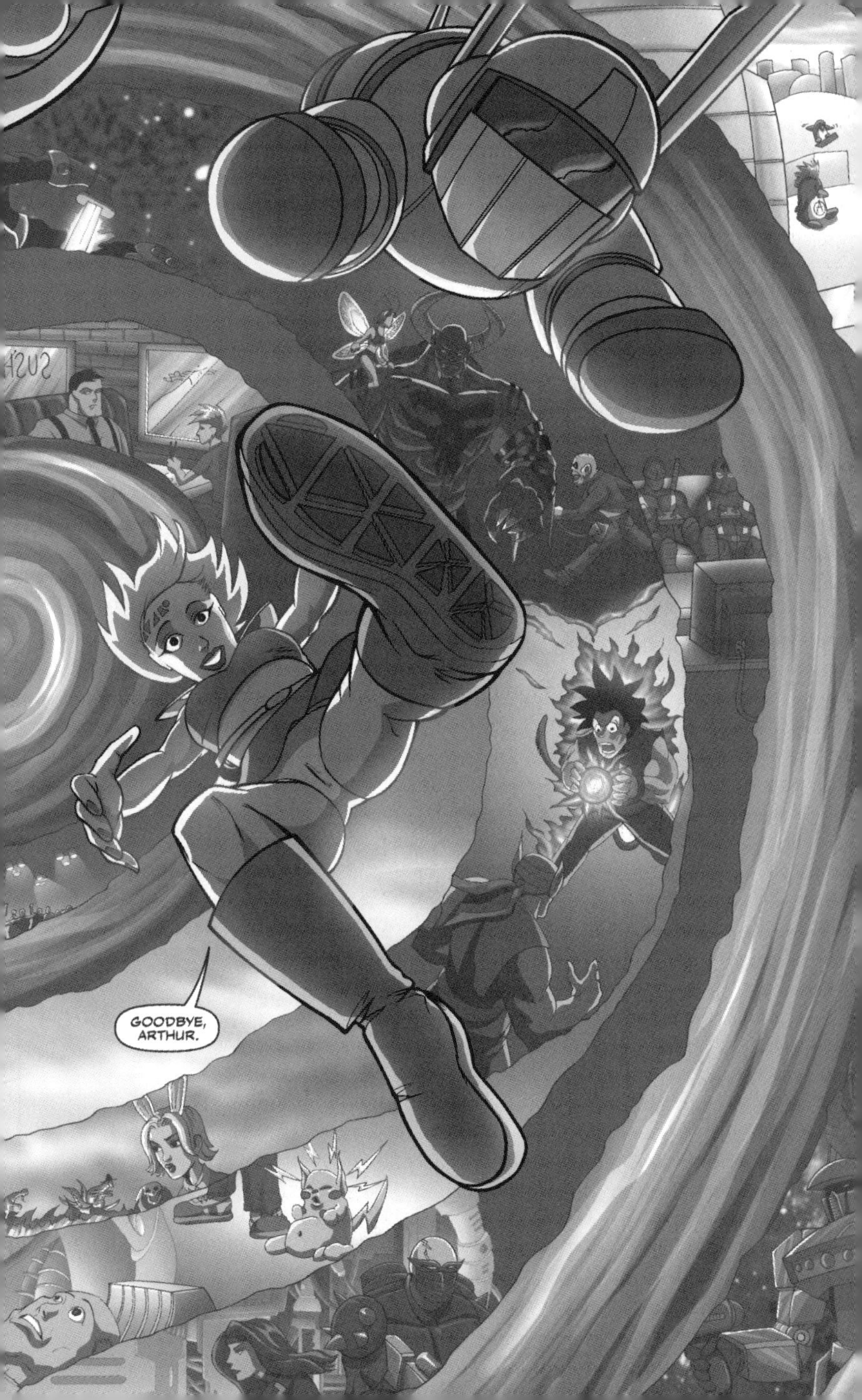
GOODBYE, ARTHUR.

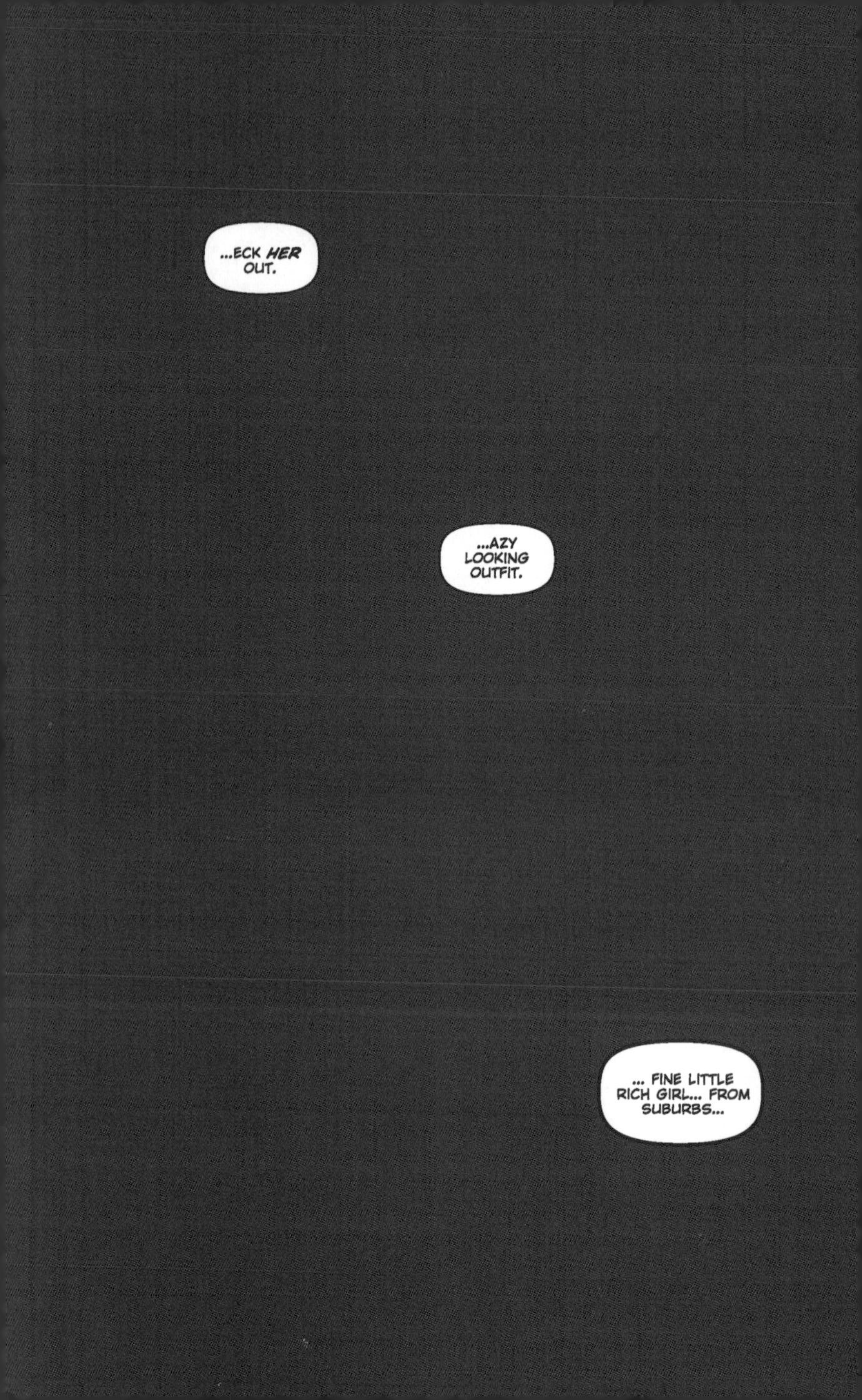
...ECK HER OUT.
...AZY LOOKING OUTFIT.
... FINE LITTLE RICH GIRL... FROM SUBURBS...

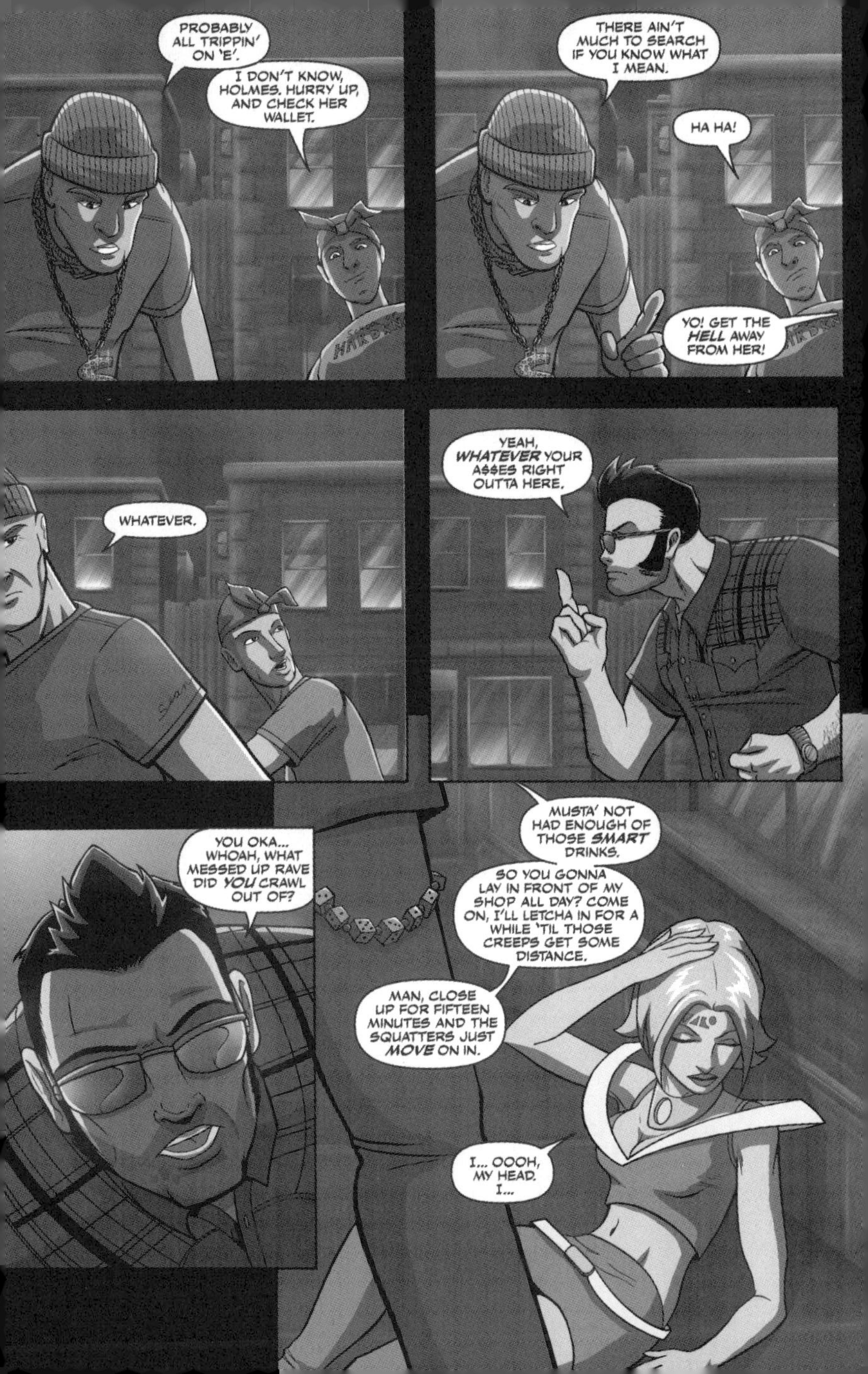
PROBABLY ALL TRIPPIN' ON 'E'.
I DON'T KNOW, HOLMES. HURRY UP, AND CHECK HER WALLET.
THERE AIN'T MUCH TO SEARCH IF YOU KNOW WHAT I MEAN.
HA HA!
YO! GET THE HELL AWAY FROM HER!
WHATEVER.
YEAH, WHATEVER YOUR A$$ES RIGHT OUTTA HERE.
YOU OKA... WHOAH, WHAT MESSED UP RAVE DID YOU CRAWL OUT OF?
MUSTA' NOT HAD ENOUGH OF THOSE SMART DRINKS.
SO YOU GONNA LAY IN FRONT OF MY SHOP ALL DAY? COME ON, I'LL LETCHA IN FOR A WHILE 'TIL THOSE CREEPS GET SOME DISTANCE.
MAN, CLOSE UP FOR FIFTEEN MINUTES AND THE SQUATTERS JUST MOVE ON IN.
I... OOOH, MY HEAD. I...

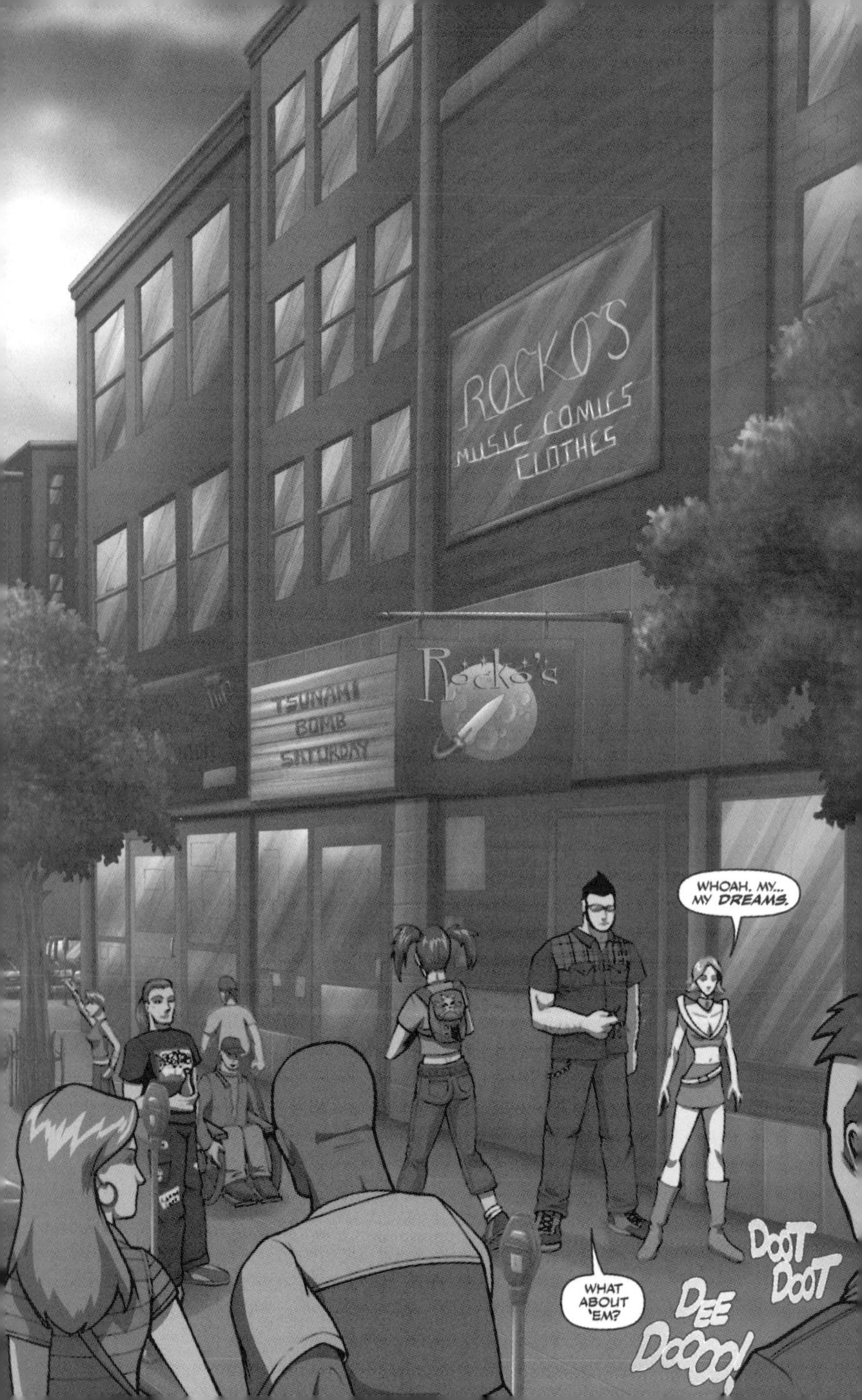
ROCKO'S
MUSIC COMICS
CLOTHES
Rocko's
TSUNAMI
BOMB
SATURDAY
WHOAH, MY... MY *DREAMS.*
WHAT ABOUT 'EM?
DOOT DOOT
DEE DOOOO!

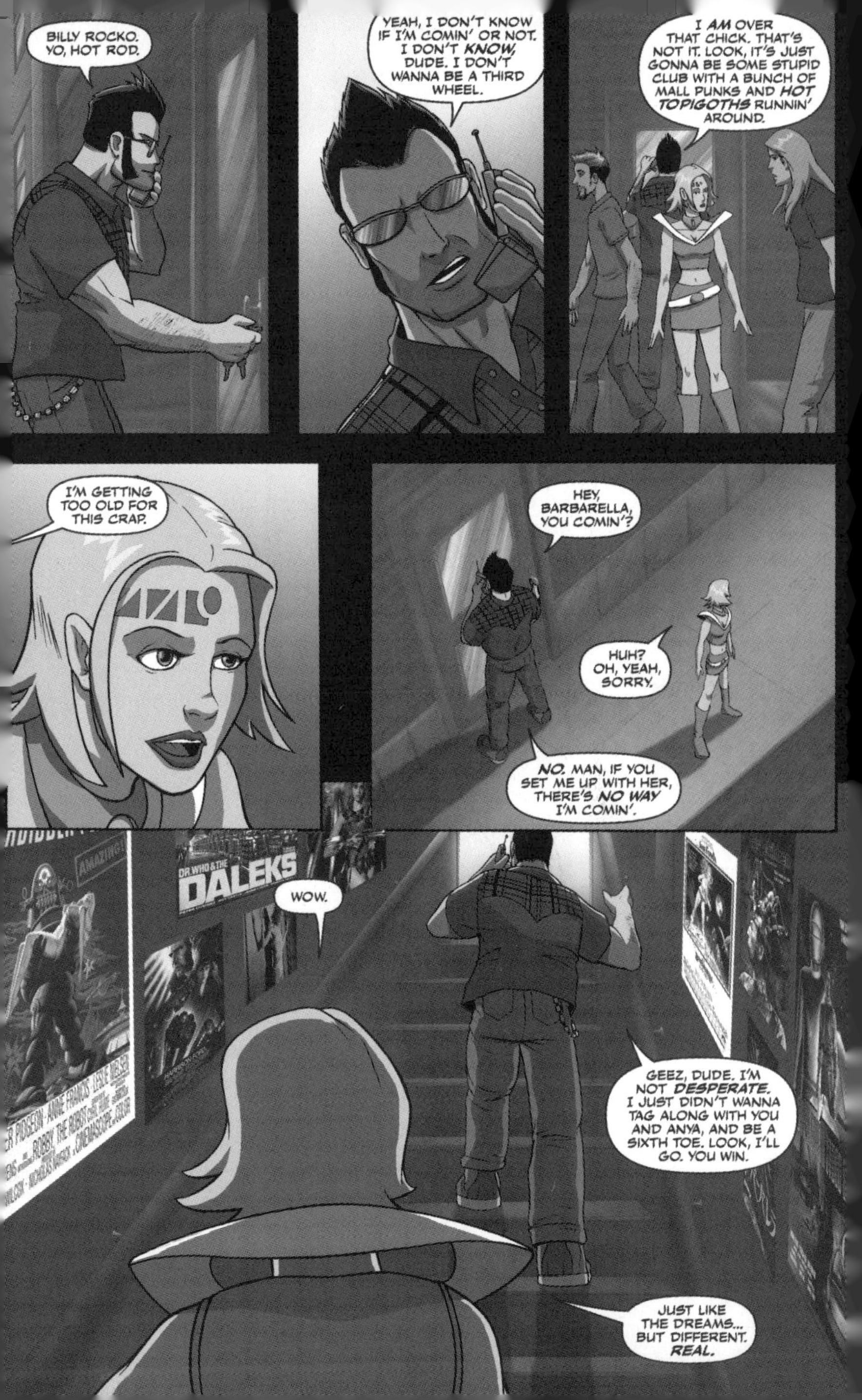
BILLY ROCKO. YO, HOT ROD.
YEAH, I DON'T KNOW IF I'M COMIN' OR NOT. I DON'T *KNOW,* DUDE. I DON'T WANNA BE A THIRD WHEEL.
I *AM* OVER THAT CHICK. THAT'S NOT IT. LOOK, IT'S JUST GONNA BE SOME STUPID CLUB WITH A BUNCH OF MALL PUNKS AND *HOT TOPIGOTHS* RUNNIN' AROUND.
I'M GETTING TOO OLD FOR THIS CRAP.
HEY, BARBARELLA, YOU COMIN'?
HUH? OH, YEAH, SORRY.
NO. MAN, IF YOU SET ME UP WITH HER, THERE'S *NO WAY* I'M COMIN'.
DR. WHO & THE DALEKS
WOW.
GEEZ, DUDE. I'M NOT *DESPERATE.* I JUST DIDN'T WANNA TAG ALONG WITH YOU AND ANYA, AND BE A SIXTH TOE. LOOK, I'LL GO. YOU WIN.
JUST LIKE THE DREAMS... BUT DIFFERENT. *REAL.*

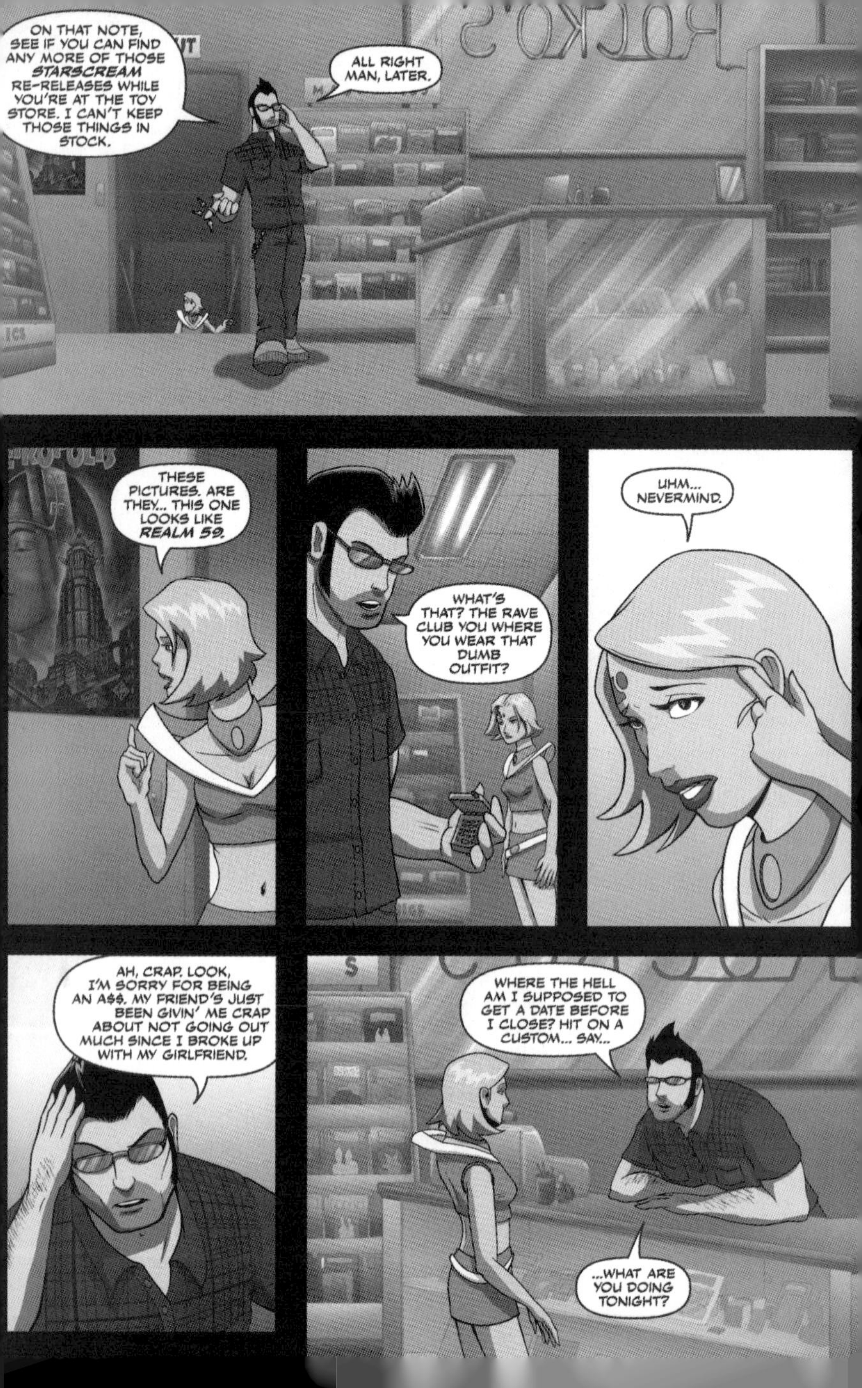
ON THAT NOTE, SEE IF YOU CAN FIND ANY MORE OF THOSE STARSCREAM RE-RELEASES WHILE YOU'RE AT THE TOY STORE. I CAN'T KEEP THOSE THINGS IN STOCK.
ALL RIGHT MAN, LATER.
THESE PICTURES. ARE THEY... THIS ONE LOOKS LIKE REALM 59.
WHAT'S THAT? THE RAVE CLUB YOU WEAR WHERE YOU WEAR THAT DUMB OUTFIT?
UHM... NEVERMIND.
AH, CRAP. LOOK, I'M SORRY FOR BEING AN A$$. MY FRIEND'S JUST BEEN GIVIN' ME CRAP ABOUT NOT GOING OUT MUCH SINCE I BROKE UP WITH MY GIRLFRIEND.
WHERE THE HELL AM I SUPPOSED TO GET A DATE BEFORE I CLOSE? HIT ON A CUSTOM... SAY...
...WHAT ARE YOU DOING TONIGHT?

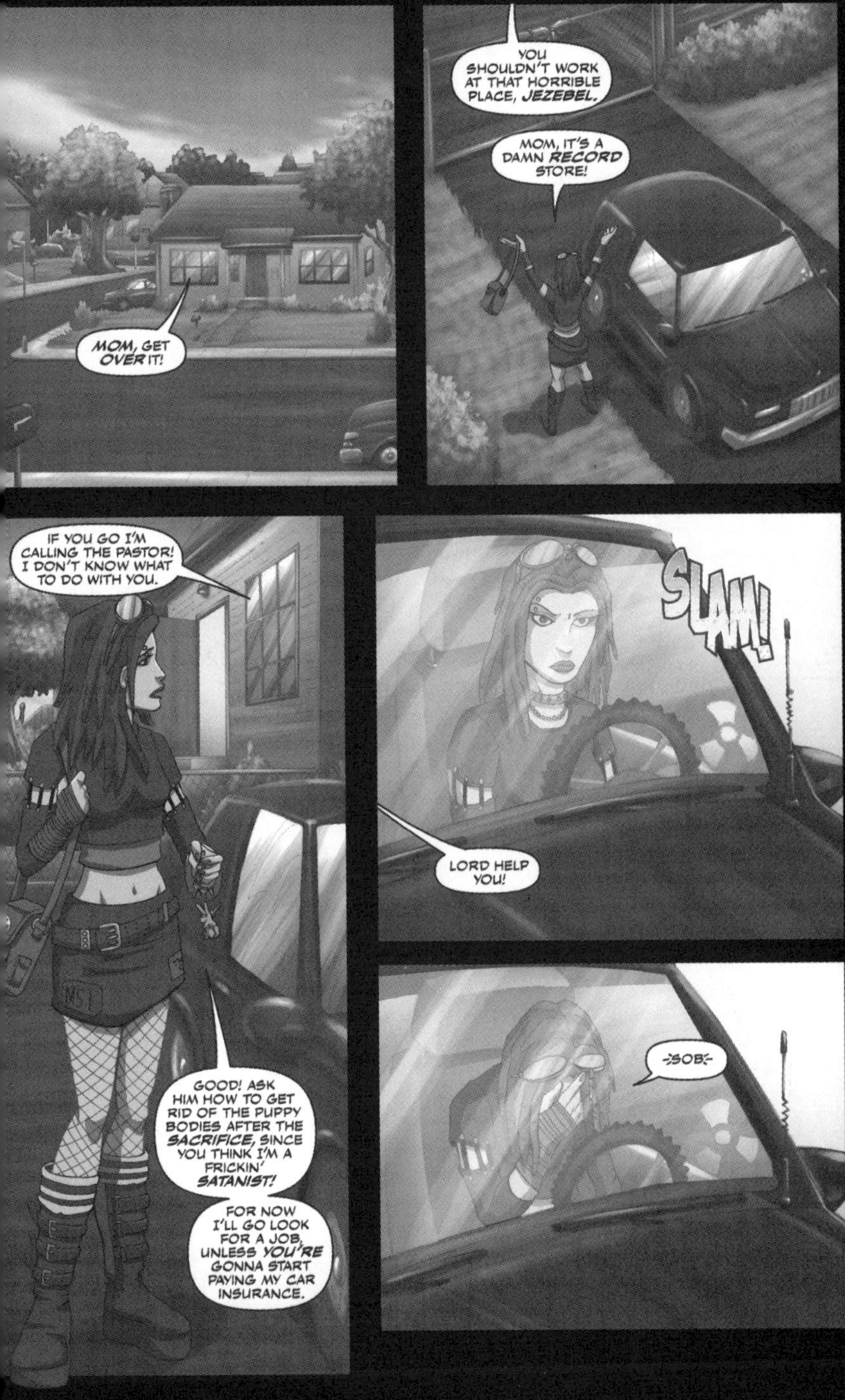
MOM, GET OVER IT!
YOU SHOULDN'T WORK AT THAT HORRIBLE PLACE, JEZEBEL.
MOM, IT'S A DAMN RECORD STORE!
IF YOU GO I'M CALLING THE PASTOR! I DON'T KNOW WHAT TO DO WITH YOU.
GOOD! ASK HIM HOW TO GET RID OF THE PUPPY BODIES AFTER THE SACRIFICE, SINCE YOU THINK I'M A FRICKIN' SATANIST!
FOR NOW I'LL GO LOOK FOR A JOB, UNLESS YOU'RE GONNA START PAYING MY CAR INSURANCE.
SLAM!
LORD HELP YOU!
-SOB-

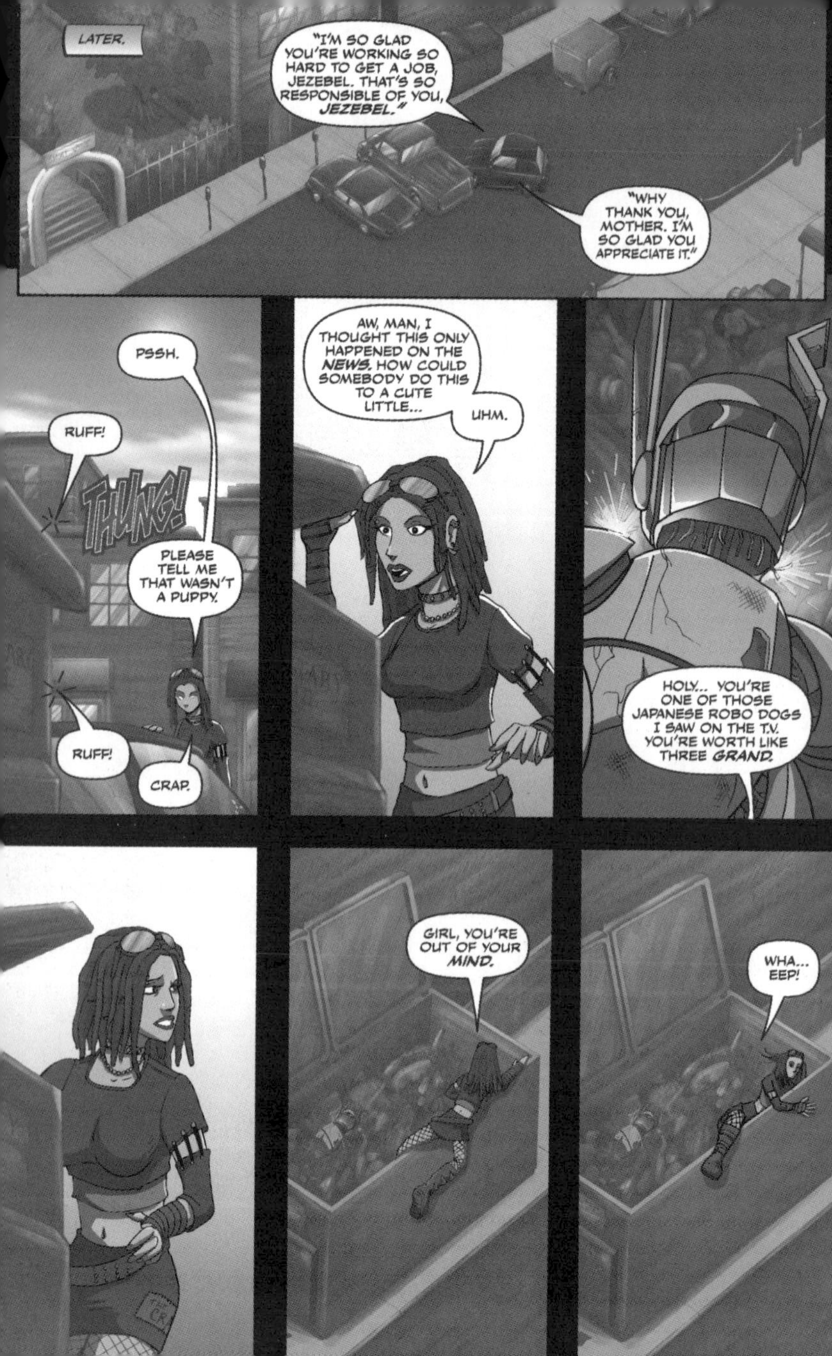
LATER.
"I'M SO GLAD YOU'RE WORKING SO HARD TO GET A JOB, JEZEBEL. THAT'S SO RESPONSIBLE OF YOU, JEZEBEL."
"WHY THANK YOU, MOTHER. I'M SO GLAD YOU APPRECIATE IT."
PSSH.
RUFF!
THUNG!
PLEASE TELL ME THAT WASN'T A PUPPY.
RUFF!
CRAP.
AW, MAN, I THOUGHT THIS ONLY HAPPENED ON THE NEWS. HOW COULD SOMEBODY DO THIS TO A CUTE LITTLE...
UHM.
HOLY... YOU'RE ONE OF THOSE JAPANESE ROBO DOGS I SAW ON THE T.V. YOU'RE WORTH LIKE THREE GRAND.
GIRL, YOU'RE OUT OF YOUR MIND.
WHA... EEP!

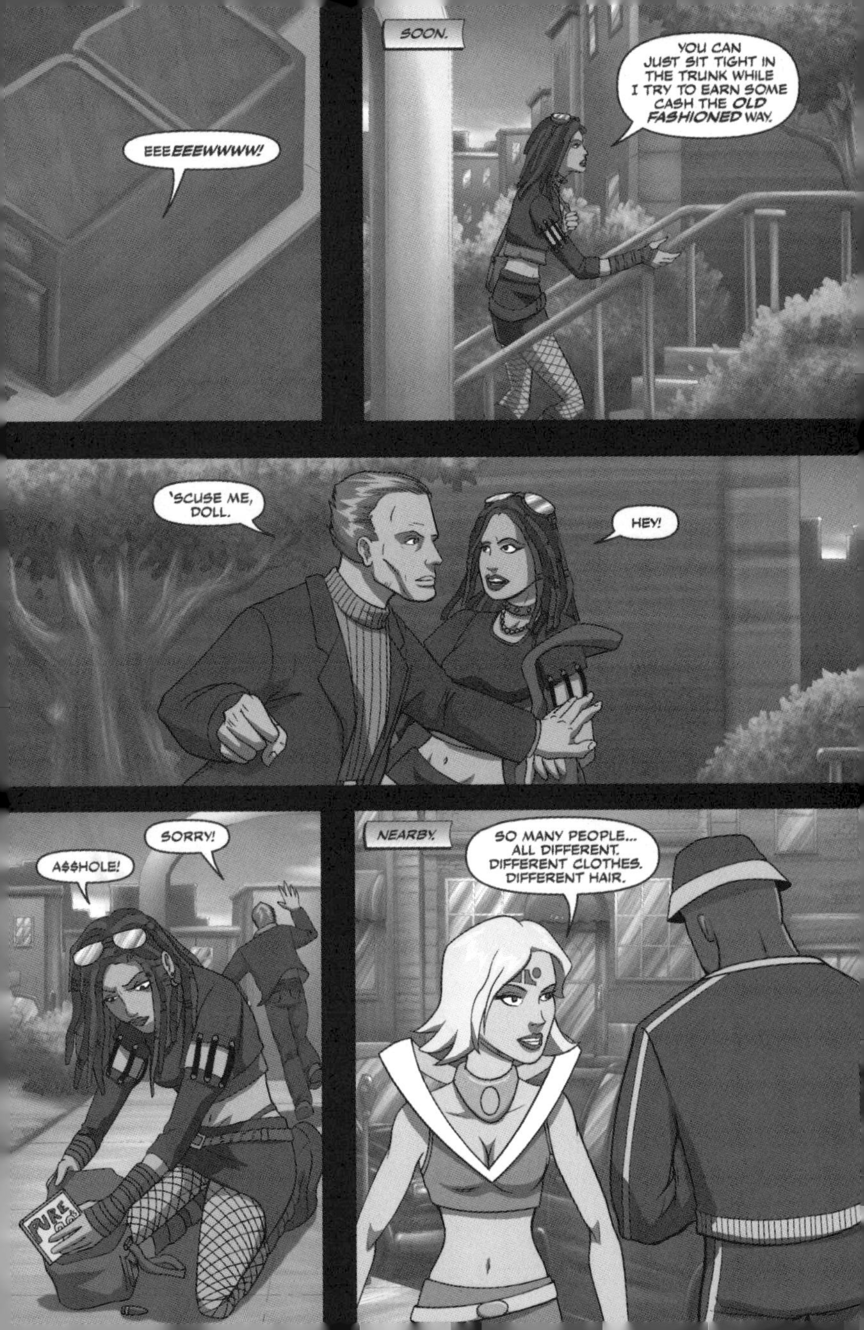
EEEEEEWWWW!
SOON.
YOU CAN JUST SIT TIGHT IN THE TRUNK WHILE I TRY TO EARN SOME CASH THE *OLD FASHIONED* WAY.
'SCUSE ME, DOLL.
HEY!
SORRY!
A$$HOLE!
NEARBY.
SO MANY PEOPLE... ALL DIFFERENT. DIFFERENT CLOTHES. DIFFERENT HAIR.

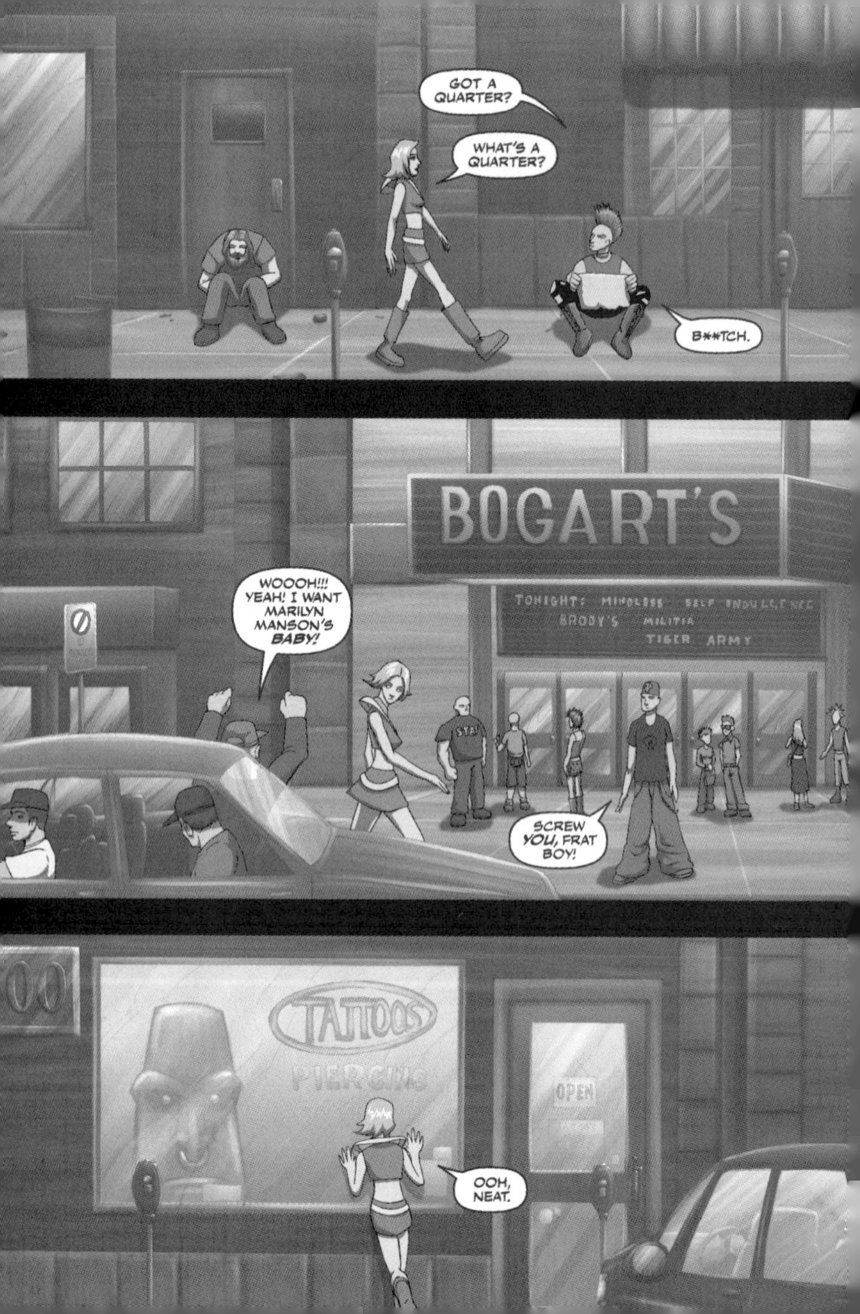
GOT A QUARTER?
WHAT'S A QUARTER?
B**TCH.
BOGART'S
TONIGHT: MINDLESS SELF INDULGENCE
BRODY'S MILITIA
TIGER ARMY
WOOOH!!! YEAH! I WANT MARILYN MANSON'S *BABY!*
SCREW *YOU,* FRAT BOY!
TATTOOS
PIERCING
OPEN
OOH, NEAT.

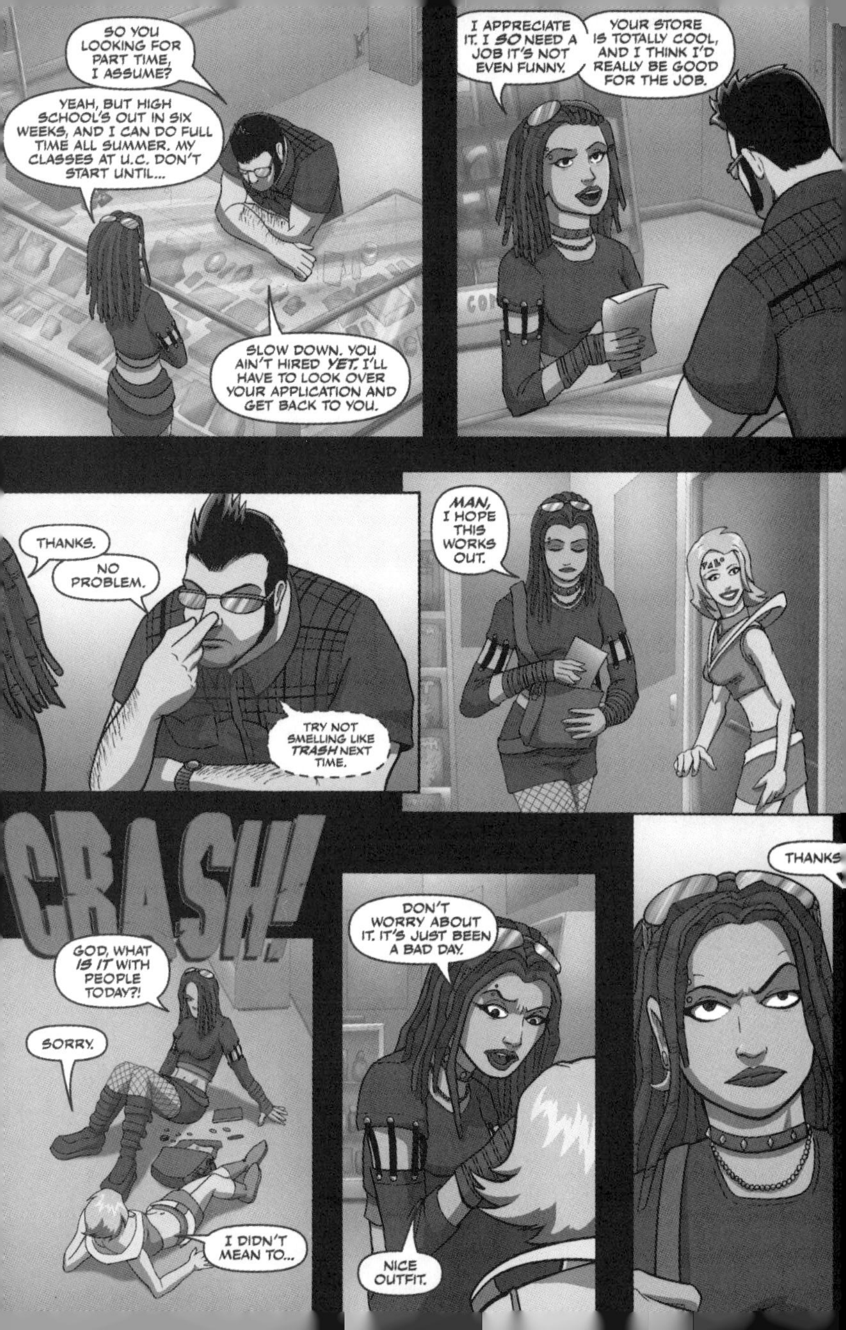
SO YOU LOOKING FOR PART TIME, I ASSUME?
YEAH, BUT HIGH SCHOOL'S OUT IN SIX WEEKS, AND I CAN DO FULL TIME ALL SUMMER. MY CLASSES AT U.C. DON'T START UNTIL...
SLOW DOWN. YOU AIN'T HIRED YET. I'LL HAVE TO LOOK OVER YOUR APPLICATION AND GET BACK TO YOU.
I APPRECIATE IT. I SO NEED A JOB IT'S NOT EVEN FUNNY.
YOUR STORE IS TOTALLY COOL, AND I THINK I'D REALLY BE GOOD FOR THE JOB.
THANKS.
NO PROBLEM.
TRY NOT SMELLING LIKE TRASH NEXT TIME.
MAN, I HOPE THIS WORKS OUT.
CRASH!
GOD, WHAT IS IT WITH PEOPLE TODAY?!
SORRY.
I DIDN'T MEAN TO...
DON'T WORRY ABOUT IT. IT'S JUST BEEN A BAD DAY.
NICE OUTFIT.
THANKS

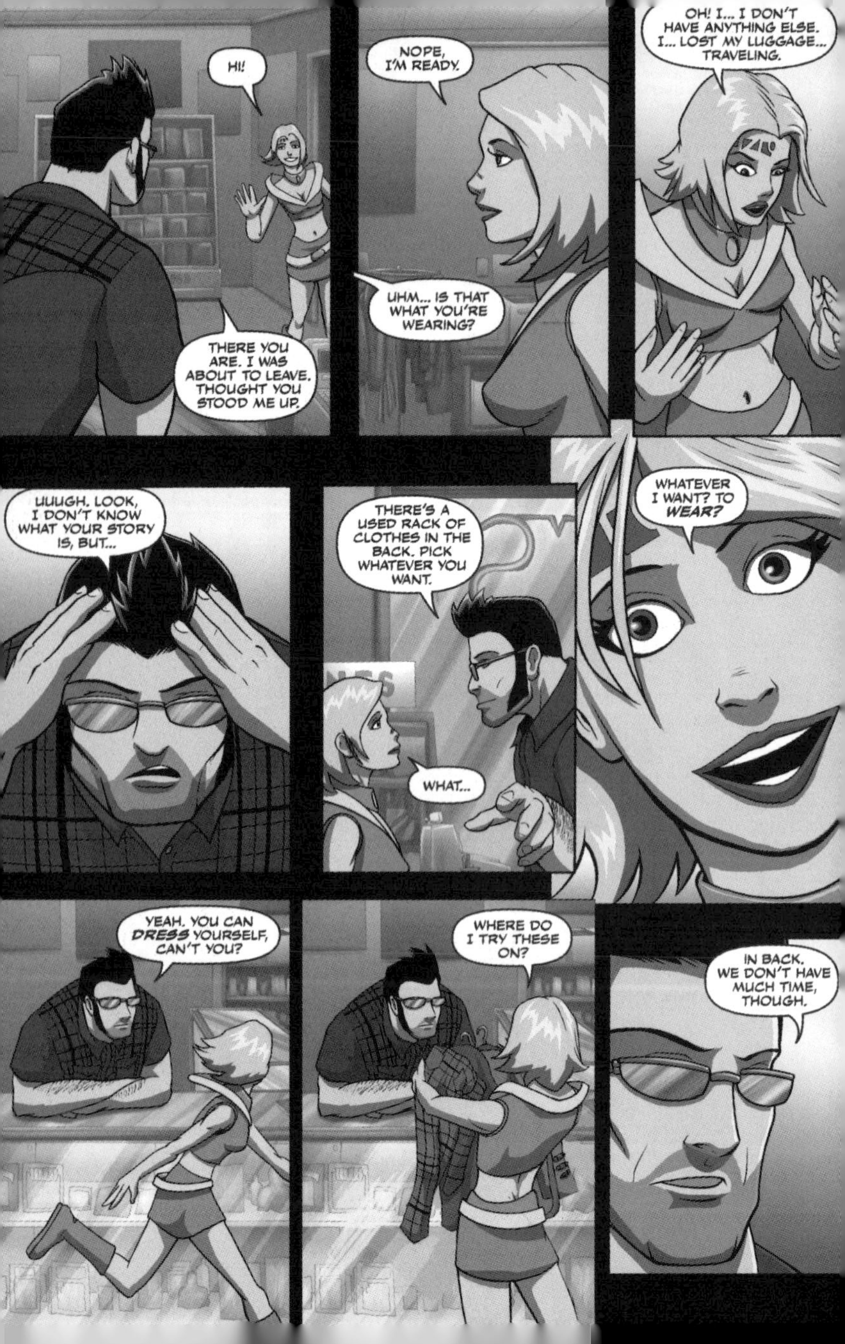
HI!
THERE YOU ARE. I WAS ABOUT TO LEAVE. THOUGHT YOU STOOD ME UP.
NOPE, I'M READY.
UHM... IS THAT WHAT YOU'RE WEARING?
OH! I... I DON'T HAVE ANYTHING ELSE. I... LOST MY LUGGAGE... TRAVELING.
UUUGH. LOOK, I DON'T KNOW WHAT YOUR STORY IS, BUT...
THERE'S A USED RACK OF CLOTHES IN THE BACK. PICK WHATEVER YOU WANT.
WHAT...
WHATEVER I WANT? TO WEAR?
YEAH. YOU CAN DRESS YOURSELF, CAN'T YOU?
WHERE DO I TRY THESE ON?
IN BACK. WE DON'T HAVE MUCH TIME, THOUGH.

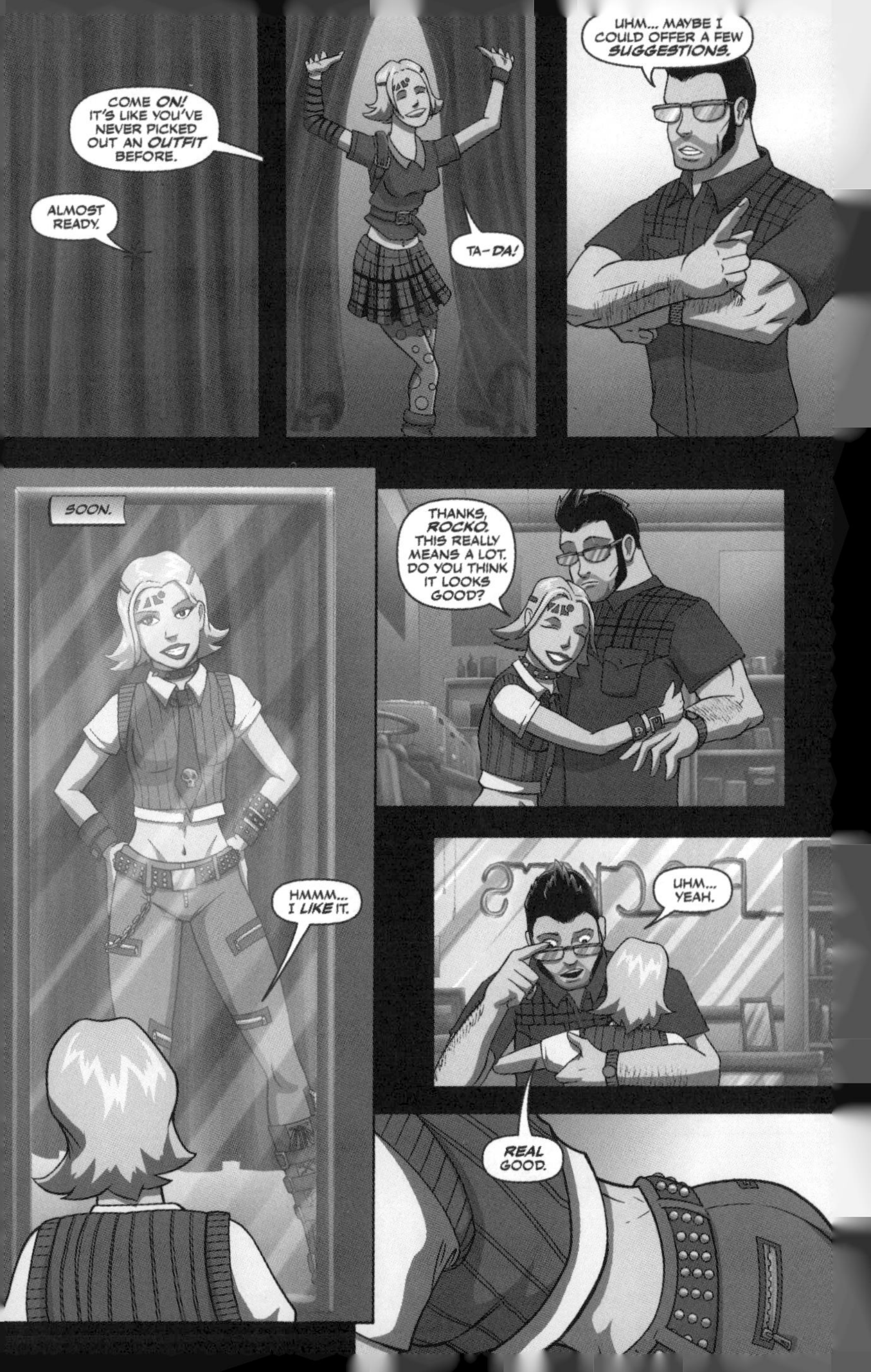
COME ON! IT'S LIKE YOU'VE NEVER PICKED OUT AN OUTFIT BEFORE.
ALMOST READY.
TA-DA!
UHM... MAYBE I COULD OFFER A FEW SUGGESTIONS.
SOON.
HMMM... I LIKE IT.
THANKS, ROCKO. THIS REALLY MEANS A LOT. DO YOU THINK IT LOOKS GOOD?
UHM... YEAH.
REAL GOOD.

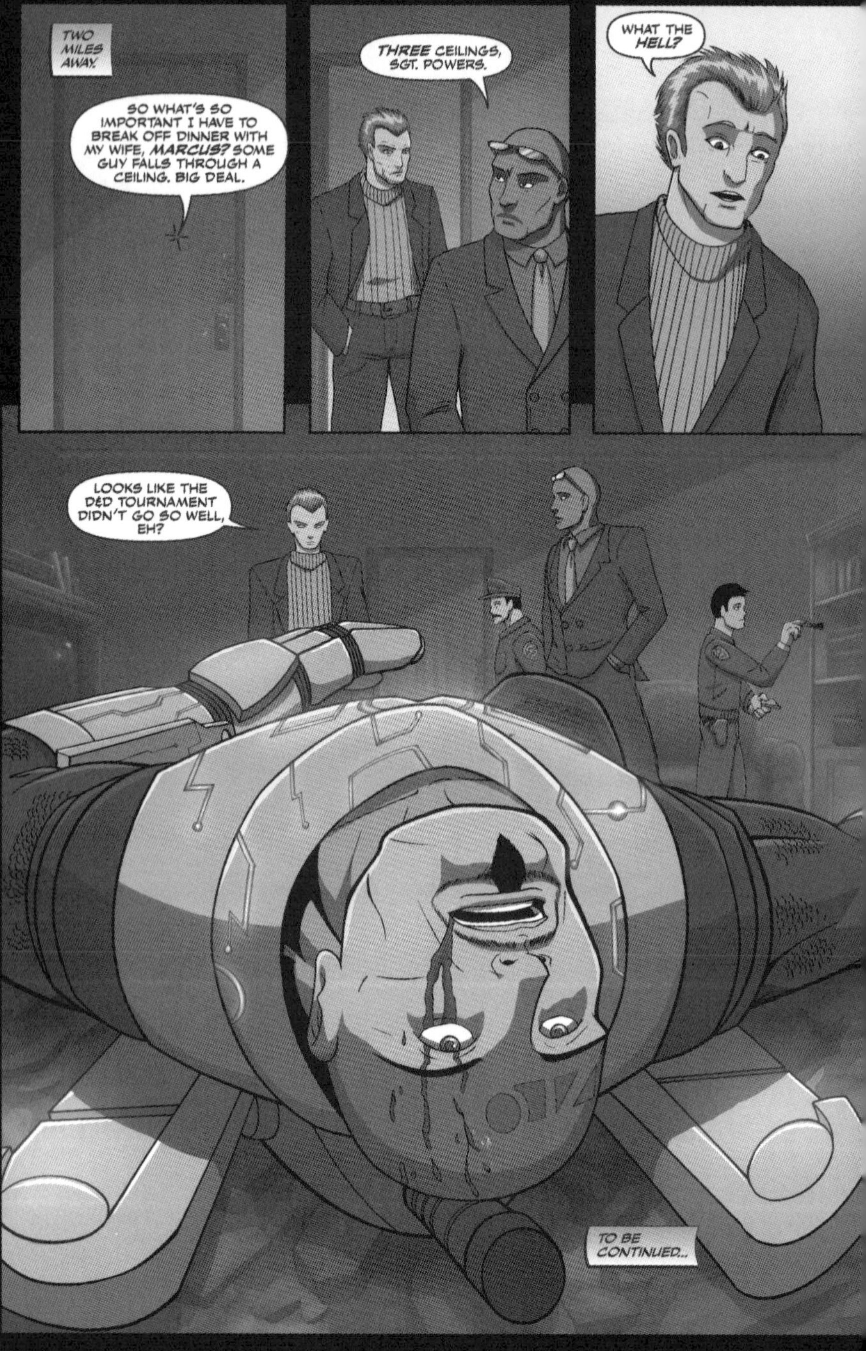
TWO MILES AWAY.
SO WHAT'S SO IMPORTANT I HAVE TO BREAK OFF DINNER WITH MY WIFE, MARCUS? SOME GUY FALLS THROUGH A CEILING. BIG DEAL.
THREE CEILINGS, SGT. POWERS.
WHAT THE HELL?
LOOKS LIKE THE D&D TOURNAMENT DIDN'T GO SO WELL, EH?
TO BE CONTINUED...

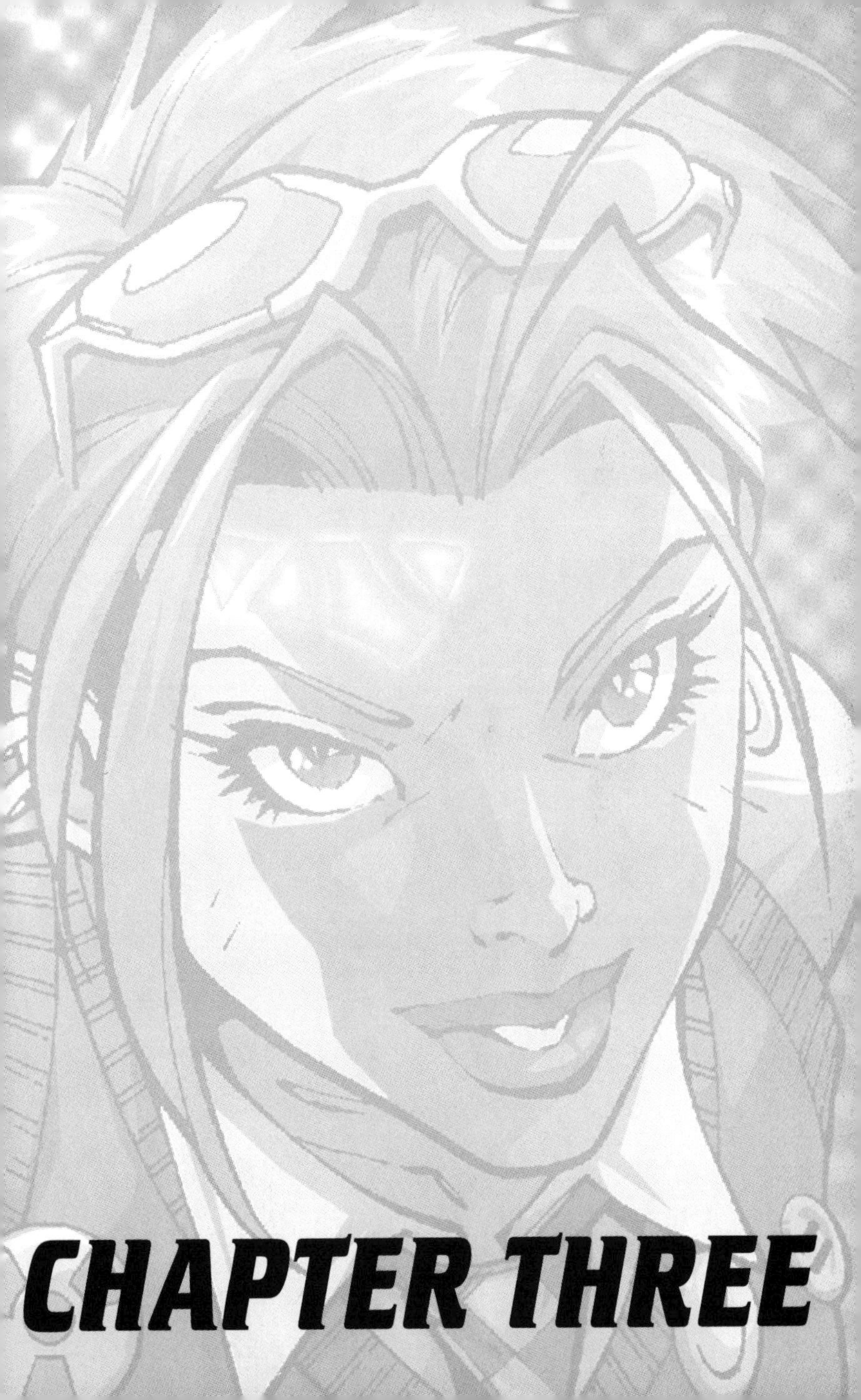

CHAPTER THREE

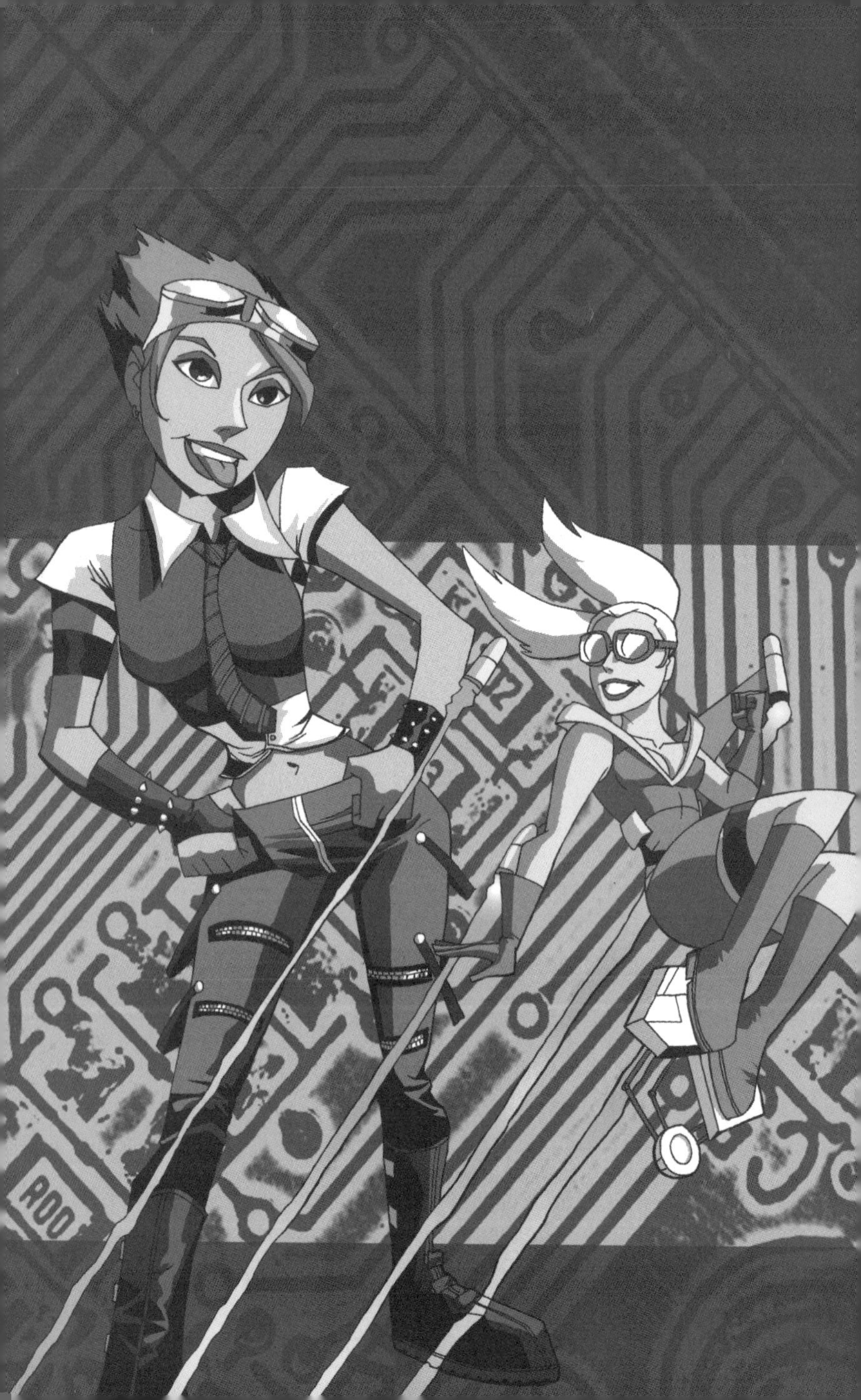
ROO

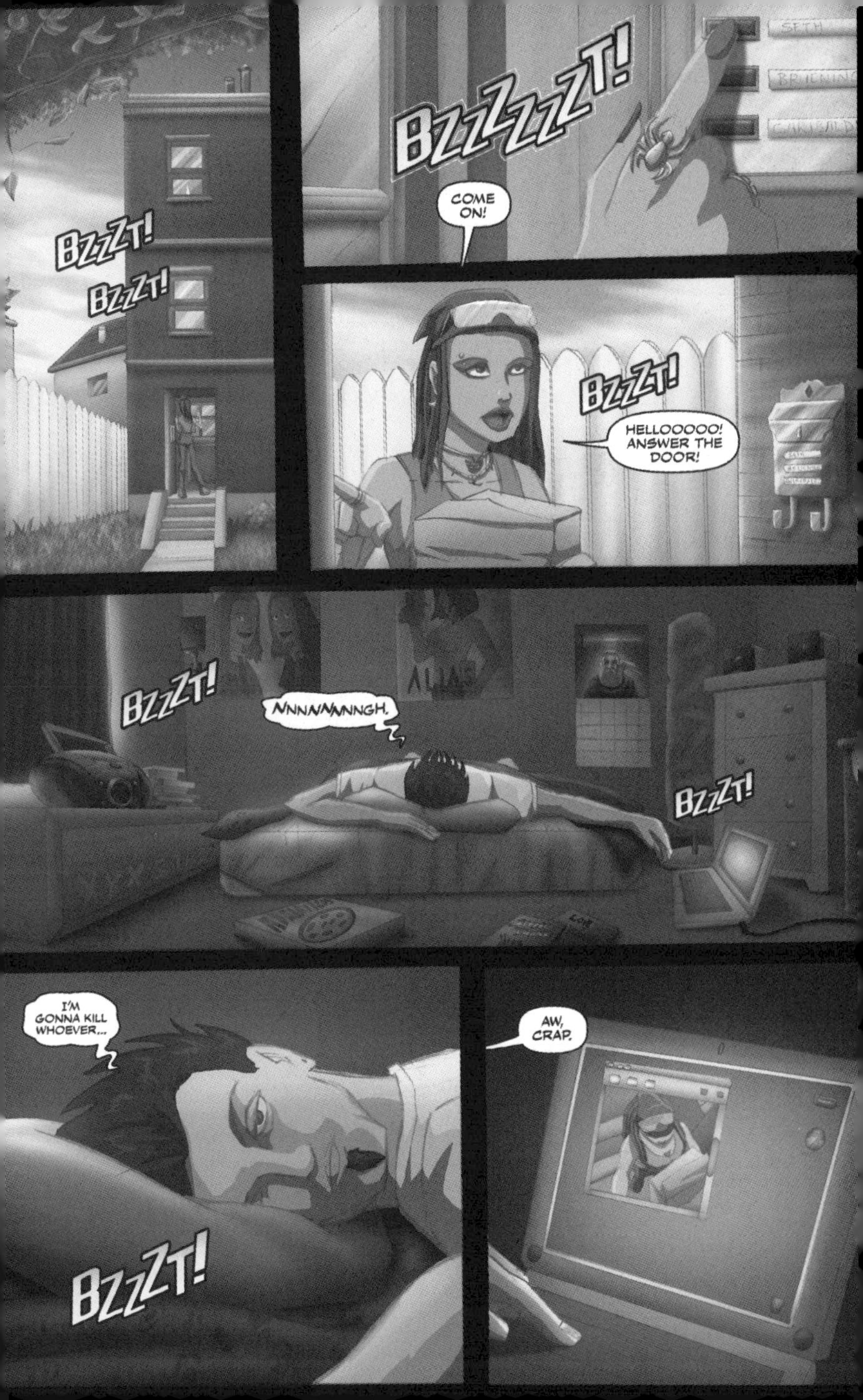
BZZZT!
BZZZT!
BZZZZZZZT!
COME ON!
BZZZT!
HELLOOOOO! ANSWER THE DOOR!
BZZZT!
NNNNNNNNGH.
BZZZT!
I'M GONNA KILL WHOEVER...
BZZZT!
AW, CRAP.

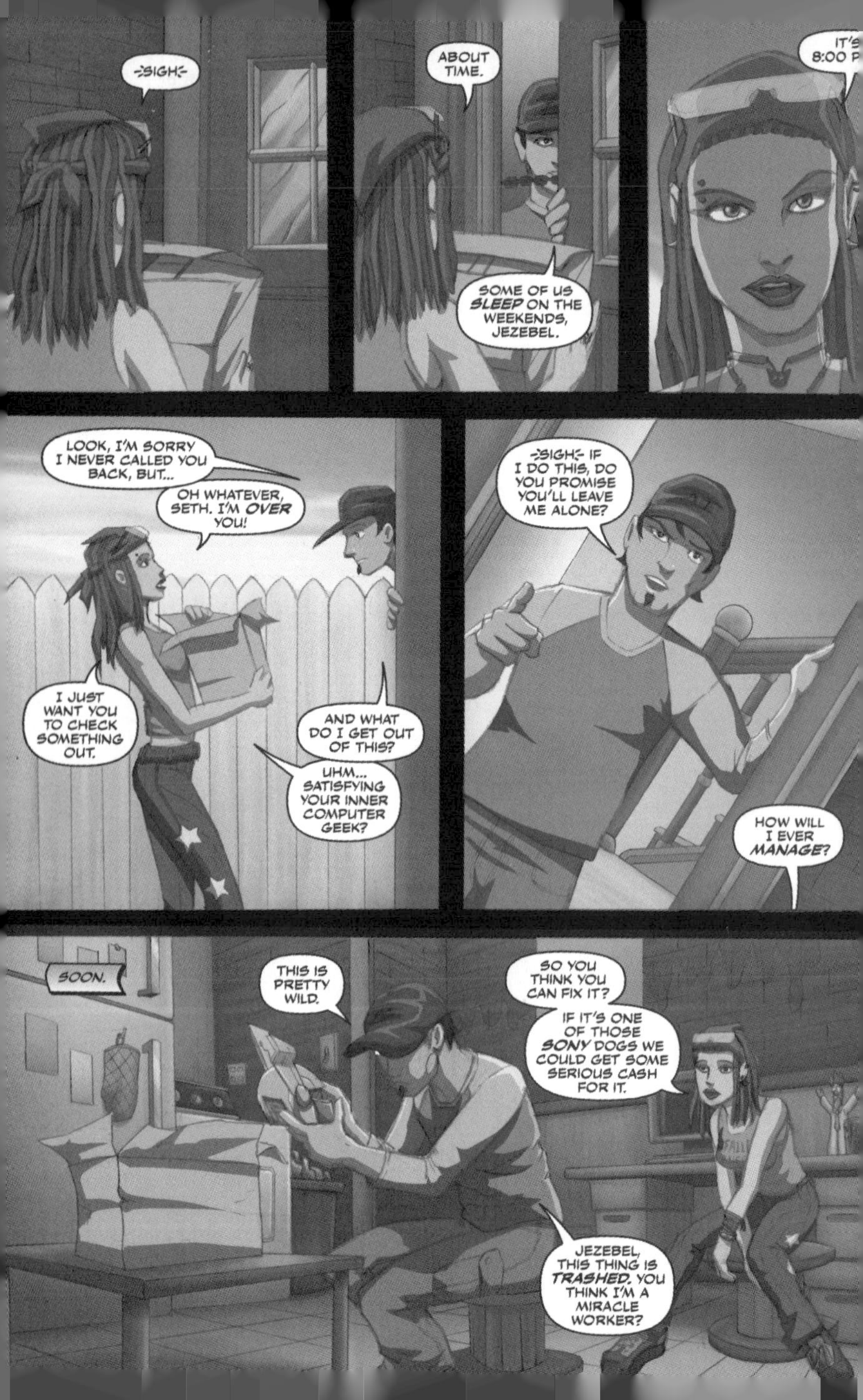
-SIGH-
ABOUT TIME.
SOME OF US *SLEEP* ON THE WEEKENDS, JEZEBEL.
IT'S 8:00 P
LOOK, I'M SORRY I NEVER CALLED YOU BACK, BUT...
OH WHATEVER, SETH. I'M *OVER* YOU!
I JUST WANT YOU TO CHECK SOMETHING OUT.
AND WHAT DO I GET OUT OF THIS?
UHM... SATISFYING YOUR INNER COMPUTER GEEK?
-SIGH- IF I DO THIS, DO YOU PROMISE YOU'LL LEAVE ME ALONE?
HOW WILL I EVER *MANAGE*?
SOON.
THIS IS PRETTY WILD.
SO YOU THINK YOU CAN FIX IT?
IF IT'S ONE OF THOSE *SONY* DOGS WE COULD GET SOME SERIOUS CASH FOR IT.
JEZEBEL, THIS THING IS *TRASHED.* YOU THINK I'M A MIRACLE WORKER?

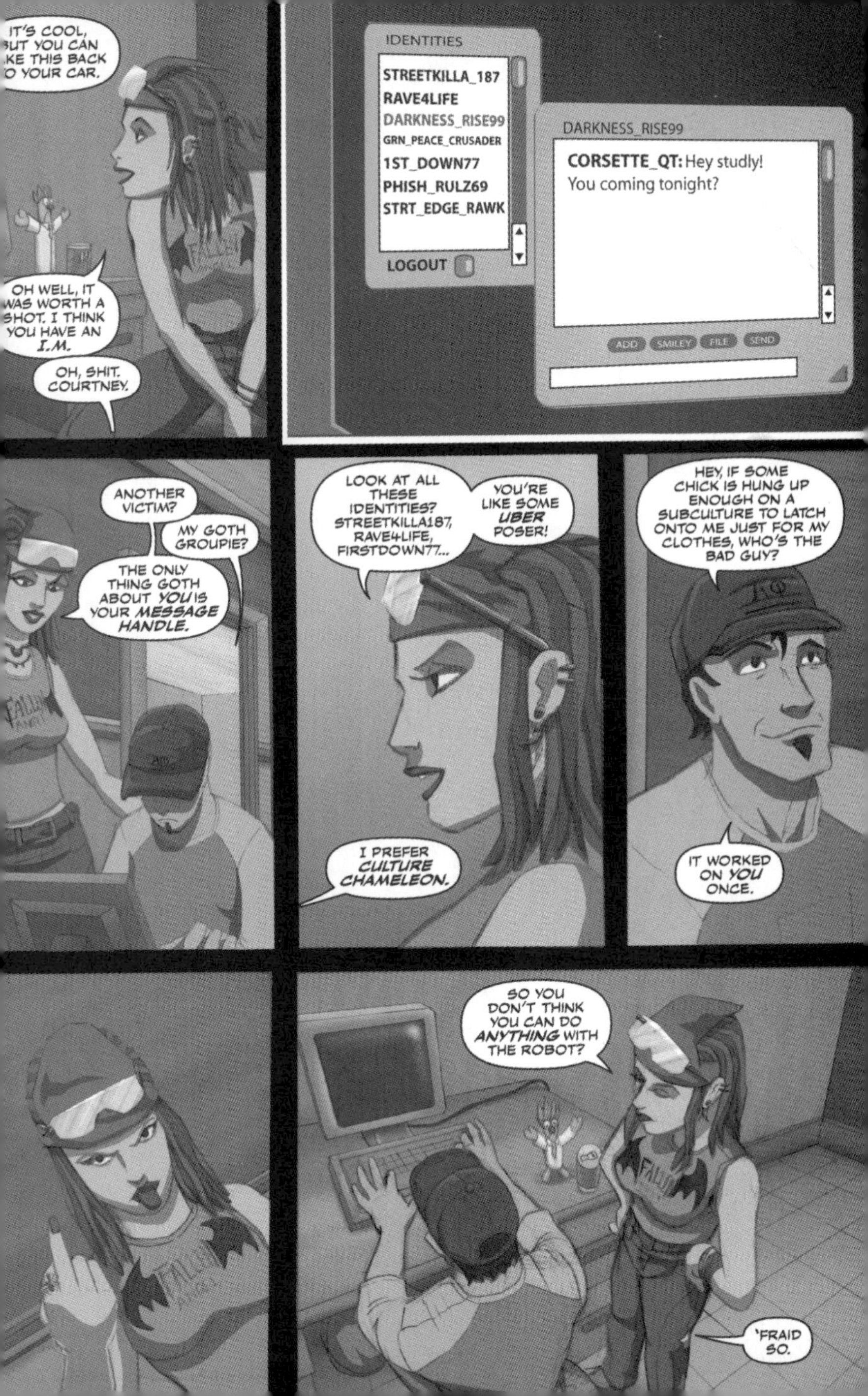
IT'S COOL, BUT YOU CAN TAKE THIS BACK TO YOUR CAR.
OH WELL, IT WAS WORTH A SHOT. I THINK YOU HAVE AN *I.M.*
OH, SHIT. COURTNEY.
IDENTITIES
STREETKILLA_187
RAVE4LIFE
DARKNESS_RISE99
GRN_PEACE_CRUSADER
1ST_DOWN77
PHISH_RULZ69
STRT_EDGE_RAWK
LOGOUT
DARKNESS_RISE99
CORSETTE_QT: Hey studly! You coming tonight?
ADD SMILEY FILE SEND
ANOTHER VICTIM?
MY GOTH GROUPIE?
THE ONLY THING GOTH ABOUT *YOU* IS YOUR *MESSAGE HANDLE.*
LOOK AT ALL THESE IDENTITIES? STREETKILLA187, RAVE4LIFE, FIRSTDOWN77...
YOU'RE LIKE SOME *UBER* POSER!
I PREFER *CULTURE CHAMELEON.*
HEY, IF SOME CHICK IS HUNG UP ENOUGH ON A SUBCULTURE TO LATCH ONTO ME JUST FOR MY CLOTHES, WHO'S THE BAD GUY?
IT WORKED ON *YOU* ONCE.
SO YOU DON'T THINK YOU CAN DO *ANYTHING* WITH THE ROBOT?
'FRAID SO.

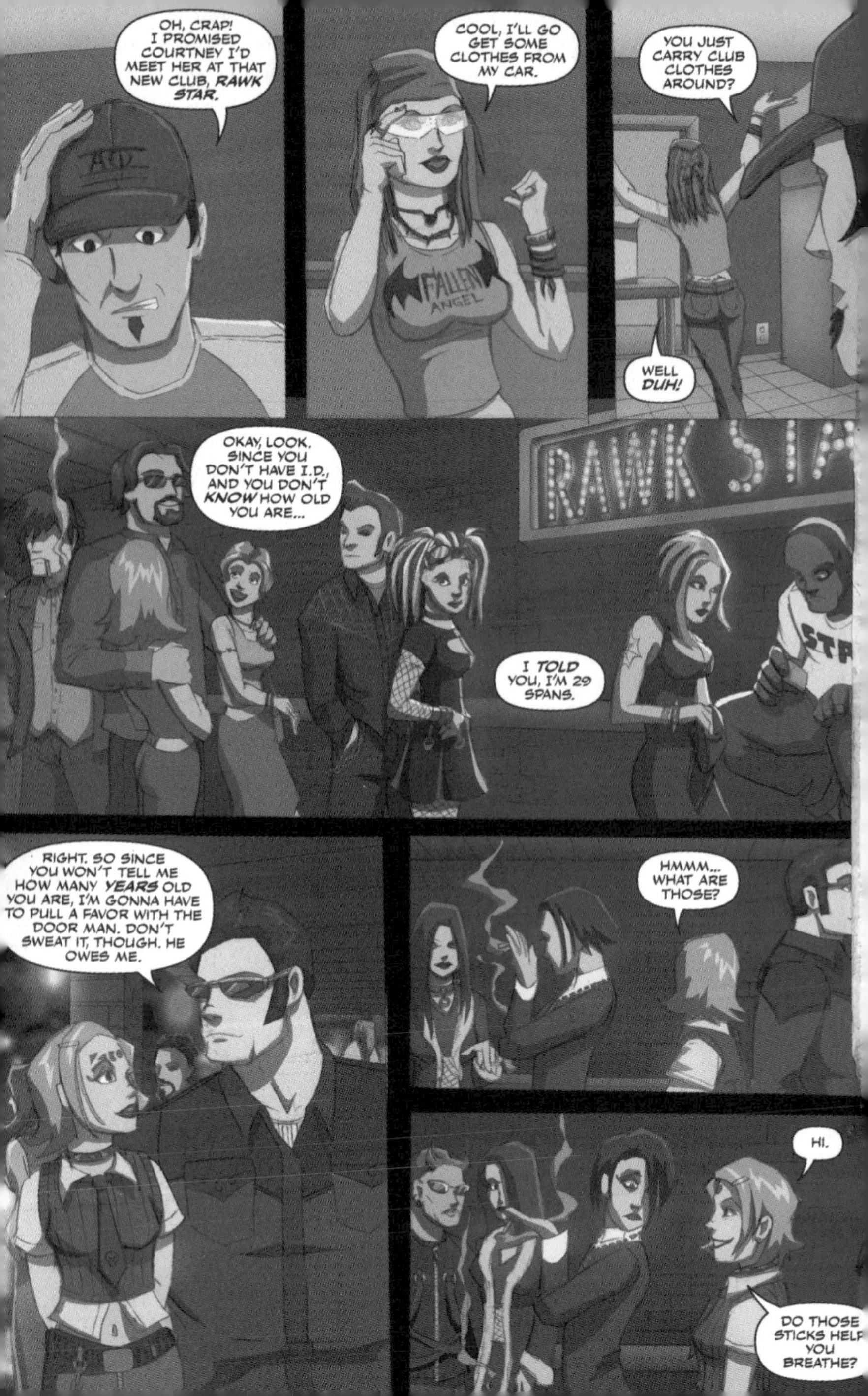
OH, CRAP! I PROMISED COURTNEY I'D MEET HER AT THAT NEW CLUB, *RAWK STAR.*
COOL, I'LL GO GET SOME CLOTHES FROM MY CAR.
YOU JUST CARRY CLUB CLOTHES AROUND?
WELL *DUH!*
OKAY, LOOK. SINCE YOU DON'T HAVE I.D., AND YOU DON'T *KNOW* HOW OLD YOU ARE...
RAWK STA
I *TOLD* YOU, I'M 29 SPANS.
RIGHT. SO SINCE YOU WON'T TELL ME HOW MANY *YEARS* OLD YOU ARE, I'M GONNA HAVE TO PULL A FAVOR WITH THE DOOR MAN. DON'T SWEAT IT, THOUGH. HE OWES ME.
HMMM... WHAT ARE THOSE?
HI.
DO THOSE STICKS HELP YOU BREATHE?

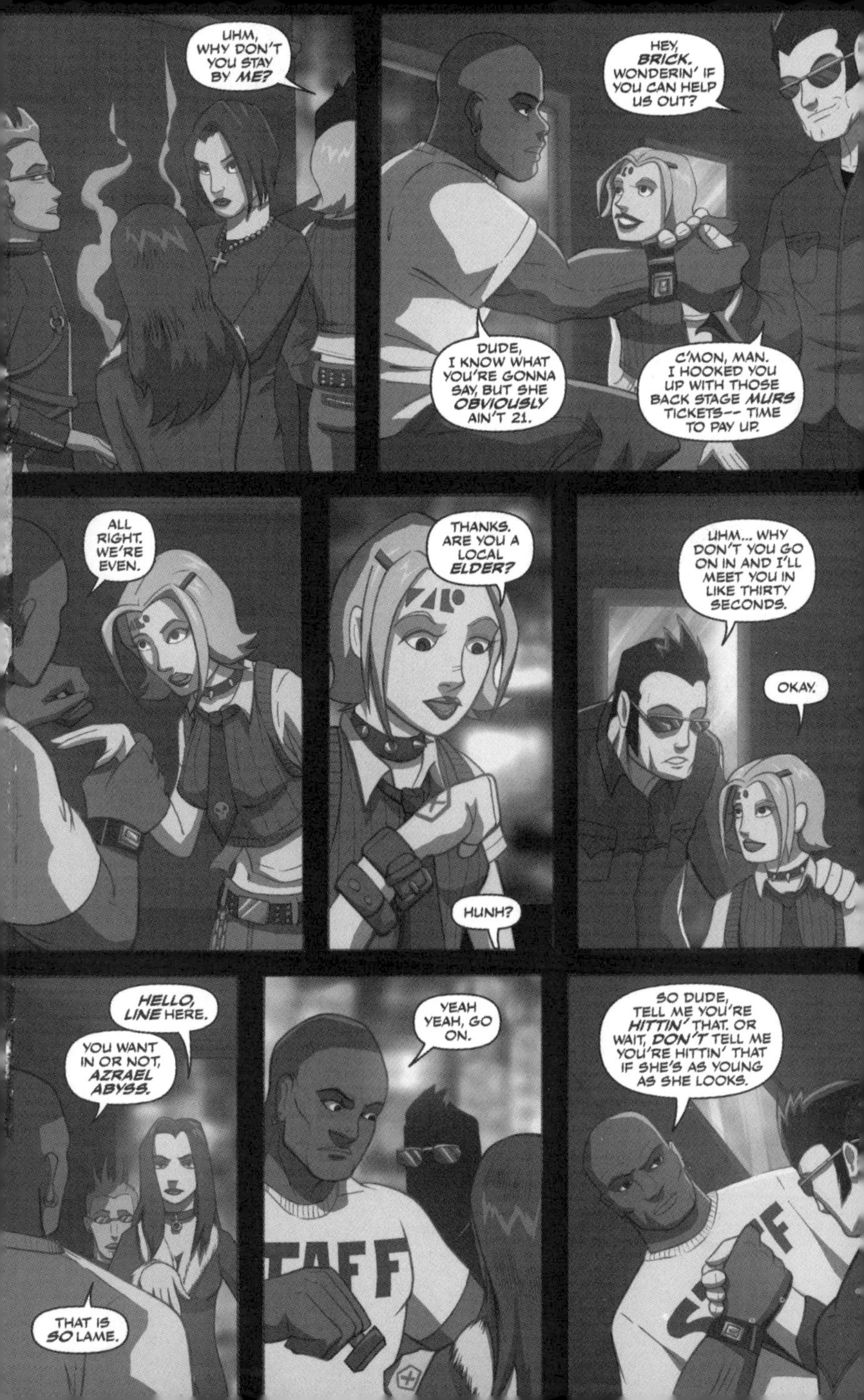
UHM, WHY DON'T YOU STAY BY ME?
HEY, BRICK. WONDERIN' IF YOU CAN HELP US OUT?
DUDE, I KNOW WHAT YOU'RE GONNA SAY, BUT SHE OBVIOUSLY AIN'T 21.
C'MON, MAN. I HOOKED YOU UP WITH THOSE BACK STAGE MURS TICKETS-- TIME TO PAY UP.
ALL RIGHT. WE'RE EVEN.
THANKS. ARE YOU A LOCAL ELDER?
HUNH?
UHM... WHY DON'T YOU GO ON IN AND I'LL MEET YOU IN LIKE THIRTY SECONDS.
OKAY.
HELLO, LINE HERE.
YOU WANT IN OR NOT, AZRAEL ABYSS.
THAT IS SO LAME.
YEAH YEAH, GO ON.
TAFF
SO DUDE, TELL ME YOU'RE HITTIN' THAT. OR WAIT, DON'T TELL ME YOU'RE HITTIN' THAT IF SHE'S AS YOUNG AS SHE LOOKS.

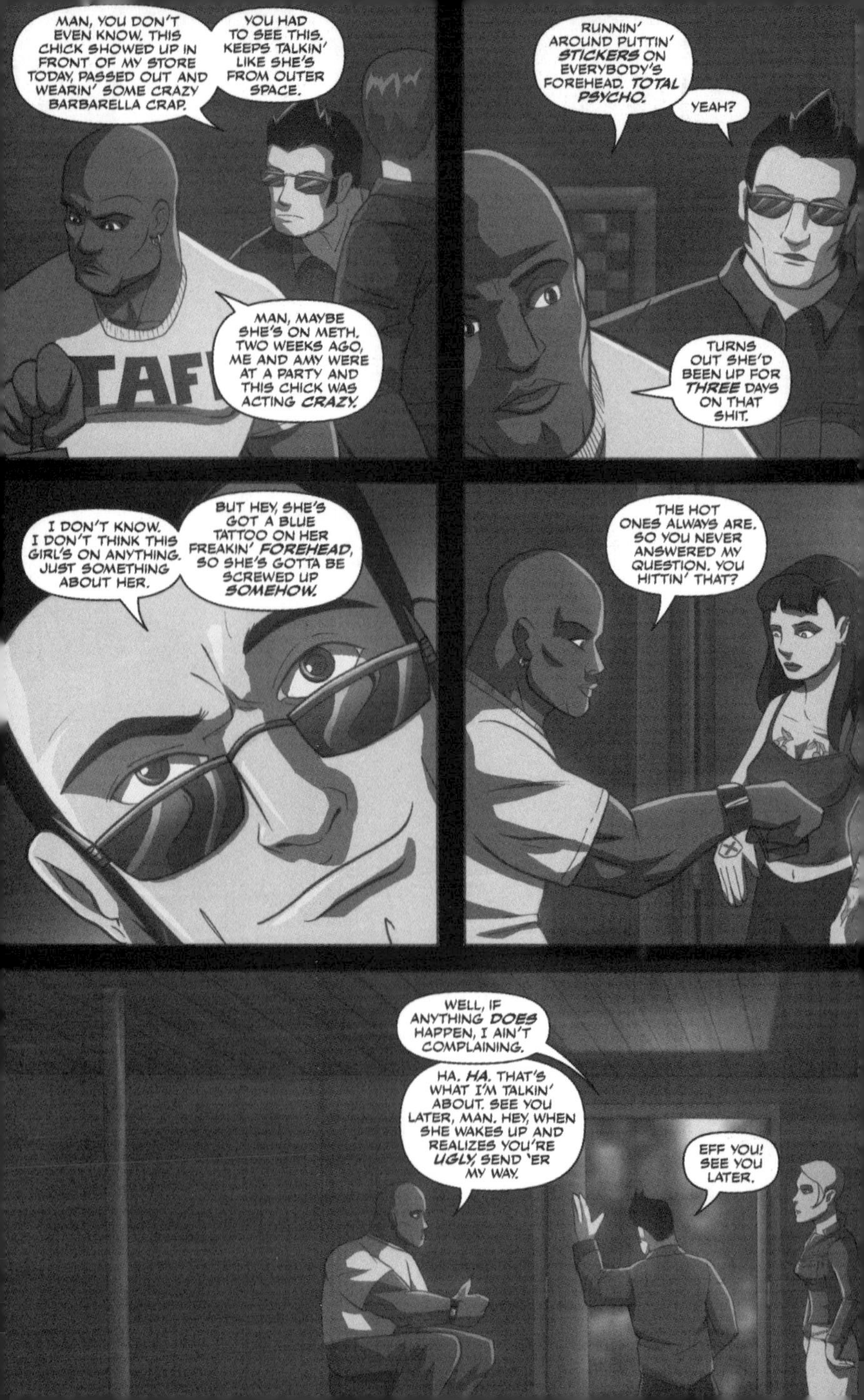
MAN, YOU DON'T EVEN KNOW. THIS CHICK SHOWED UP IN FRONT OF MY STORE TODAY, PASSED OUT AND WEARIN' SOME CRAZY BARBARELLA CRAP.
YOU HAD TO SEE THIS. KEEPS TALKIN' LIKE SHE'S FROM OUTER SPACE.
TAF
MAN, MAYBE SHE'S ON METH. TWO WEEKS AGO, ME AND AMY WERE AT A PARTY AND THIS CHICK WAS ACTING *CRAZY*.
RUNNIN' AROUND PUTTIN' ***STICKERS*** ON EVERYBODY'S FOREHEAD. ***TOTAL PSYCHO.***
YEAH?
TURNS OUT SHE'D BEEN UP FOR *THREE* DAYS ON THAT SHIT.
I DON'T KNOW. I DON'T THINK THIS GIRL'S ON ANYTHING. JUST SOMETHING ABOUT HER.
BUT HEY, SHE'S GOT A BLUE TATTOO ON HER FREAKIN' ***FOREHEAD***, SO SHE'S GOTTA BE SCREWED UP ***SOMEHOW.***
THE HOT ONES ALWAYS ARE. SO YOU NEVER ANSWERED MY QUESTION. YOU HITTIN' THAT?
WELL, IF ANYTHING ***DOES*** HAPPEN, I AIN'T COMPLAINING.
HA. ***HA.*** THAT'S WHAT I'M TALKIN' ABOUT. SEE YOU LATER, MAN. HEY, WHEN SHE WAKES UP AND REALIZES YOU'RE ***UGLY***, SEND 'ER MY WAY.
EFF YOU! SEE YOU LATER.

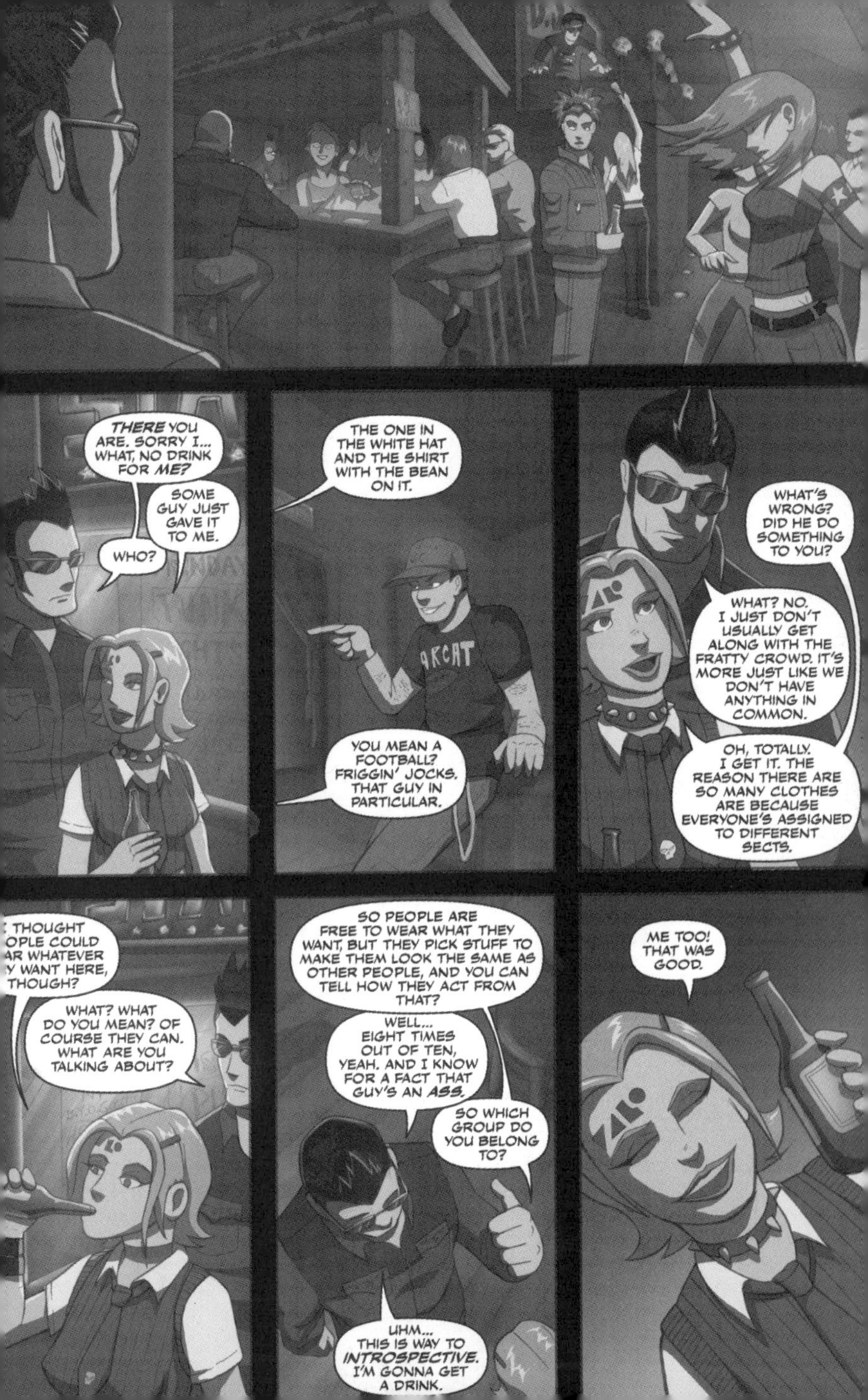
THERE YOU ARE. SORRY I... WHAT, NO DRINK FOR ME?
SOME GUY JUST GAVE IT TO ME.
WHO?
THE ONE IN THE WHITE HAT AND THE SHIRT WITH THE BEAN ON IT.
YOU MEAN A FOOTBALL? FRIGGIN' JOCKS. THAT GUY IN PARTICULAR.
WHAT'S WRONG? DID HE DO SOMETHING TO YOU?
WHAT? NO. I JUST DON'T USUALLY GET ALONG WITH THE FRATTY CROWD. IT'S MORE JUST LIKE WE DON'T HAVE ANYTHING IN COMMON.
OH, TOTALLY. I GET IT. THE REASON THERE ARE SO MANY CLOTHES ARE BECAUSE EVERYONE'S ASSIGNED TO DIFFERENT SECTS.
THOUGHT OPLE COULD AR WHATEVER Y WANT HERE, THOUGH?
WHAT? WHAT DO YOU MEAN? OF COURSE THEY CAN. WHAT ARE YOU TALKING ABOUT?
SO PEOPLE ARE FREE TO WEAR WHAT THEY WANT, BUT THEY PICK STUFF TO MAKE THEM LOOK THE SAME AS OTHER PEOPLE, AND YOU CAN TELL HOW THEY ACT FROM THAT?
WELL... EIGHT TIMES OUT OF TEN, YEAH. AND I KNOW FOR A FACT THAT GUY'S AN ASS.
SO WHICH GROUP DO YOU BELONG TO?
UHM... THIS IS WAY TO INTROSPECTIVE. I'M GONNA GET A DRINK.
ME TOO! THAT WAS GOOD.

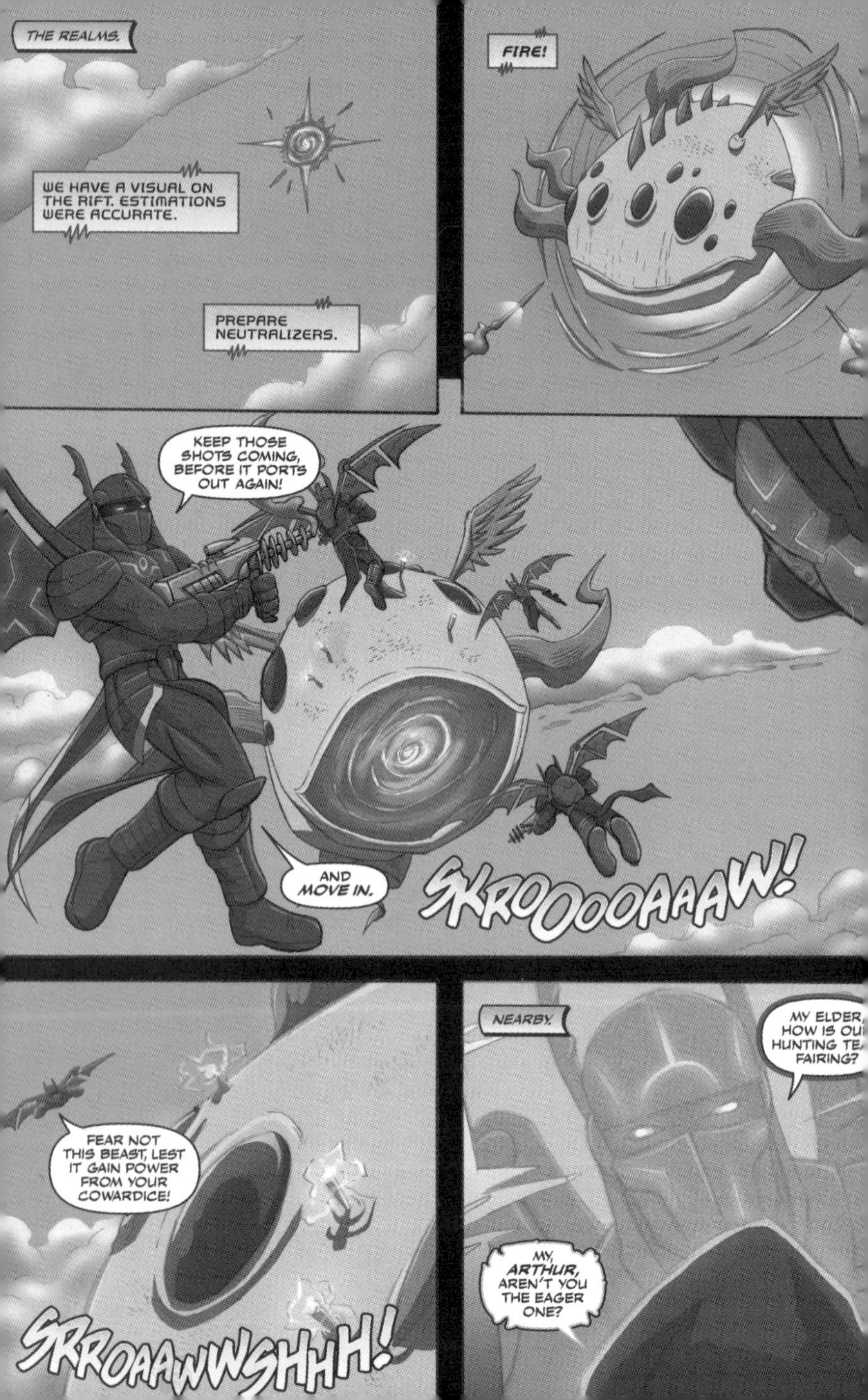
THE REALMS.
WE HAVE A VISUAL ON THE RIFT. ESTIMATIONS WERE ACCURATE.
PREPARE NEUTRALIZERS.
FIRE!
KEEP THOSE SHOTS COMING, BEFORE IT PORTS OUT AGAIN!
AND MOVE IN.
SKROOOOOAAAW!
FEAR NOT THIS BEAST, LEST IT GAIN POWER FROM YOUR COWARDICE!
SRROAAWWSHHH!
NEARBY.
MY ELDER, HOW IS OU HUNTING TE FAIRING?
MY, ARTHUR, AREN'T YOU THE EAGER ONE?

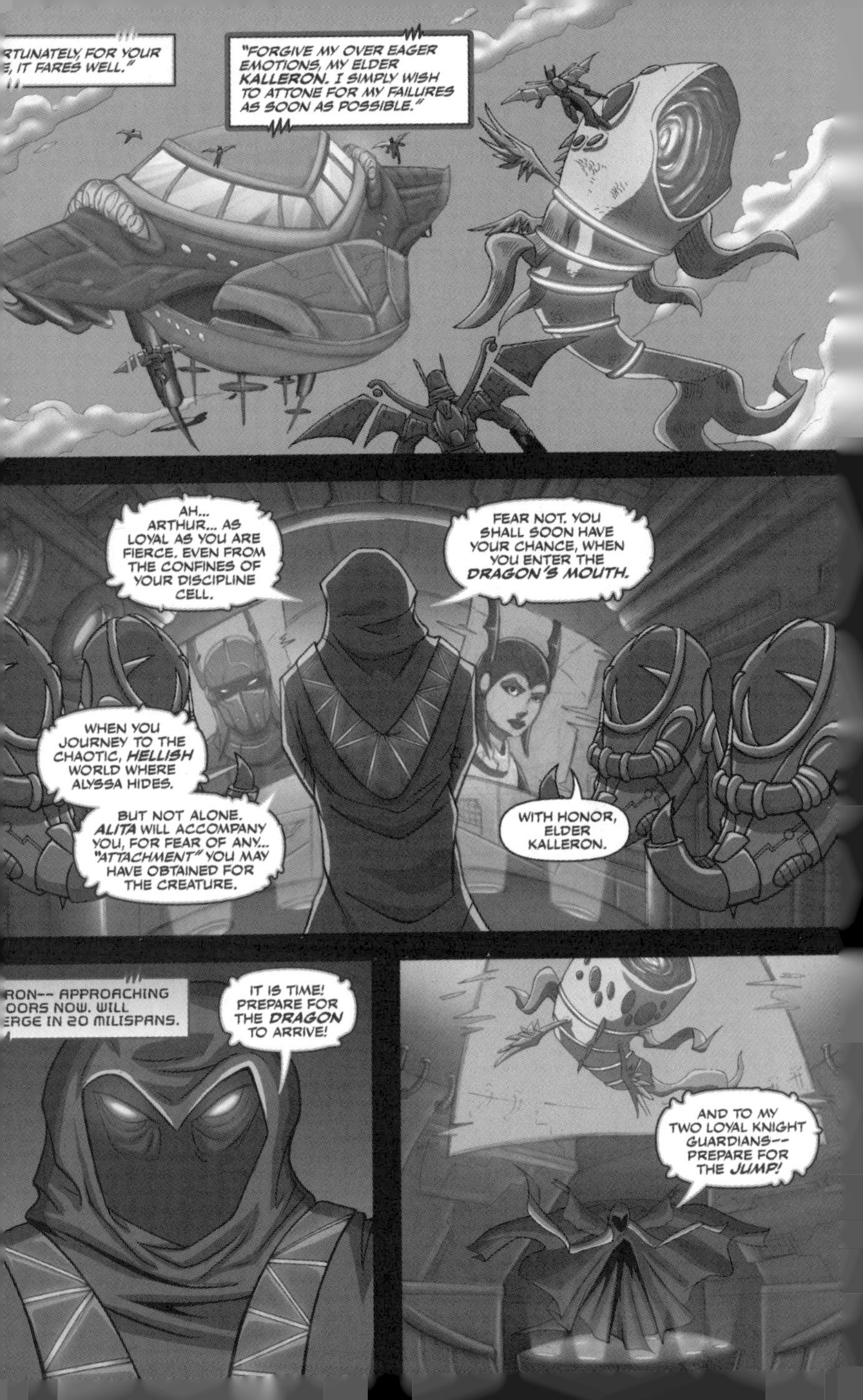
"...RTUNATELY, FOR YOUR ...E, IT FARES WELL."
"FORGIVE MY OVER EAGER EMOTIONS, MY ELDER KALLERON. I SIMPLY WISH TO ATTONE FOR MY FAILURES AS SOON AS POSSIBLE."
AH... ARTHUR... AS LOYAL AS YOU ARE FIERCE. EVEN FROM THE CONFINES OF YOUR DISCIPLINE CELL.
FEAR NOT. YOU SHALL SOON HAVE YOUR CHANCE, WHEN YOU ENTER THE DRAGON'S MOUTH.
WHEN YOU JOURNEY TO THE CHAOTIC, HELLISH WORLD WHERE ALYSSA HIDES.
BUT NOT ALONE. ALITA WILL ACCOMPANY YOU, FOR FEAR OF ANY... "ATTACHMENT" YOU MAY HAVE OBTAINED FOR THE CREATURE.
WITH HONOR, ELDER KALLERON.
...RON-- APPROACHING ...OORS NOW. WILL ...ERGE IN 20 MILISPANS.
IT IS TIME! PREPARE FOR THE DRAGON TO ARRIVE!
AND TO MY TWO LOYAL KNIGHT GUARDIANS-- PREPARE FOR THE JUMP!

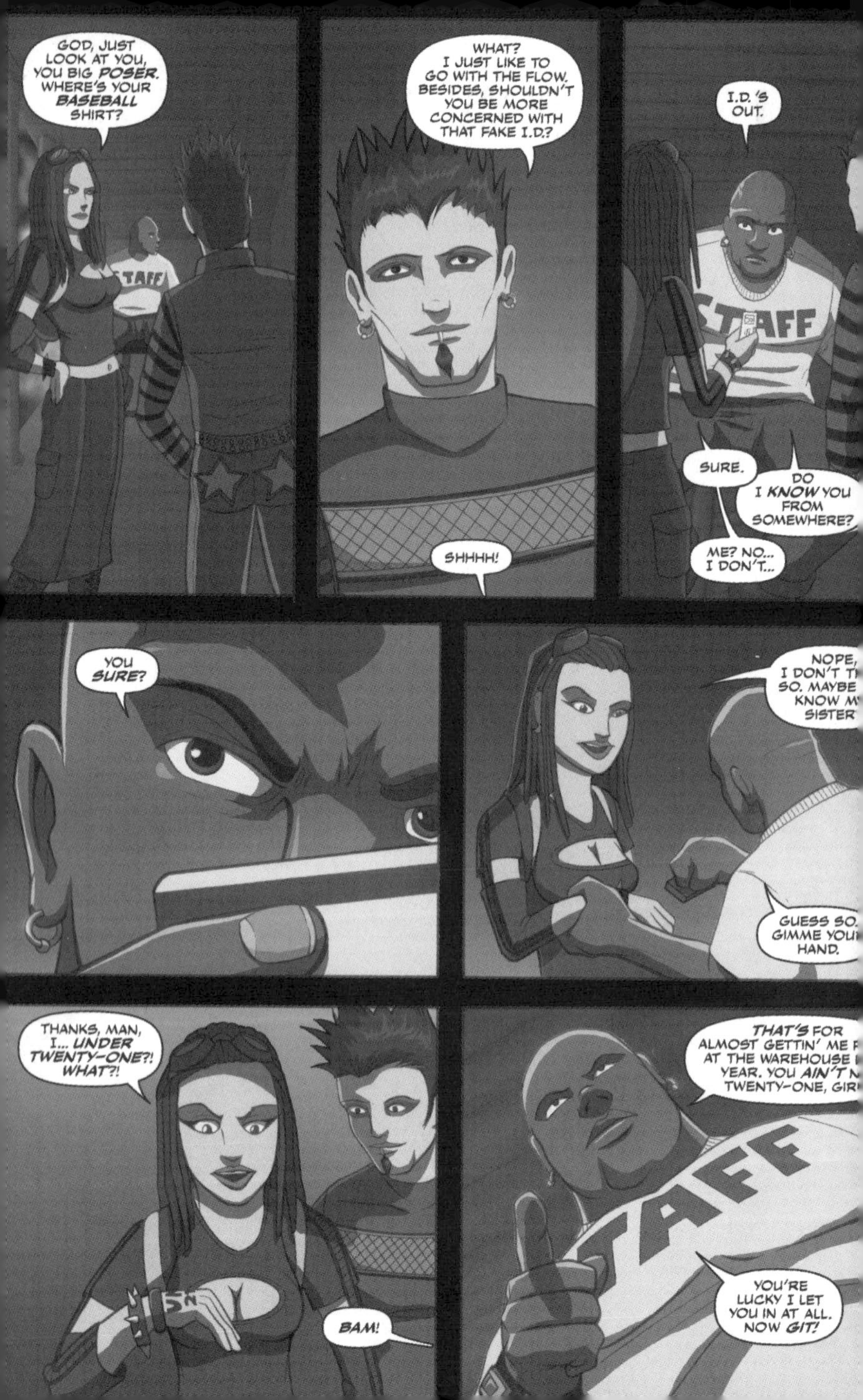
GOD, JUST LOOK AT YOU, YOU BIG *POSER*. WHERE'S YOUR *BASEBALL* SHIRT?
STAFF
WHAT? I JUST LIKE TO GO WITH THE FLOW. BESIDES, SHOULDN'T YOU BE MORE CONCERNED WITH THAT FAKE I.D.?
SHHHH!
I.D.'S OUT.
STAFF
SURE.
DO I *KNOW* YOU FROM SOMEWHERE?
ME? NO... I DON'T...
YOU *SURE*?
NOPE, I DON'T T SO. MAYBE KNOW M SISTER
GUESS SO. GIMME YOU HAND.
THANKS, MAN, I... *UNDER TWENTY-ONE*?! *WHAT*?!
BAM!
THAT'S FOR ALMOST GETTIN' ME F AT THE WAREHOUSE YEAR. YOU *AIN'T* N TWENTY-ONE, GIR
STAFF
YOU'RE LUCKY I LET YOU IN AT ALL. NOW *GIT!*

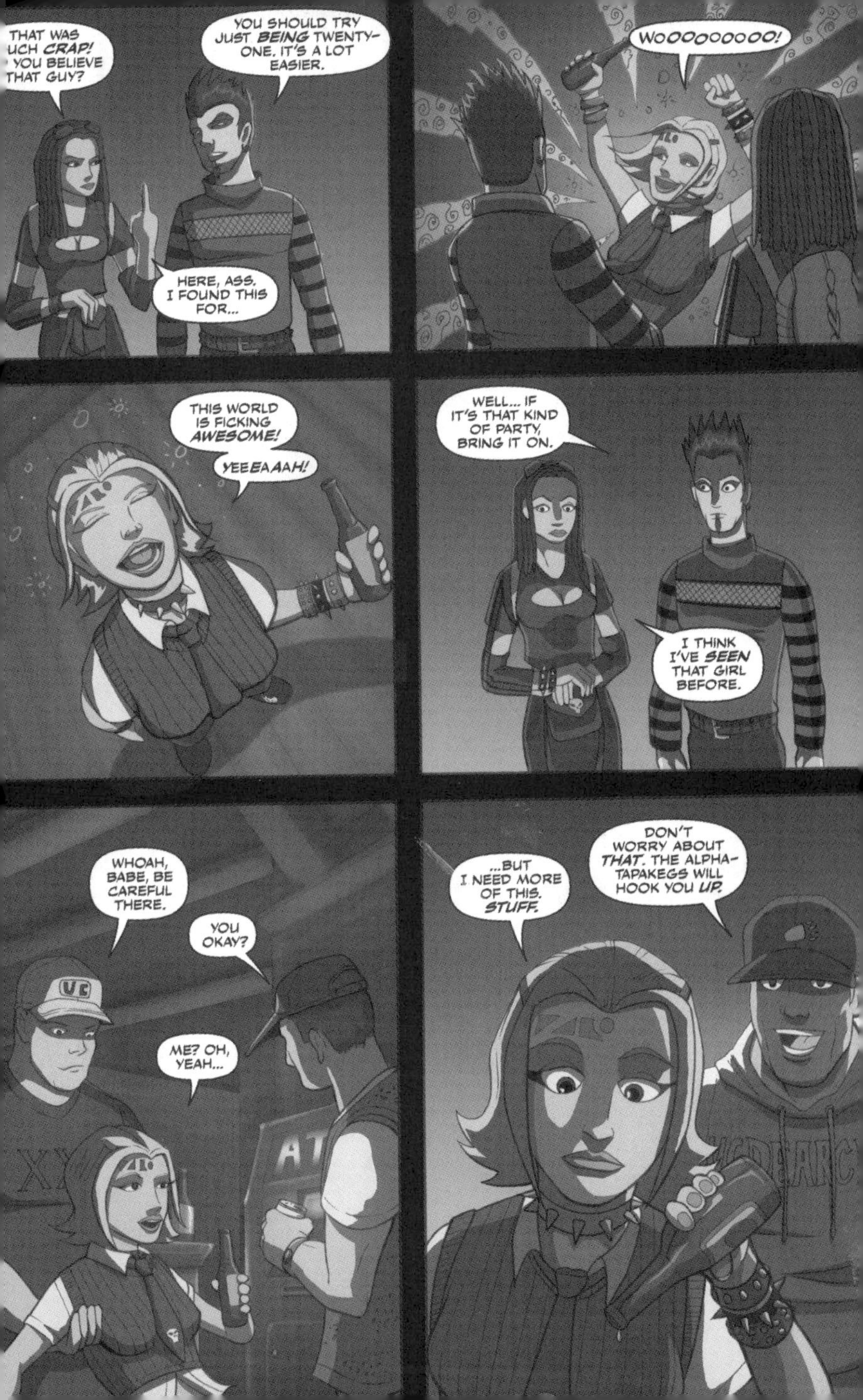
THAT WAS UCH CRAP! YOU BELIEVE THAT GUY?
YOU SHOULD TRY JUST BEING TWENTY-ONE. IT'S A LOT EASIER.
HERE, ASS. I FOUND THIS FOR...
WOOOOOOOOO!
THIS WORLD IS FICKING AWESOME!
YEEEAAAH!
WELL... IF IT'S THAT KIND OF PARTY, BRING IT ON.
I THINK I'VE SEEN THAT GIRL BEFORE.
WHOAH, BABE, BE CAREFUL THERE.
YOU OKAY?
ME? OH, YEAH...
...BUT I NEED MORE OF THIS. STUFF.
DON'T WORRY ABOUT THAT. THE ALPHA-TAPAKEGS WILL HOOK YOU UP.

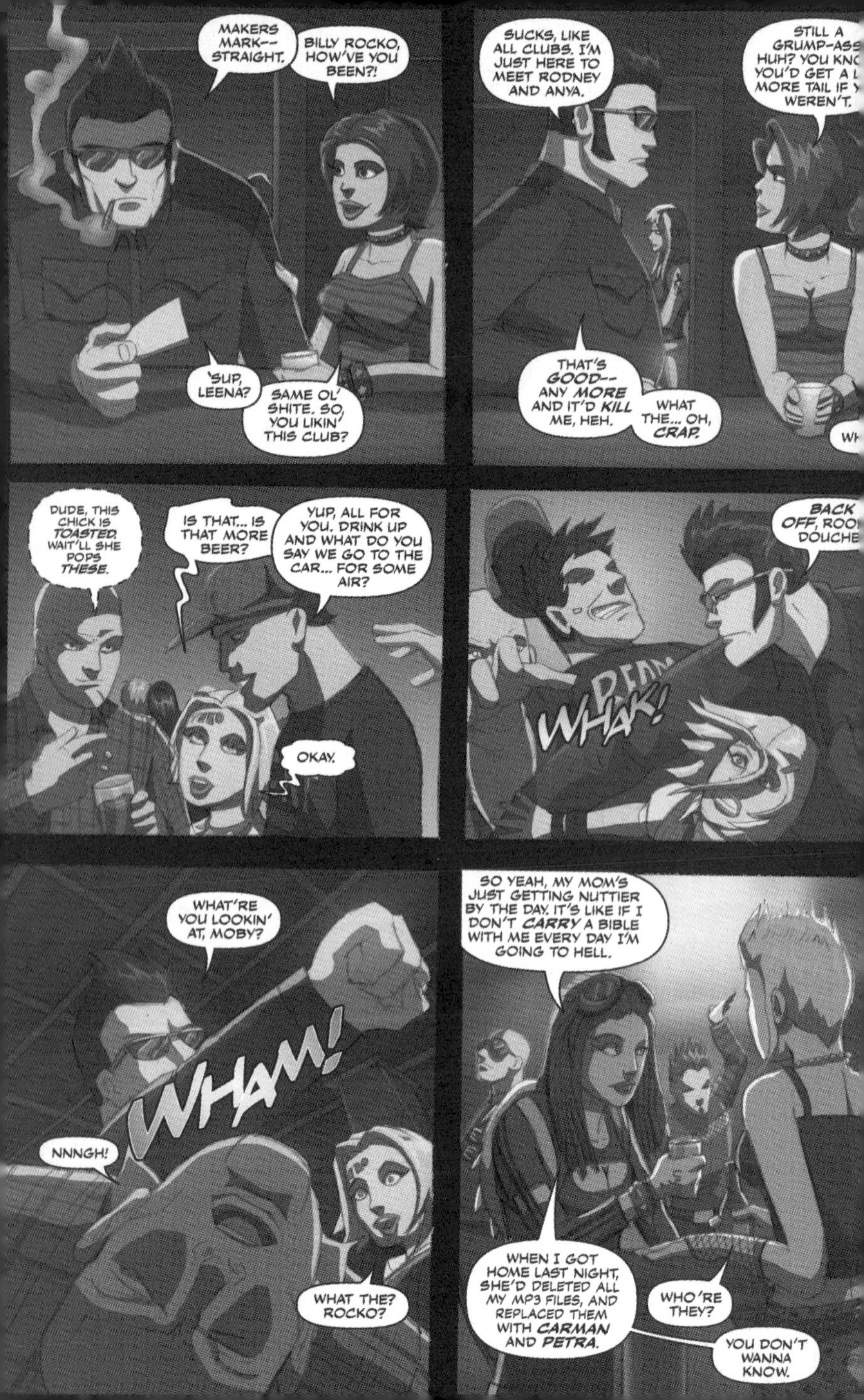
MAKERS MARK-- STRAIGHT.
BILLY ROCKO, HOW'VE YOU BEEN?!
'SUP, LEENA?
SAME OL' SHITE. SO, YOU LIKIN' THIS CLUB?
SUCKS, LIKE ALL CLUBS. I'M JUST HERE TO MEET RODNEY AND ANYA.
STILL A GRUMP-ASS HUH? YOU KNO YOU'D GET A L MORE TAIL IF Y WEREN'T.
THAT'S *GOOD*-- ANY *MORE* AND IT'D *KILL* ME, HEH.
WHAT THE... OH, *CRAP.*
WH
DUDE, THIS CHICK IS *TOASTED.* WAIT'LL SHE POPS *THESE.*
IS THAT... IS THAT MORE BEER?
YUP, ALL FOR YOU. DRINK UP AND WHAT DO YOU SAY WE GO TO THE CAR... FOR SOME AIR?
OKAY.
BACK OFF, ROO DOUCHE
WHAK!
WHAT'RE YOU LOOKIN' AT, MOBY?
WHAM!
NNNGH!
WHAT THE? ROCKO?
SO YEAH, MY MOM'S JUST GETTING NUTTIER BY THE DAY. IT'S LIKE IF I DON'T *CARRY* A BIBLE WITH ME EVERY DAY I'M GOING TO HELL.
WHEN I GOT HOME LAST NIGHT, SHE'D DELETED ALL MY MP3 FILES, AND REPLACED THEM WITH *CARMAN* AND *PETRA.*
WHO'RE THEY?
YOU DON'T WANNA KNOW.

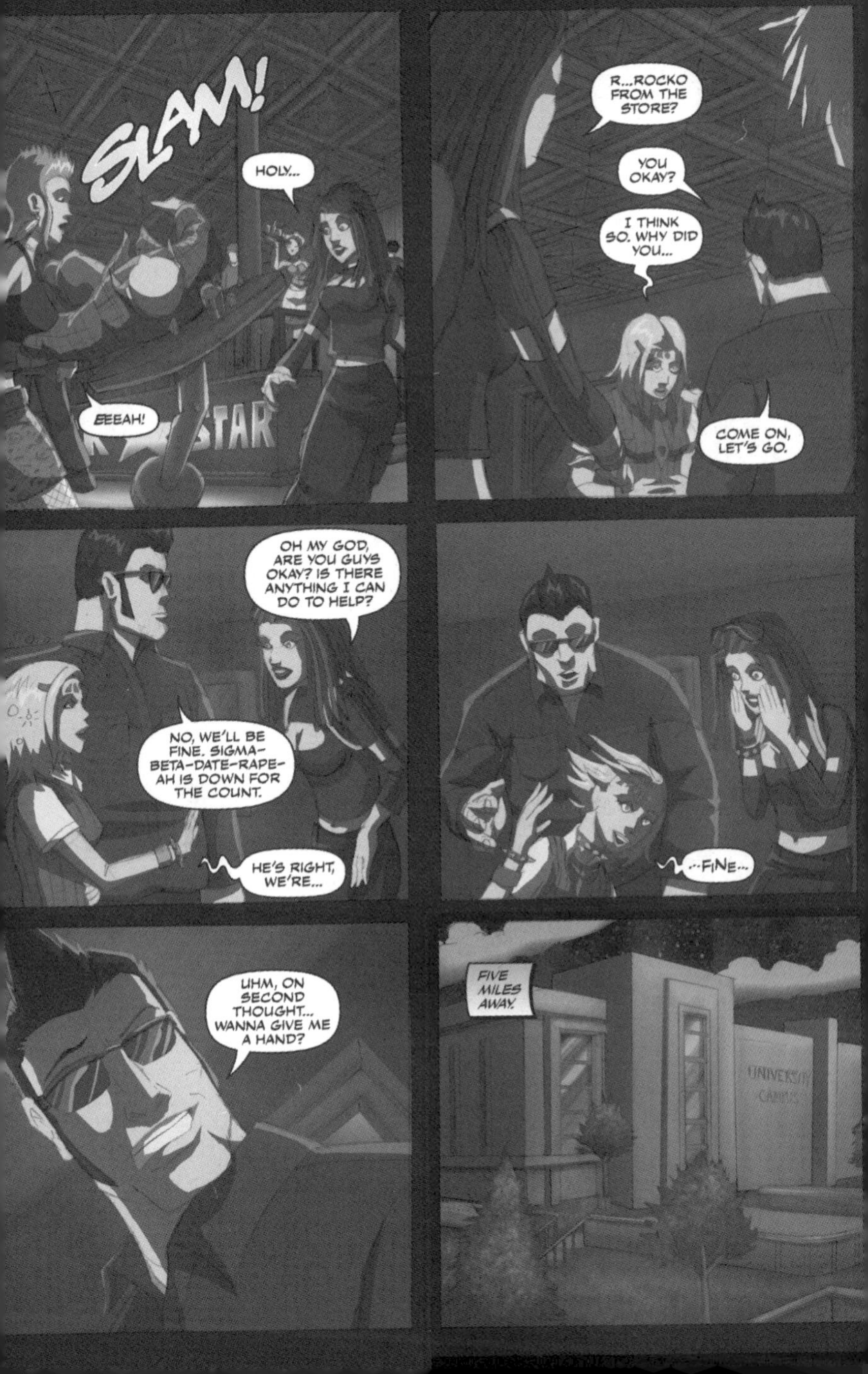
SLAM!
HOLY...
EEEAH!
STAR
R...ROCKO FROM THE STORE?
YOU OKAY?
I THINK SO. WHY DID YOU...
COME ON, LET'S GO.
OH MY GOD, ARE YOU GUYS OKAY? IS THERE ANYTHING I CAN DO TO HELP?
NO, WE'LL BE FINE. SIGMA-BETA-DATE-RAPE-AH IS DOWN FOR THE COUNT.
HE'S RIGHT, WE'RE...
...FINE...
UHM, ON SECOND THOUGHT... WANNA GIVE ME A HAND?
FIVE MILES AWAY.

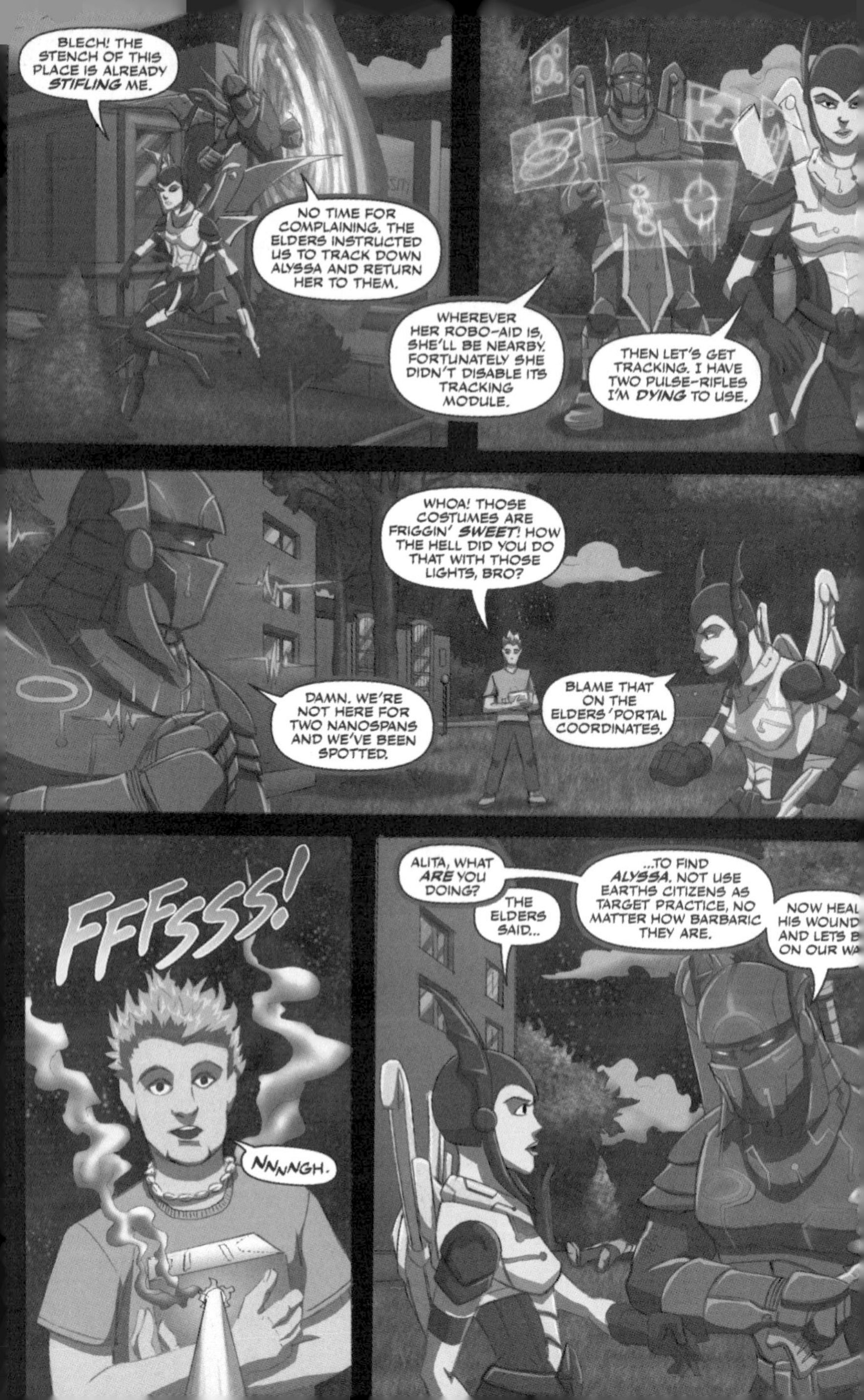
BLECH! THE STENCH OF THIS PLACE IS ALREADY *STIFLING* ME.
NO TIME FOR COMPLAINING. THE ELDERS INSTRUCTED US TO TRACK DOWN ALYSSA AND RETURN HER TO THEM.
WHEREVER HER ROBO-AID IS, SHE'LL BE NEARBY. FORTUNATELY SHE DIDN'T DISABLE ITS TRACKING MODULE.
THEN LET'S GET TRACKING. I HAVE TWO PULSE-RIFLES I'M *DYING* TO USE.
WHOA! THOSE COSTUMES ARE FRIGGIN' *SWEET*! HOW THE HELL DID YOU DO THAT WITH THOSE LIGHTS, BRO?
DAMN. WE'RE NOT HERE FOR TWO NANOSPANS AND WE'VE BEEN SPOTTED.
BLAME THAT ON THE ELDERS' PORTAL COORDINATES.
FFFSSS!
NNNNGH.
ALITA, WHAT *ARE* YOU DOING?
THE ELDERS SAID...
...TO FIND *ALYSSA*. NOT USE EARTHS CITIZENS AS TARGET PRACTICE, NO MATTER HOW BARBARIC THEY ARE.
NOW HEAL HIS WOUND AND LETS B ON OUR WA

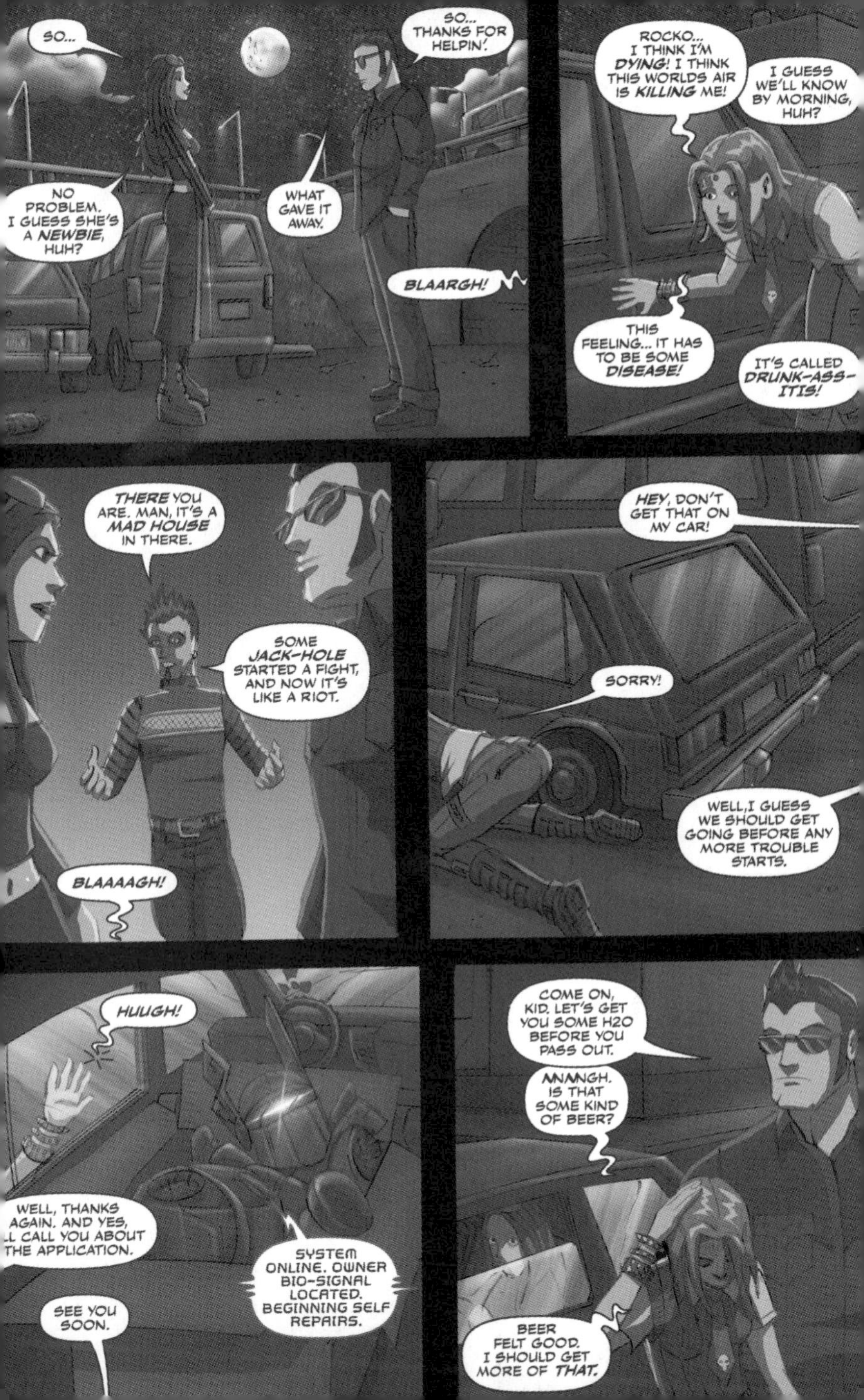

SO...
NO PROBLEM. I GUESS SHE'S A NEWBIE, HUH?
SO... THANKS FOR HELPIN'.
WHAT GAVE IT AWAY.
BLAARGH!
ROCKO... I THINK I'M DYING! I THINK THIS WORLDS AIR IS KILLING ME!
I GUESS WE'LL KNOW BY MORNING, HUH?
THIS FEELING... IT HAS TO BE SOME DISEASE!
IT'S CALLED DRUNK-ASS-ITIS!
THERE YOU ARE. MAN, IT'S A MAD HOUSE IN THERE.
SOME JACK-HOLE STARTED A FIGHT, AND NOW IT'S LIKE A RIOT.
BLAAAAGH!
HEY, DON'T GET THAT ON MY CAR!
SORRY!
WELL, I GUESS WE SHOULD GET GOING BEFORE ANY MORE TROUBLE STARTS.
HUUGH!
WELL, THANKS AGAIN. AND YES, LL CALL YOU ABOUT THE APPLICATION.
SYSTEM ONLINE. OWNER BIO-SIGNAL LOCATED. BEGINNING SELF REPAIRS.
SEE YOU SOON.
COME ON, KID. LET'S GET YOU SOME H2O BEFORE YOU PASS OUT.
NNNNGH. IS THAT SOME KIND OF BEER?
BEER FELT GOOD. I SHOULD GET MORE OF THAT.

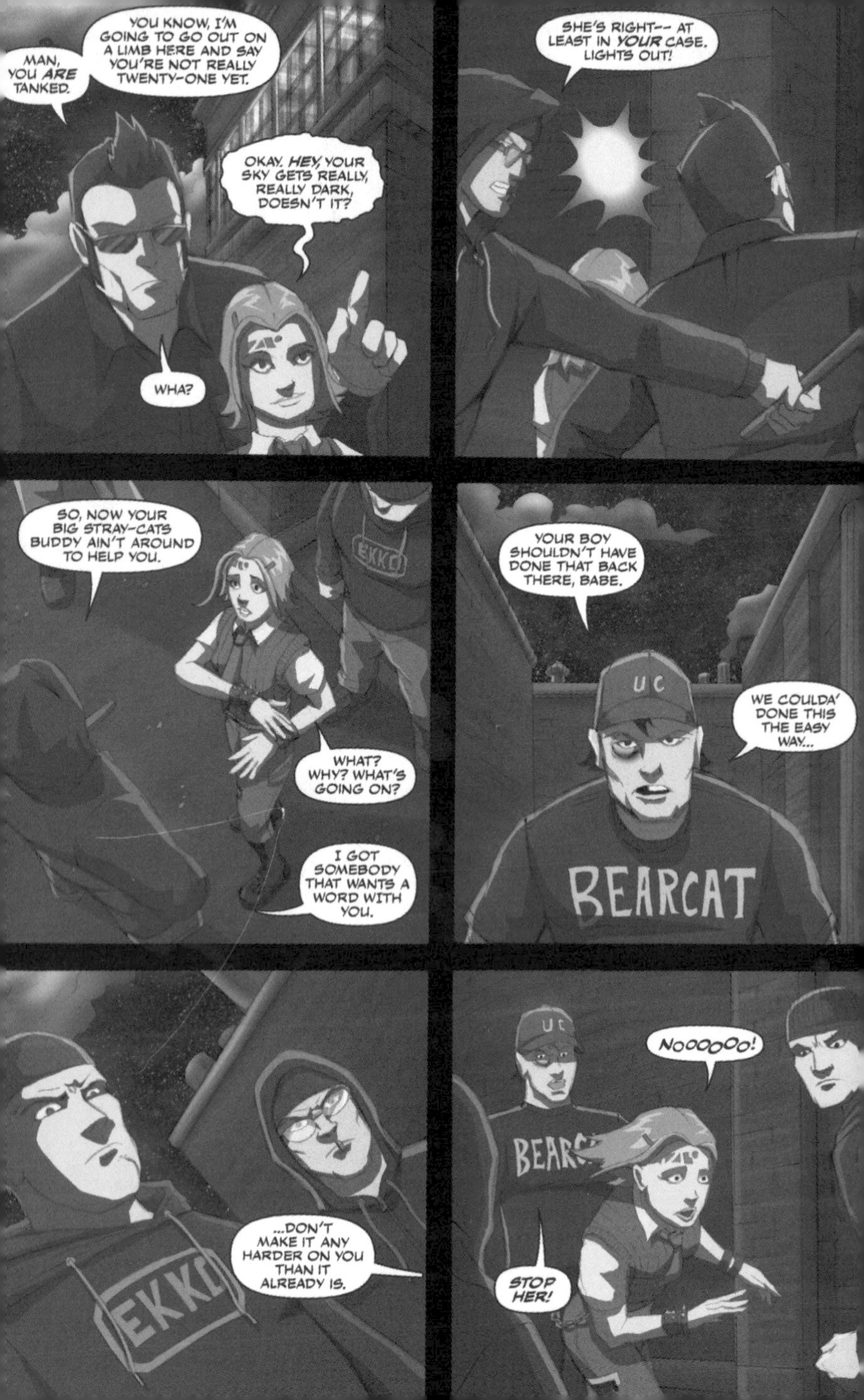
MAN, YOU *ARE* TANKED.
YOU KNOW, I'M GOING TO GO OUT ON A LIMB HERE AND SAY YOU'RE NOT REALLY TWENTY-ONE YET.
OKAY. *HEY,* YOUR SKY GETS REALLY, REALLY DARK, DOESN'T IT?
WHA?
SHE'S RIGHT-- AT LEAST IN *YOUR* CASE. LIGHTS OUT!
SO, NOW YOUR BIG STRAY-CATS BUDDY AIN'T AROUND TO HELP YOU.
WHAT? WHY? WHAT'S GOING ON?
I GOT SOMEBODY THAT WANTS A WORD WITH YOU.
YOUR BOY SHOULDN'T HAVE DONE THAT BACK THERE, BABE.
WE COULDA' DONE THIS THE EASY WAY...
...DON'T MAKE IT ANY HARDER ON YOU THAN IT ALREADY IS.
NOOOOOO!
STOP HER!

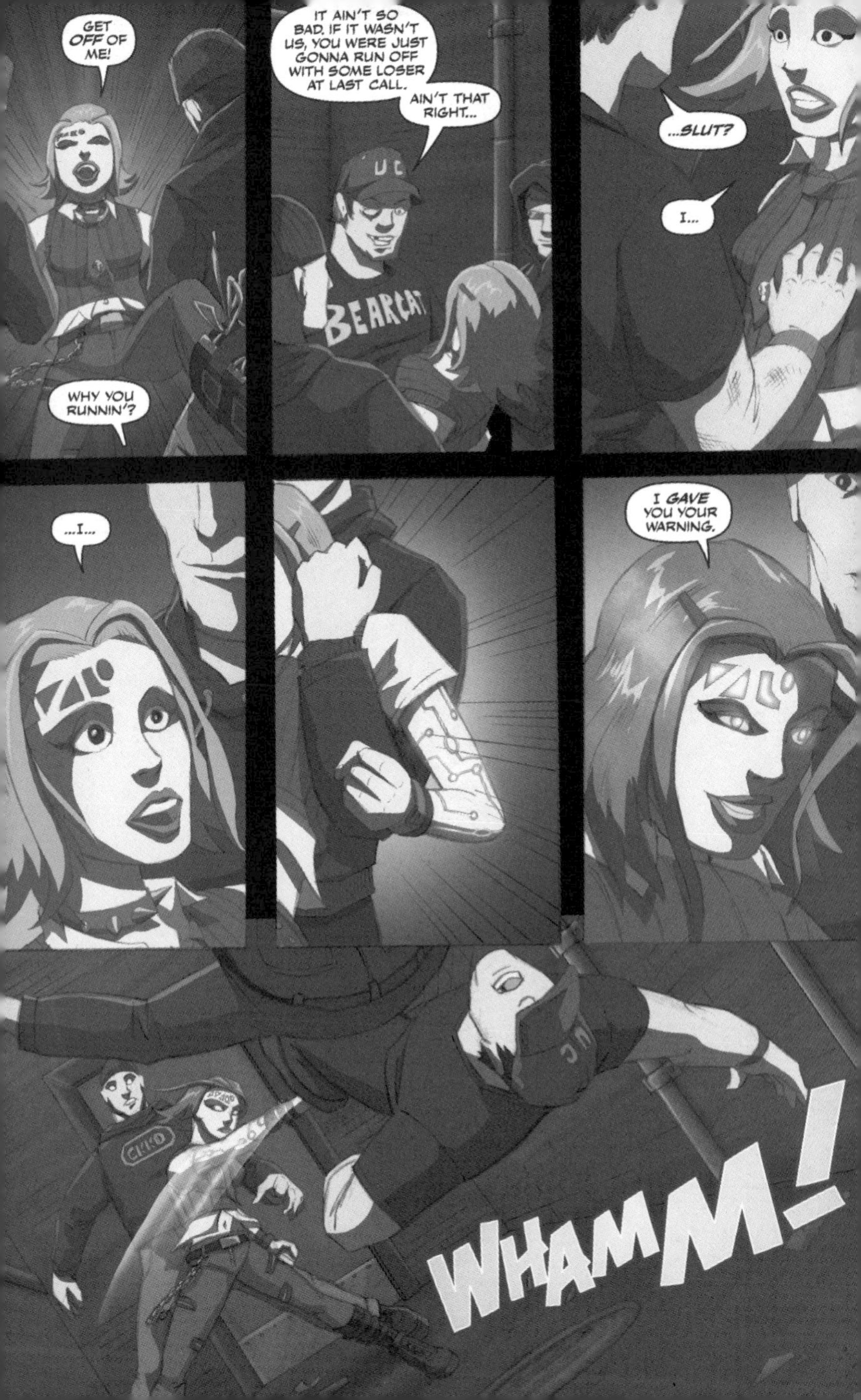
GET OFF OF ME!
WHY YOU RUNNIN'?
IT AIN'T SO BAD. IF IT WASN'T US, YOU WERE JUST GONNA RUN OFF WITH SOME LOSER AT LAST CALL.
AIN'T THAT RIGHT...
BEARCAT
...SLUT?
I...
...I...
I GAVE YOU YOUR WARNING.
WHAMM!

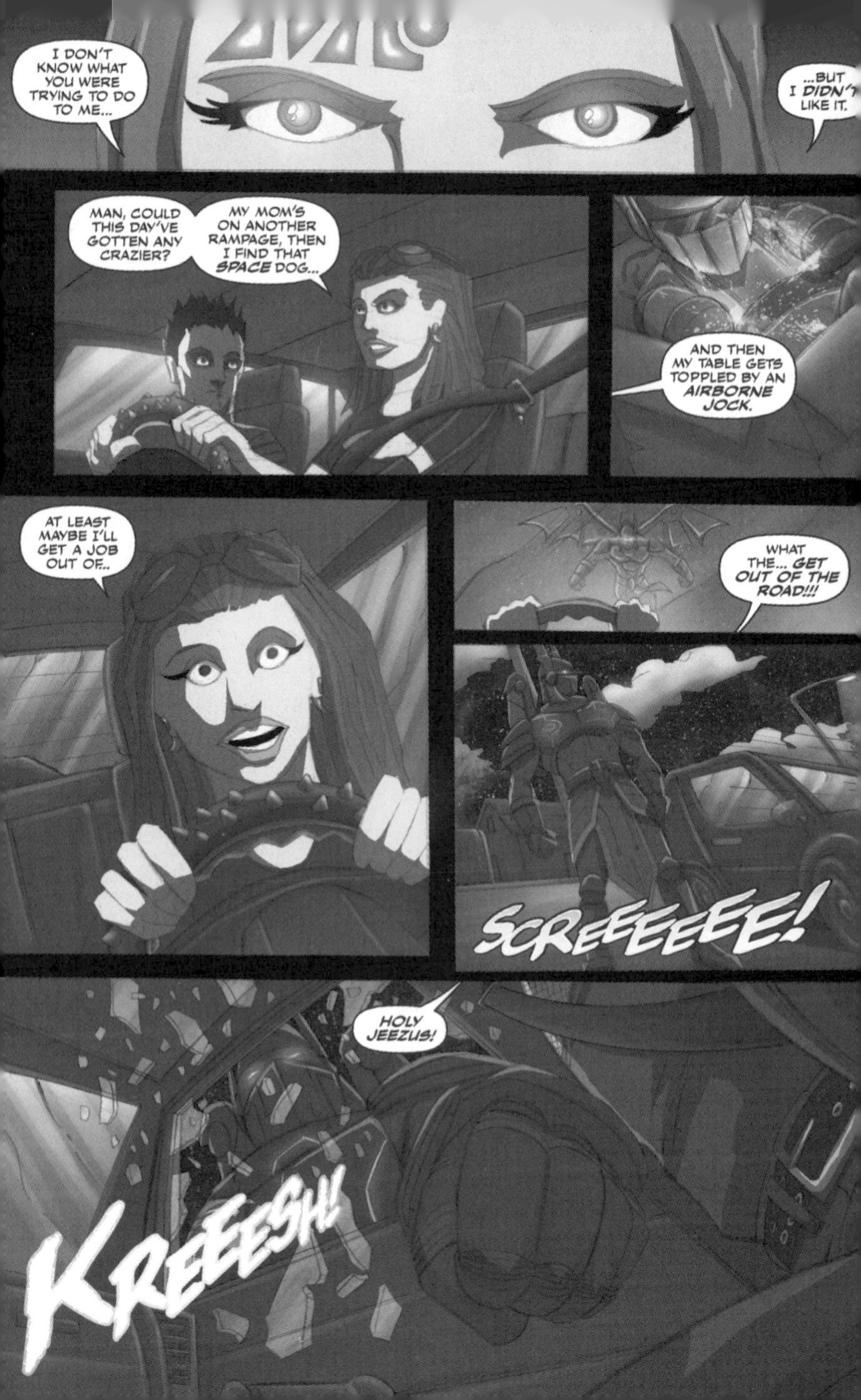
I DON'T KNOW WHAT YOU WERE TRYING TO DO TO ME...
...BUT I DIDN'T LIKE IT.
MAN, COULD THIS DAY'VE GOTTEN ANY CRAZIER?
MY MOM'S ON ANOTHER RAMPAGE, THEN I FIND THAT SPACE DOG...
AND THEN MY TABLE GETS TOPPLED BY AN AIRBORNE JOCK.
AT LEAST MAYBE I'LL GET A JOB OUT OF..
WHAT THE... GET OUT OF THE ROAD!!!
SCREEEEEEE!
HOLY JEEZUS!
KREEEESH!

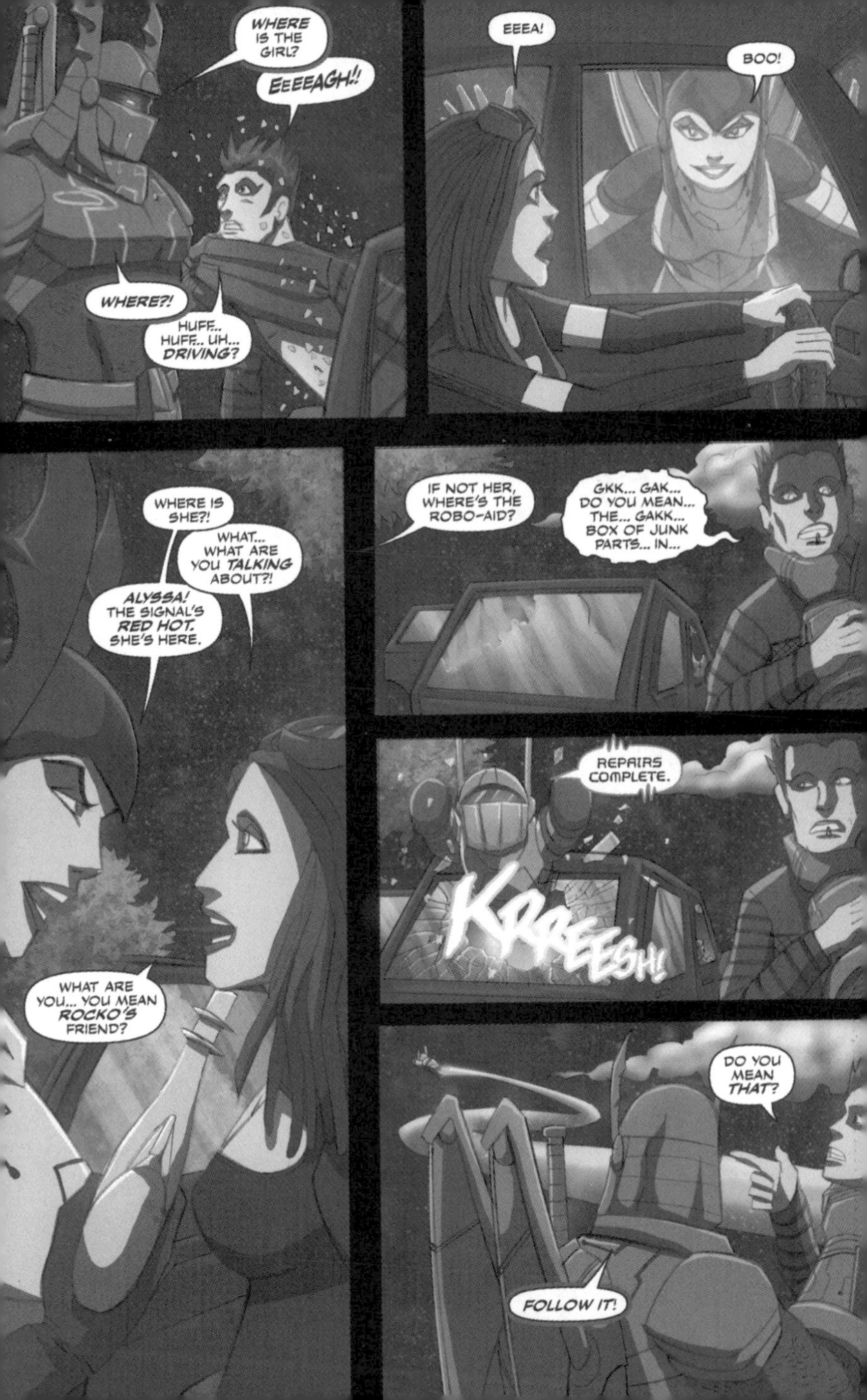
WHERE IS THE GIRL?
EEEEAGH!!
WHERE?!
HUFF.. HUFF.. UH... DRIVING?
EEEA!
BOO!
WHERE IS SHE?!
WHAT... WHAT ARE YOU TALKING ABOUT?!
ALYSSA! THE SIGNAL'S RED HOT. SHE'S HERE.
WHAT ARE YOU... YOU MEAN ROCKO'S FRIEND?
IF NOT HER, WHERE'S THE ROBO-AID?
GKK... GAK... DO YOU MEAN... THE... GAKK... BOX OF JUNK PARTS... IN...
REPAIRS COMPLETE.
KRREEESH!
DO YOU MEAN THAT?
FOLLOW IT!

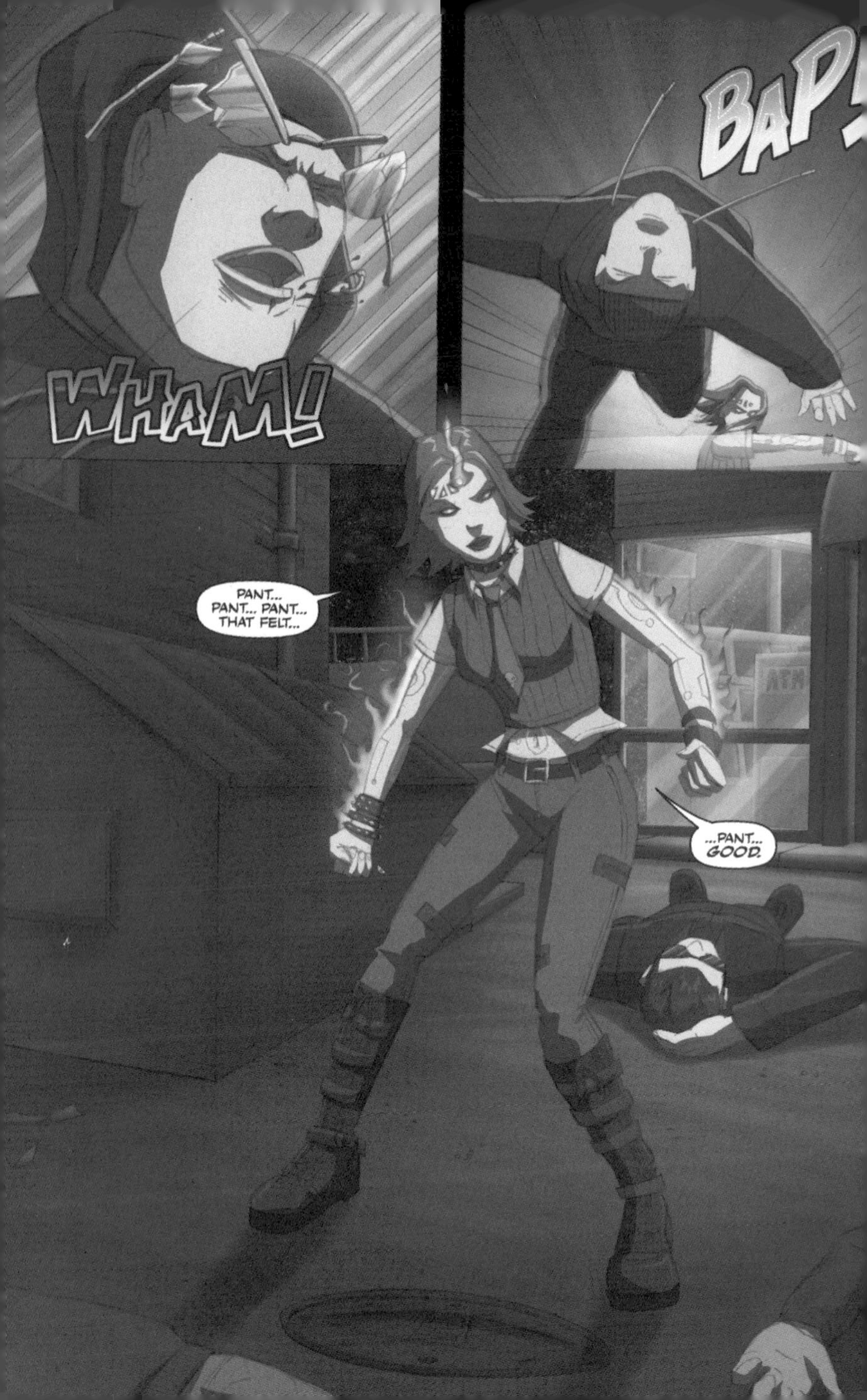
WHAM!
BAP!
PANT... PANT... PANT... THAT FELT...
...PANT... GOOD.

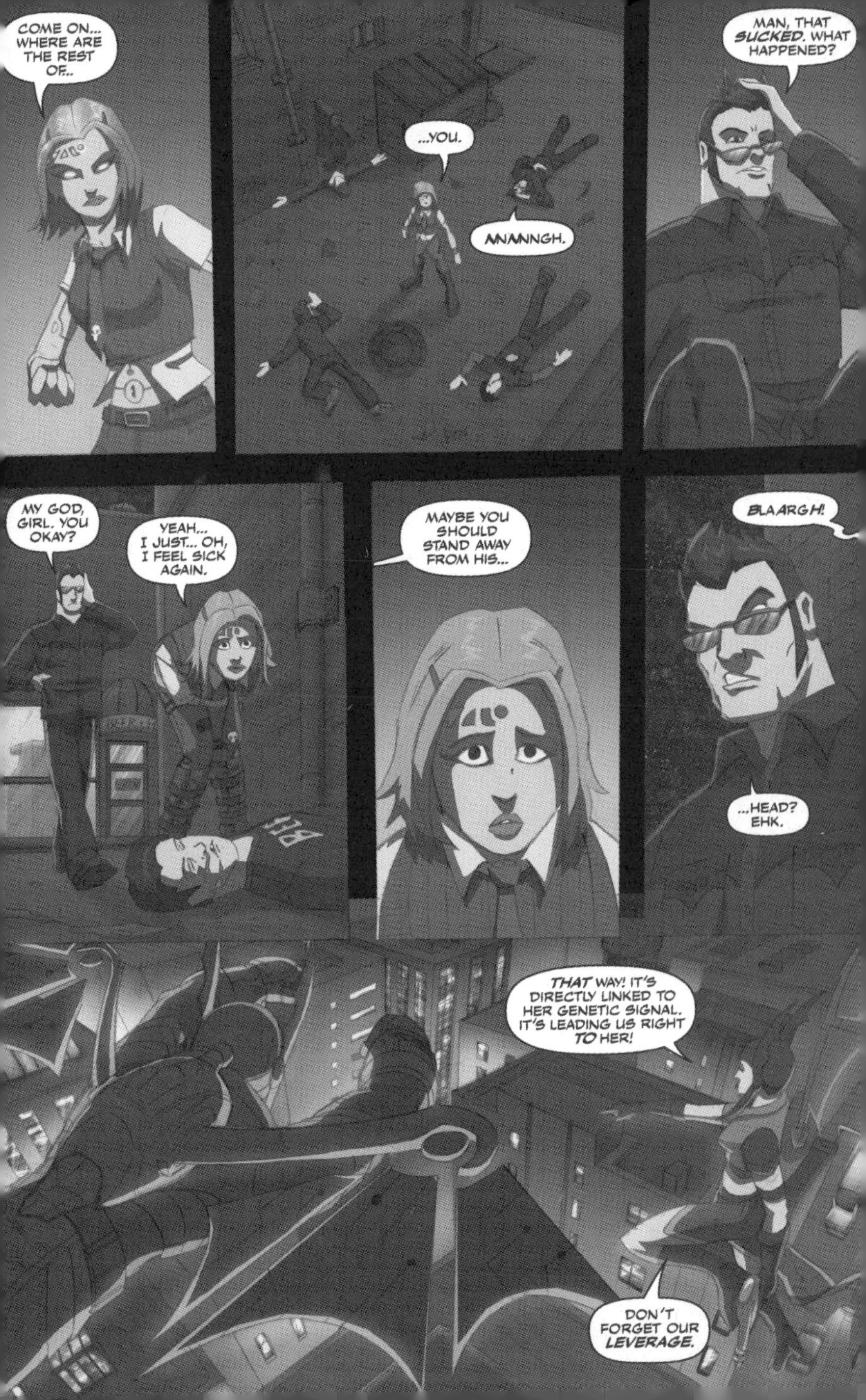
COME ON... WHERE ARE THE REST OF...
...YOU.
MNNNGH.
MAN, THAT *SUCKED*. WHAT HAPPENED?
MY GOD, GIRL. YOU OKAY?
YEAH... I JUST... OH, I FEEL SICK AGAIN.
MAYBE YOU SHOULD STAND AWAY FROM HIS...
BLAARGH!
...HEAD? EHK.
THAT WAY! IT'S DIRECTLY LINKED TO HER GENETIC SIGNAL. IT'S LEADING US RIGHT *TO* HER!
DON'T FORGET OUR *LEVERAGE*.

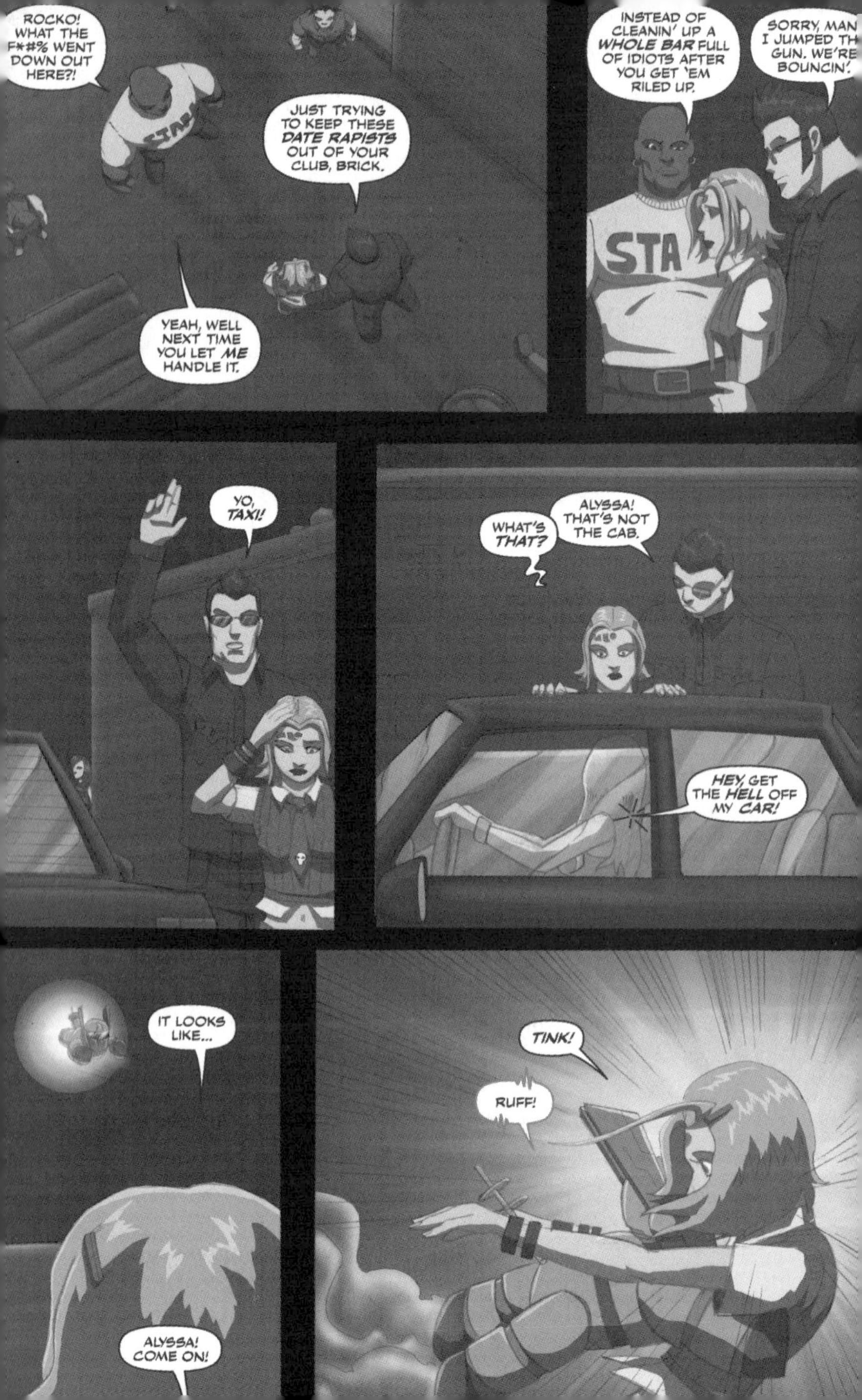
ROCKO! WHAT THE F*#% WENT DOWN OUT HERE?!
JUST TRYING TO KEEP THESE DATE RAPISTS OUT OF YOUR CLUB, BRICK.
YEAH, WELL NEXT TIME YOU LET ME HANDLE IT.
INSTEAD OF CLEANIN' UP A WHOLE BAR FULL OF IDIOTS AFTER YOU GET 'EM RILED UP.
SORRY, MAN I JUMPED TH GUN. WE'RE BOUNCIN'.
YO, TAXI!
ALYSSA! THAT'S NOT THE CAB.
WHAT'S THAT?
HEY, GET THE HELL OFF MY CAR!
IT LOOKS LIKE...
ALYSSA! COME ON!
TINK!
RUFF!

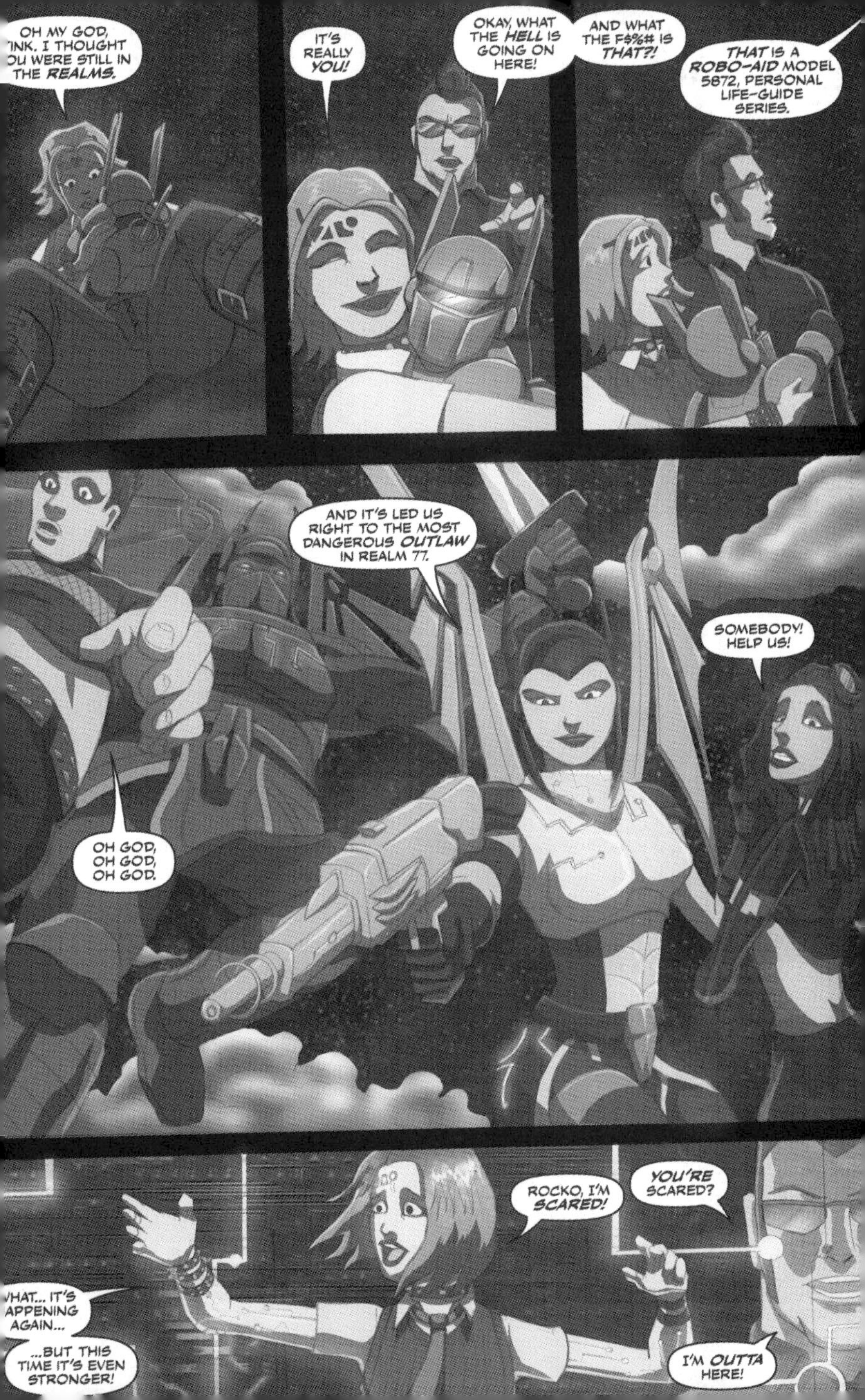
OH MY GOD, TINK. I THOUGHT YOU WERE STILL IN THE REALMS.
IT'S REALLY YOU!
OKAY, WHAT THE HELL IS GOING ON HERE!
AND WHAT THE F$%# IS THAT?!
THAT IS A ROBO-AID MODEL 5872, PERSONAL LIFE-GUIDE SERIES.
AND IT'S LED US RIGHT TO THE MOST DANGEROUS OUTLAW IN REALM 77.
SOMEBODY! HELP US!
OH GOD, OH GOD, OH GOD.
ROCKO, I'M SCARED!
YOU'RE SCARED?
WHAT... IT'S HAPPENING AGAIN...
...BUT THIS TIME IT'S EVEN STRONGER!
I'M OUTTA HERE!

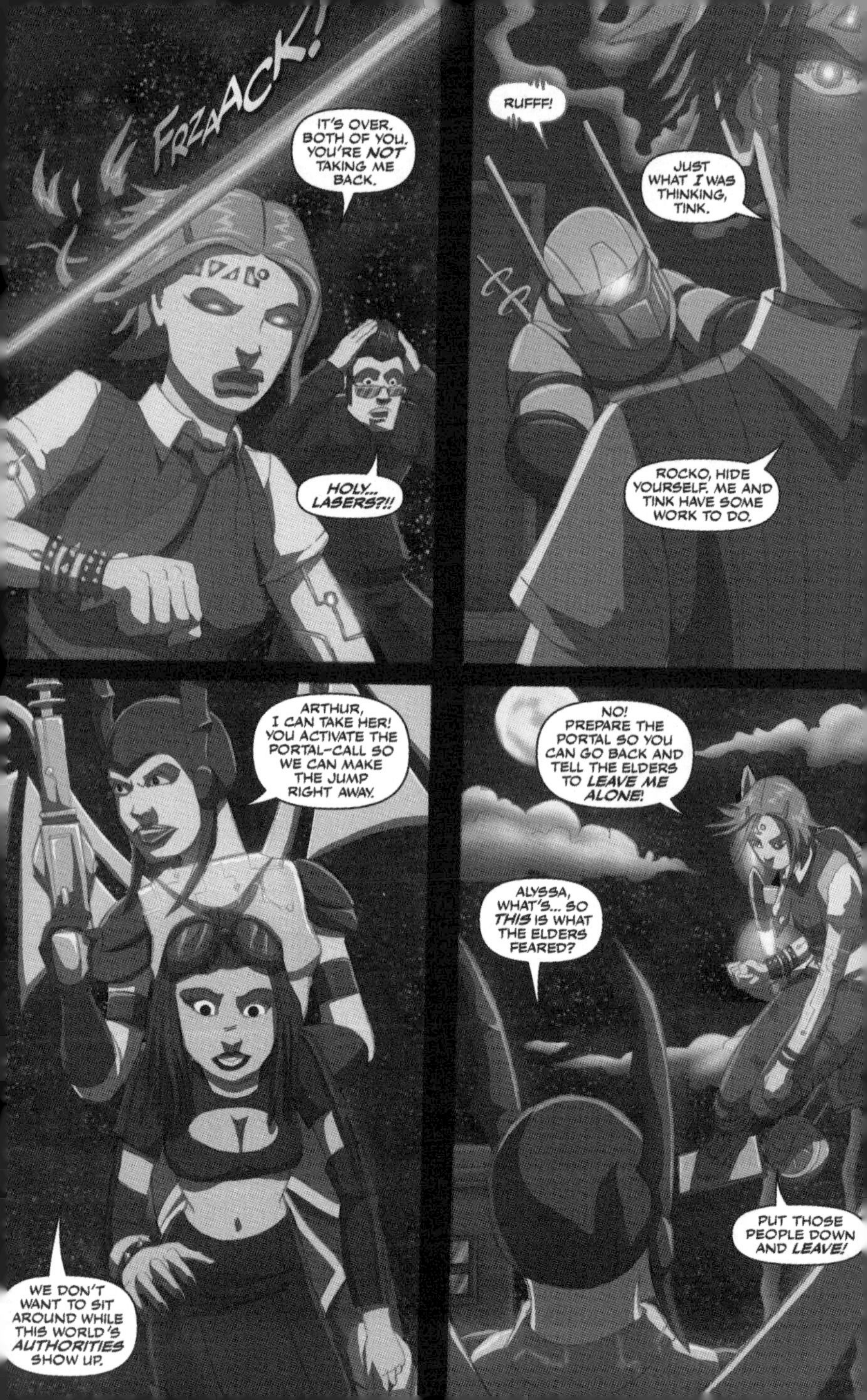
FRZAACK!
IT'S OVER. BOTH OF YOU. YOU'RE NOT TAKING ME BACK.
HOLY... LASERS?!!
RUFFF!
JUST WHAT I WAS THINKING, TINK.
ROCKO, HIDE YOURSELF. ME AND TINK HAVE SOME WORK TO DO.
ARTHUR, I CAN TAKE HER! YOU ACTIVATE THE PORTAL-CALL SO WE CAN MAKE THE JUMP RIGHT AWAY.
WE DON'T WANT TO SIT AROUND WHILE THIS WORLD'S AUTHORITIES SHOW UP.
NO! PREPARE THE PORTAL SO YOU CAN GO BACK AND TELL THE ELDERS TO LEAVE ME ALONE!
ALYSSA, WHAT'S... SO THIS IS WHAT THE ELDERS FEARED?
PUT THOSE PEOPLE DOWN AND LEAVE!

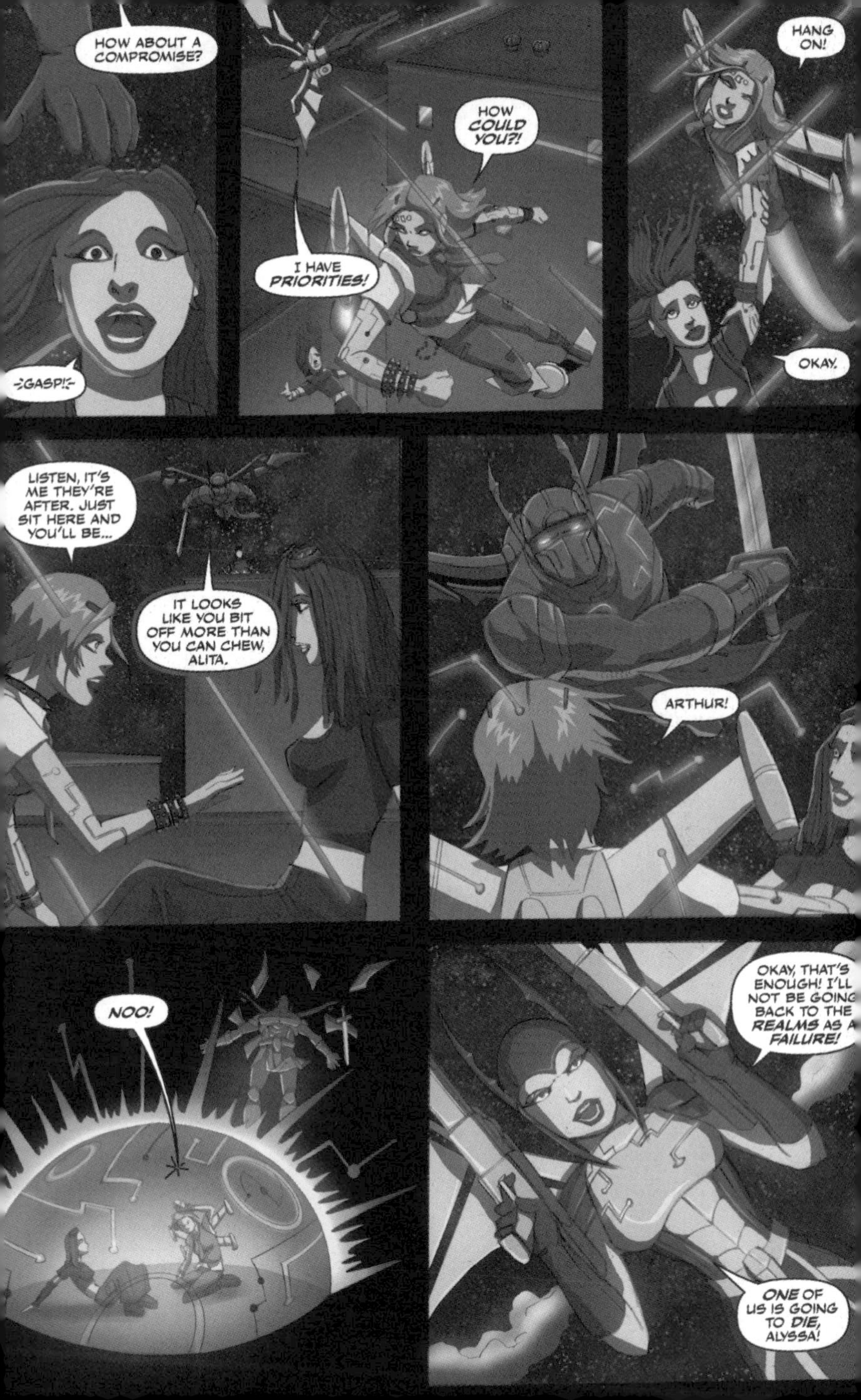
HOW ABOUT A COMPROMISE?
-GASP!-
HOW COULD YOU?!
I HAVE PRIORITIES!
HANG ON!
OKAY.
LISTEN, IT'S ME THEY'RE AFTER. JUST SIT HERE AND YOU'LL BE...
IT LOOKS LIKE YOU BIT OFF MORE THAN YOU CAN CHEW, ALITA.
ARTHUR!
NOO!
OKAY, THAT'S ENOUGH! I'LL NOT BE GOING BACK TO THE REALMS AS A FAILURE!
ONE OF US IS GOING TO DIE, ALYSSA!

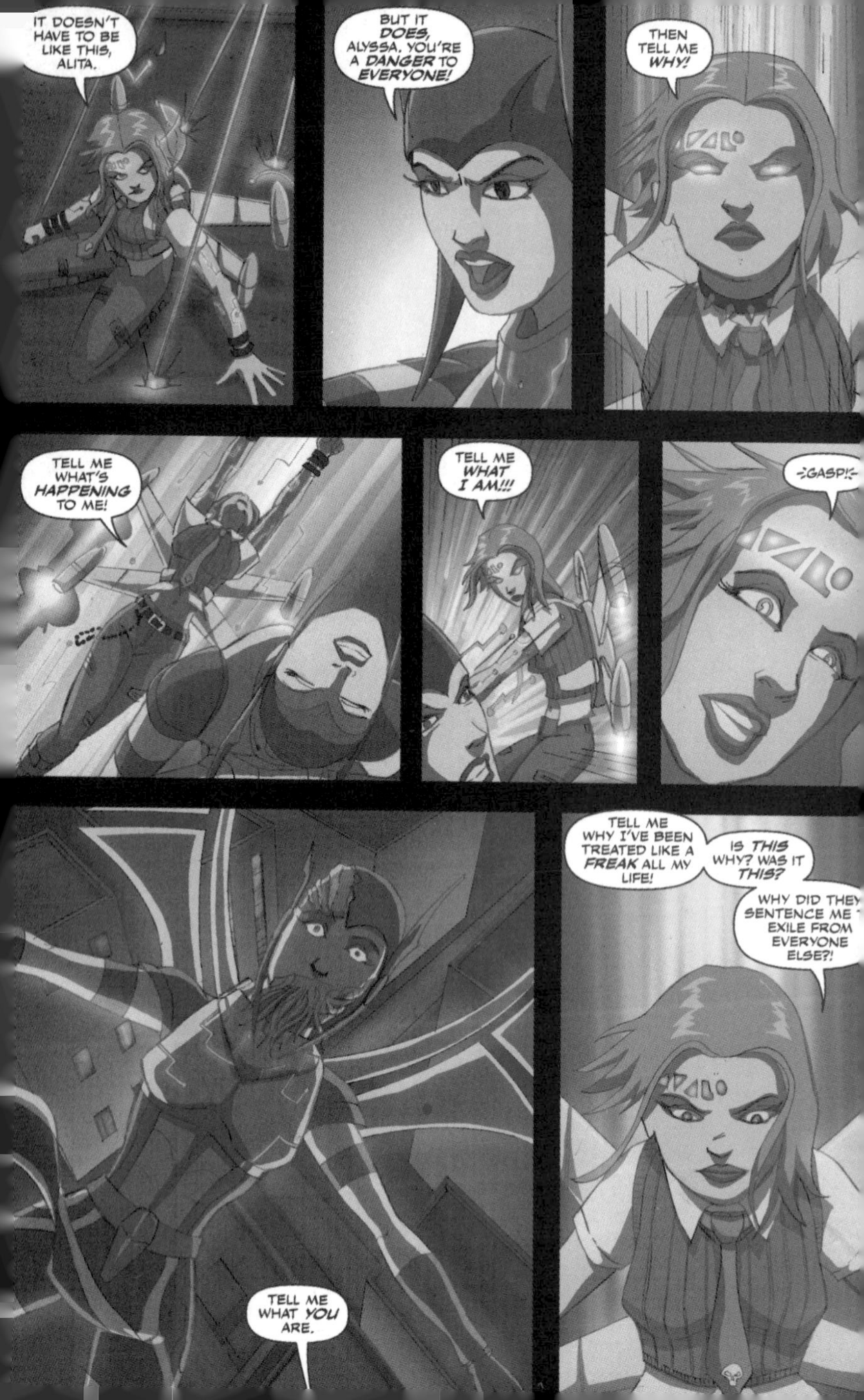
IT DOESN'T HAVE TO BE LIKE THIS, ALITA.
BUT IT DOES, ALYSSA. YOU'RE A DANGER TO EVERYONE!
THEN TELL ME WHY!
TELL ME WHAT'S HAPPENING TO ME!
TELL ME WHAT I AM!!!
GASP!
TELL ME WHAT YOU ARE.
TELL ME WHY I'VE BEEN TREATED LIKE A FREAK ALL MY LIFE!
IS THIS WHY? WAS IT THIS?
WHY DID THEY SENTENCE ME TO EXILE FROM EVERYONE ELSE?!

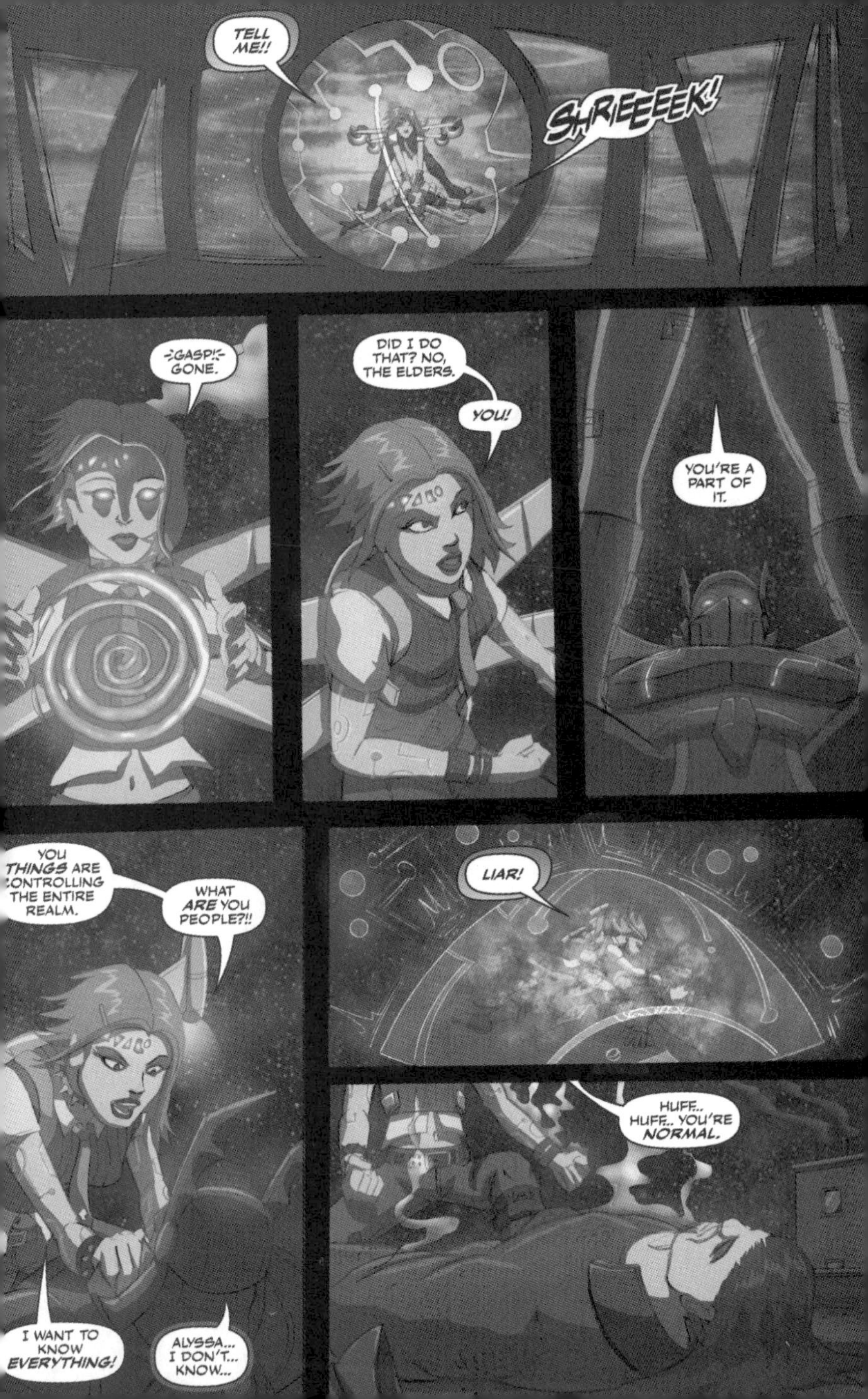
TELL ME!!
SHRIEEEEK!
-GASP!- GONE.
DID I DO THAT? NO, THE ELDERS.
YOU!
YOU'RE A PART OF IT.
YOU THINGS ARE CONTROLLING THE ENTIRE REALM.
WHAT ARE YOU PEOPLE?!!
I WANT TO KNOW EVERYTHING!
ALYSSA... I DON'T... KNOW...
LIAR!
HUFF.. HUFF.. YOU'RE NORMAL.

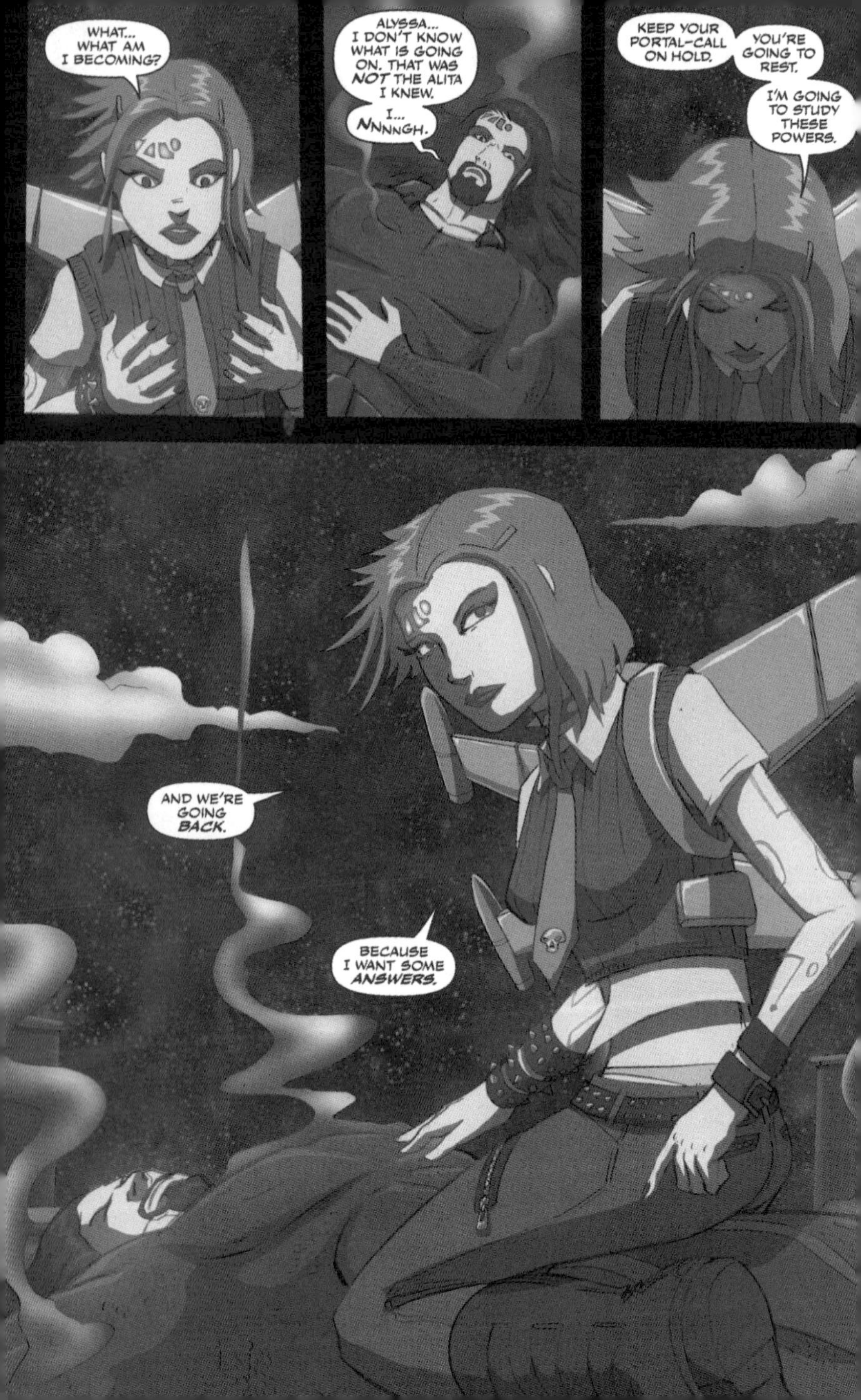
WHAT... WHAT AM I BECOMING?
ALYSSA... I DON'T KNOW WHAT IS GOING ON. THAT WAS NOT THE ALITA I KNEW.
I... NNNNGH.
KEEP YOUR PORTAL-CALL ON HOLD.
YOU'RE GOING TO REST.
I'M GOING TO STUDY THESE POWERS.
AND WE'RE GOING BACK.
BECAUSE I WANT SOME ANSWERS.

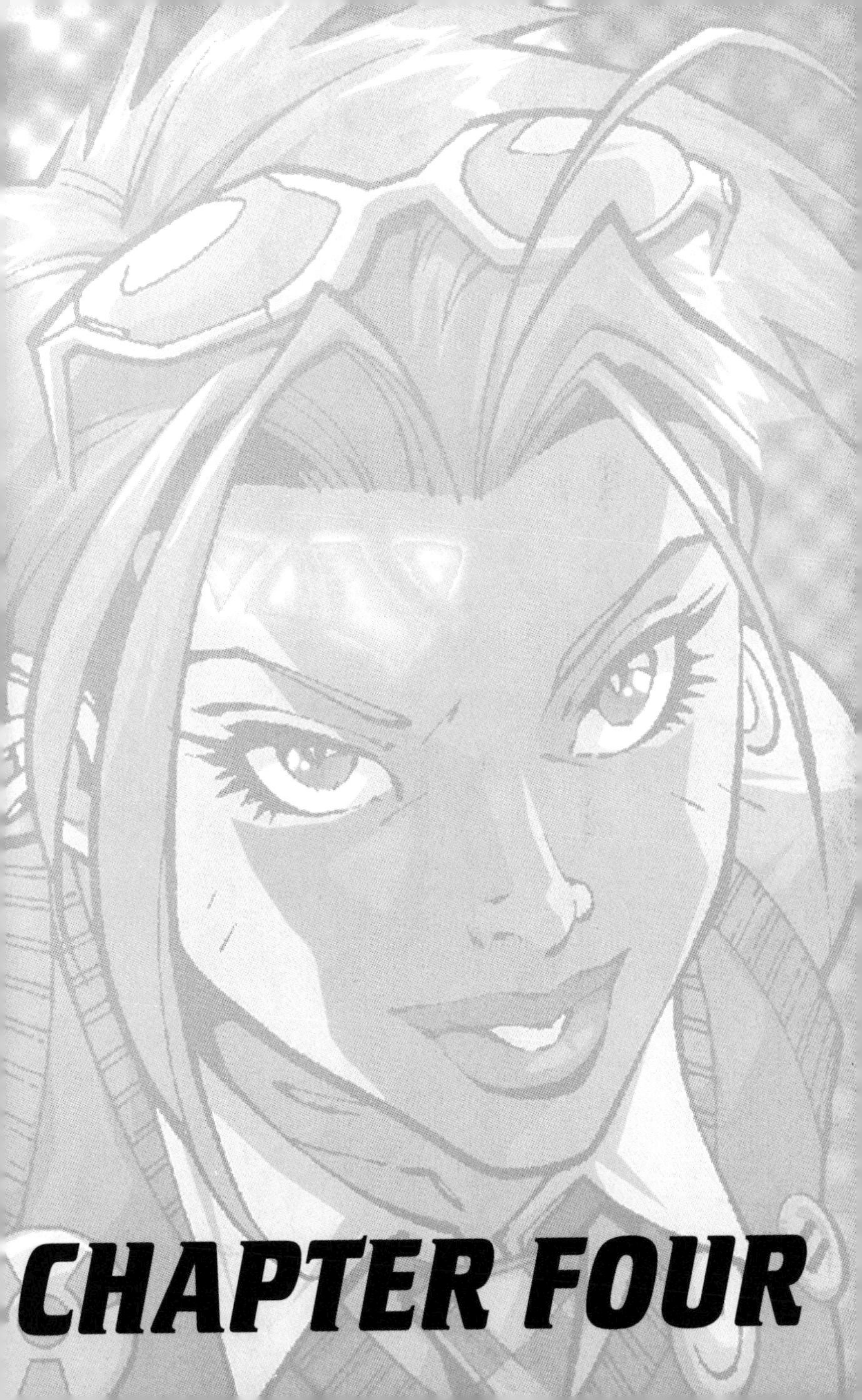

CHAPTER FOUR

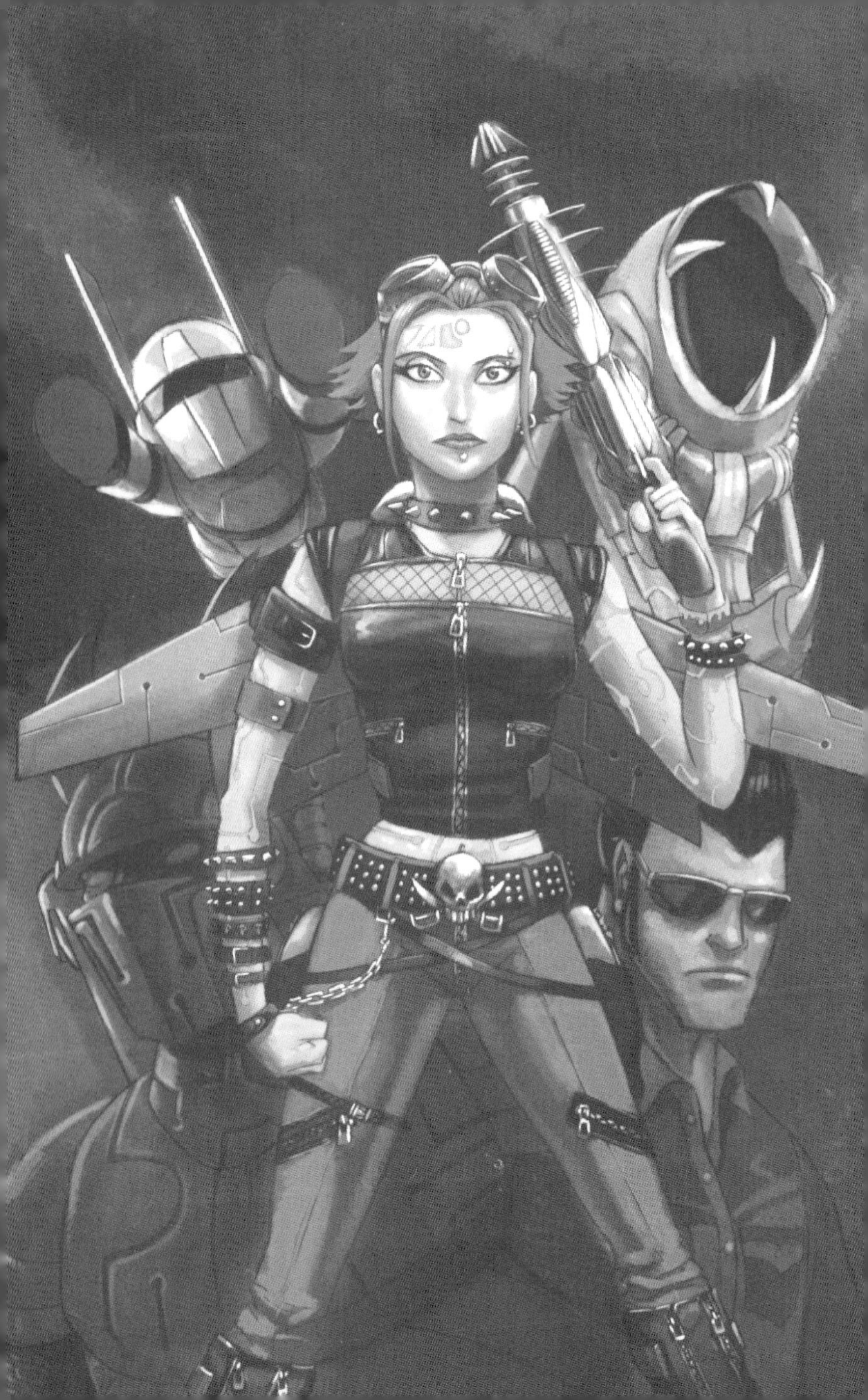

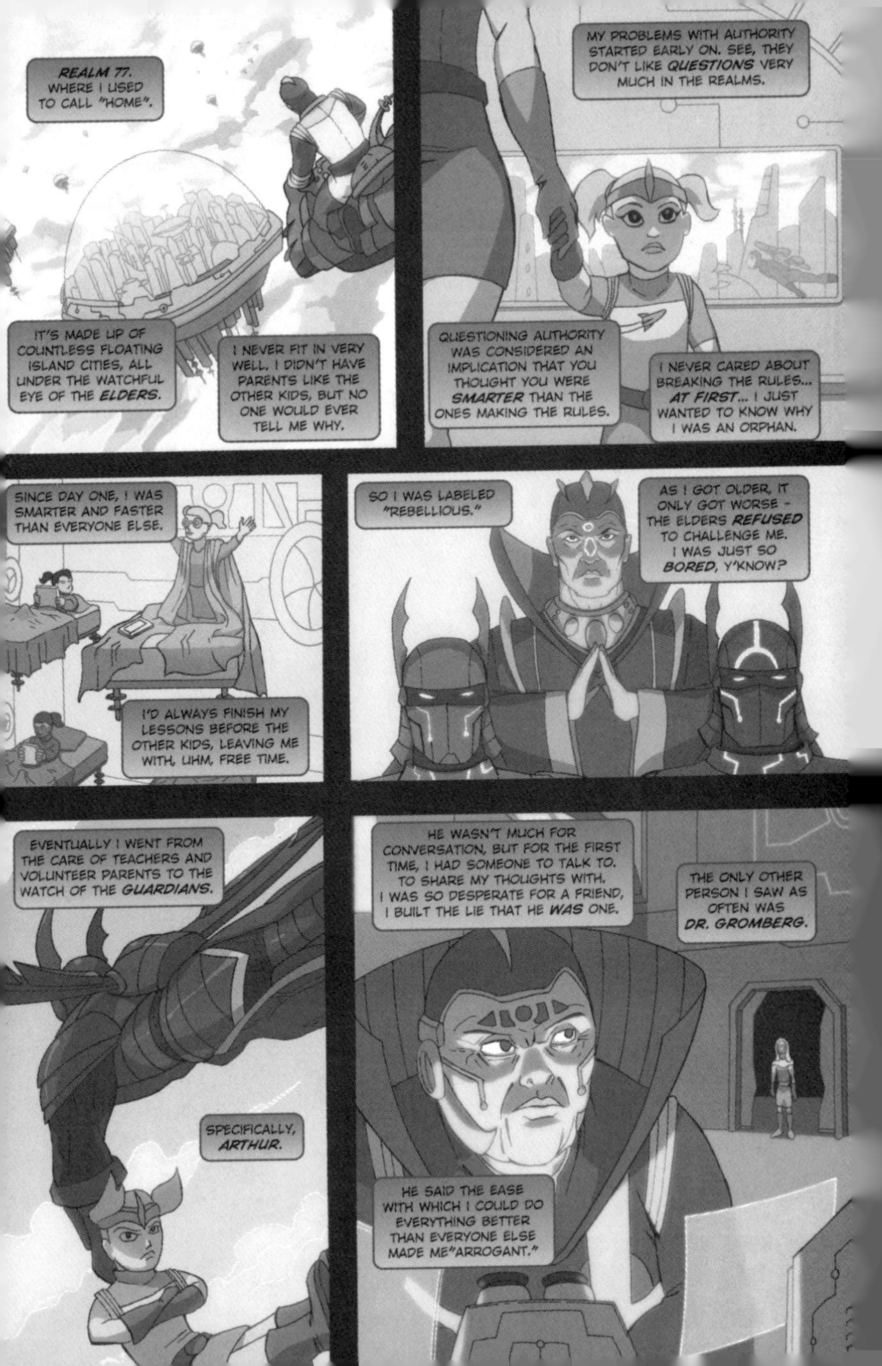
REALM 77. WHERE I USED TO CALL "HOME".
IT'S MADE UP OF COUNTLESS FLOATING ISLAND CITIES, ALL UNDER THE WATCHFUL EYE OF THE ELDERS.
I NEVER FIT IN VERY WELL. I DIDN'T HAVE PARENTS LIKE THE OTHER KIDS, BUT NO ONE WOULD EVER TELL ME WHY.
MY PROBLEMS WITH AUTHORITY STARTED EARLY ON. SEE, THEY DON'T LIKE QUESTIONS VERY MUCH IN THE REALMS.
QUESTIONING AUTHORITY WAS CONSIDERED AN IMPLICATION THAT YOU THOUGHT YOU WERE SMARTER THAN THE ONES MAKING THE RULES.
I NEVER CARED ABOUT BREAKING THE RULES... AT FIRST... I JUST WANTED TO KNOW WHY I WAS AN ORPHAN.
SINCE DAY ONE, I WAS SMARTER AND FASTER THAN EVERYONE ELSE.
I'D ALWAYS FINISH MY LESSONS BEFORE THE OTHER KIDS, LEAVING ME WITH, UHM, FREE TIME.
SO I WAS LABELED "REBELLIOUS."
AS I GOT OLDER, IT ONLY GOT WORSE - THE ELDERS REFUSED TO CHALLENGE ME. I WAS JUST SO BORED, Y'KNOW?
EVENTUALLY I WENT FROM THE CARE OF TEACHERS AND VOLUNTEER PARENTS TO THE WATCH OF THE GUARDIANS.
SPECIFICALLY, ARTHUR.
HE WASN'T MUCH FOR CONVERSATION, BUT FOR THE FIRST TIME, I HAD SOMEONE TO TALK TO. TO SHARE MY THOUGHTS WITH. I WAS SO DESPERATE FOR A FRIEND, I BUILT THE LIE THAT HE WAS ONE.
THE ONLY OTHER PERSON I SAW AS OFTEN WAS DR. GROMBERG.
HE SAID THE EASE WITH WHICH I COULD DO EVERYTHING BETTER THAN EVERYONE ELSE MADE ME "ARROGANT."

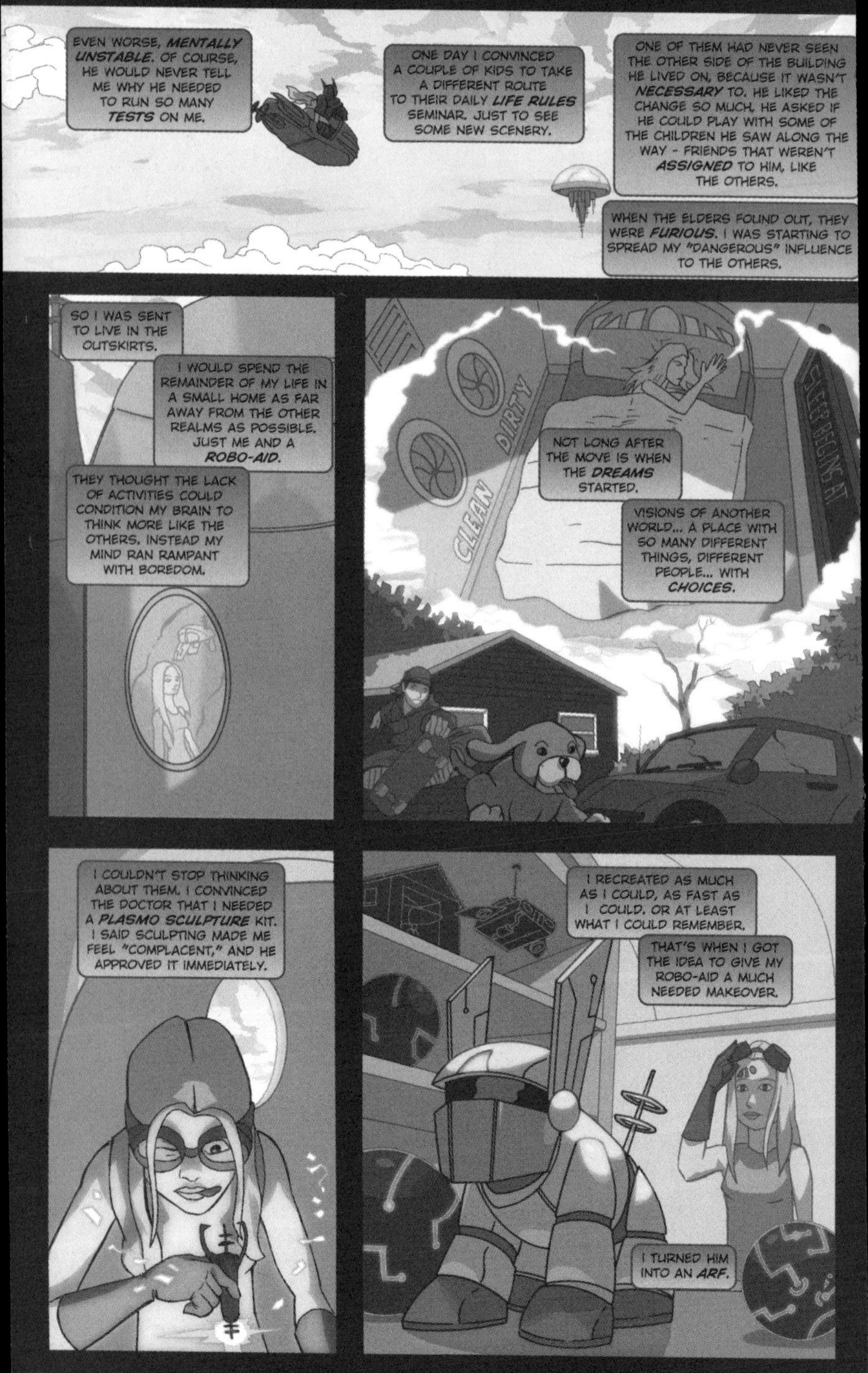
EVEN WORSE, MENTALLY UNSTABLE. OF COURSE, HE WOULD NEVER TELL ME WHY HE NEEDED TO RUN SO MANY TESTS ON ME.
ONE DAY I CONVINCED A COUPLE OF KIDS TO TAKE A DIFFERENT ROUTE TO THEIR DAILY LIFE RULES SEMINAR. JUST TO SEE SOME NEW SCENERY.
ONE OF THEM HAD NEVER SEEN THE OTHER SIDE OF THE BUILDING HE LIVED ON, BECAUSE IT WASN'T NECESSARY TO. HE LIKED THE CHANGE SO MUCH, HE ASKED IF HE COULD PLAY WITH SOME OF THE CHILDREN HE SAW ALONG THE WAY - FRIENDS THAT WEREN'T ASSIGNED TO HIM, LIKE THE OTHERS.
WHEN THE ELDERS FOUND OUT, THEY WERE FURIOUS. I WAS STARTING TO SPREAD MY "DANGEROUS" INFLUENCE TO THE OTHERS.
SO I WAS SENT TO LIVE IN THE OUTSKIRTS.
I WOULD SPEND THE REMAINDER OF MY LIFE IN A SMALL HOME AS FAR AWAY FROM THE OTHER REALMS AS POSSIBLE. JUST ME AND A ROBO-AID.
THEY THOUGHT THE LACK OF ACTIVITIES COULD CONDITION MY BRAIN TO THINK MORE LIKE THE OTHERS. INSTEAD MY MIND RAN RAMPANT WITH BOREDOM.
DIRTY
CLEAN
NOT LONG AFTER THE MOVE IS WHEN THE DREAMS STARTED.
VISIONS OF ANOTHER WORLD... A PLACE WITH SO MANY DIFFERENT THINGS, DIFFERENT PEOPLE... WITH CHOICES.
I COULDN'T STOP THINKING ABOUT THEM. I CONVINCED THE DOCTOR THAT I NEEDED A PLASMO SCULPTURE KIT. I SAID SCULPTING MADE ME FEEL "COMPLACENT," AND HE APPROVED IT IMMEDIATELY.
I RECREATED AS MUCH AS I COULD, AS FAST AS I COULD. OR AT LEAST WHAT I COULD REMEMBER.
THAT'S WHEN I GOT THE IDEA TO GIVE MY ROBO-AID A MUCH NEEDED MAKEOVER.
I TURNED HIM INTO AN ARF.

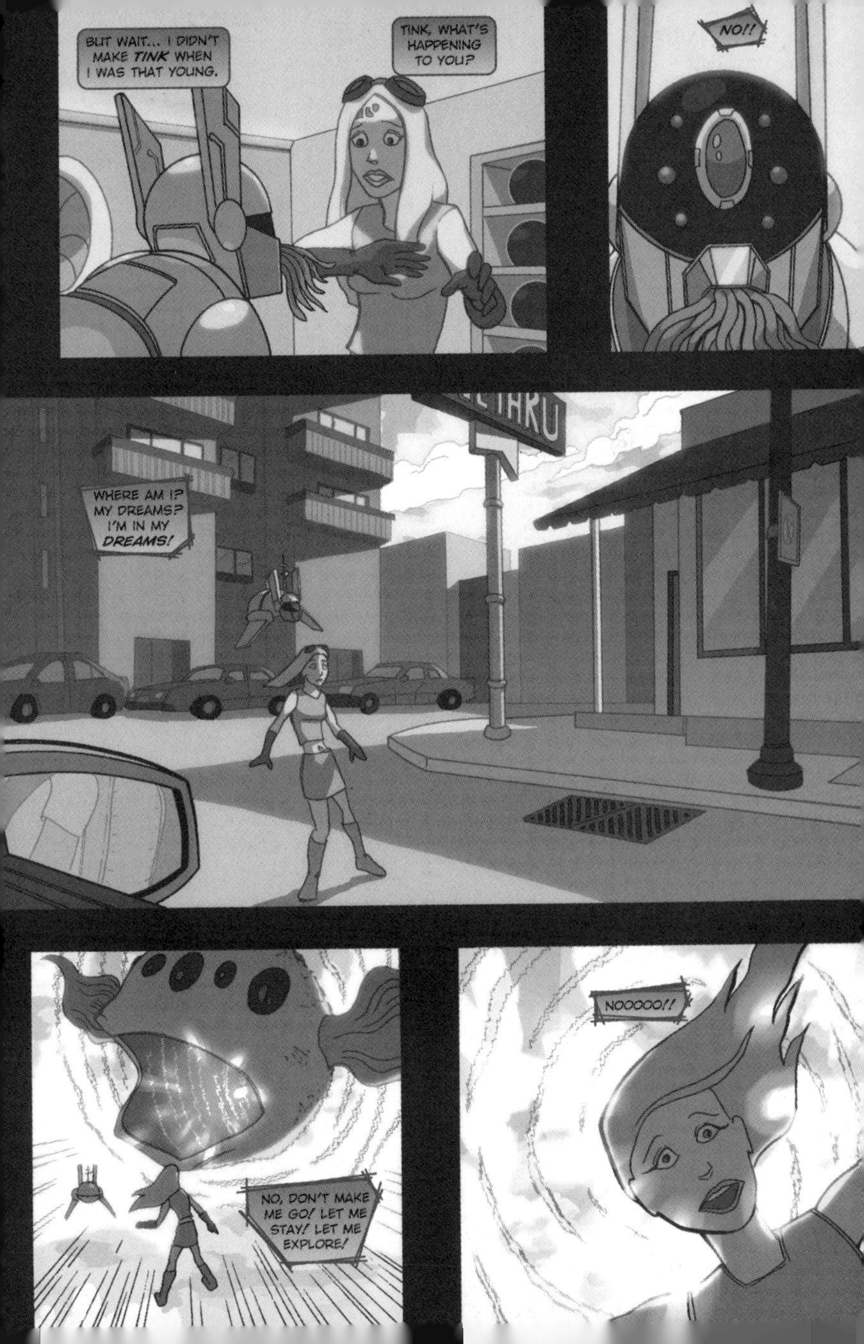
BUT WAIT... I DIDN'T MAKE *TINK* WHEN I WAS THAT YOUNG.
TINK, WHAT'S HAPPENING TO YOU?
NO!!
WHERE AM I? MY DREAMS? I'M IN MY *DREAMS!*
NO, DON'T MAKE ME GO! LET ME STAY! LET ME EXPLORE!
NOOOOO!!

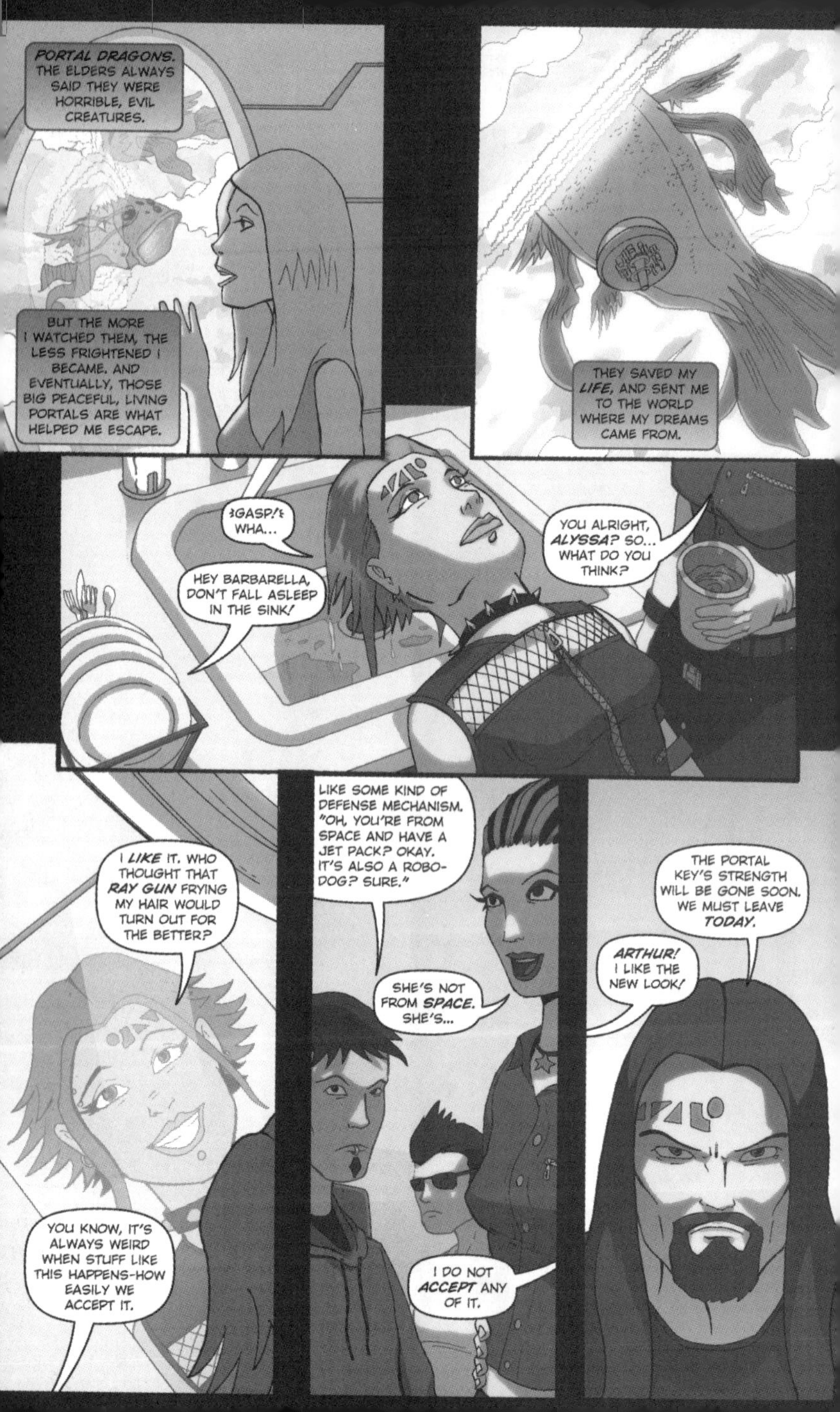
PORTAL DRAGONS. THE ELDERS ALWAYS SAID THEY WERE HORRIBLE, EVIL CREATURES.
BUT THE MORE I WATCHED THEM, THE LESS FRIGHTENED I BECAME. AND EVENTUALLY, THOSE BIG PEACEFUL, LIVING PORTALS ARE WHAT HELPED ME ESCAPE.
THEY SAVED MY LIFE, AND SENT ME TO THE WORLD WHERE MY DREAMS CAME FROM.
GASP! WHA...
HEY BARBARELLA, DON'T FALL ASLEEP IN THE SINK!
YOU ALRIGHT, ALYSSA? SO... WHAT DO YOU THINK?
I LIKE IT. WHO THOUGHT THAT RAY GUN FRYING MY HAIR WOULD TURN OUT FOR THE BETTER?
YOU KNOW, IT'S ALWAYS WEIRD WHEN STUFF LIKE THIS HAPPENS-HOW EASILY WE ACCEPT IT.
LIKE SOME KIND OF DEFENSE MECHANISM. "OH, YOU'RE FROM SPACE AND HAVE A JET PACK? OKAY. IT'S ALSO A ROBO-DOG? SURE."
SHE'S NOT FROM SPACE. SHE'S...
I DO NOT ACCEPT ANY OF IT.
THE PORTAL KEY'S STRENGTH WILL BE GONE SOON. WE MUST LEAVE TODAY.
ARTHUR! I LIKE THE NEW LOOK!

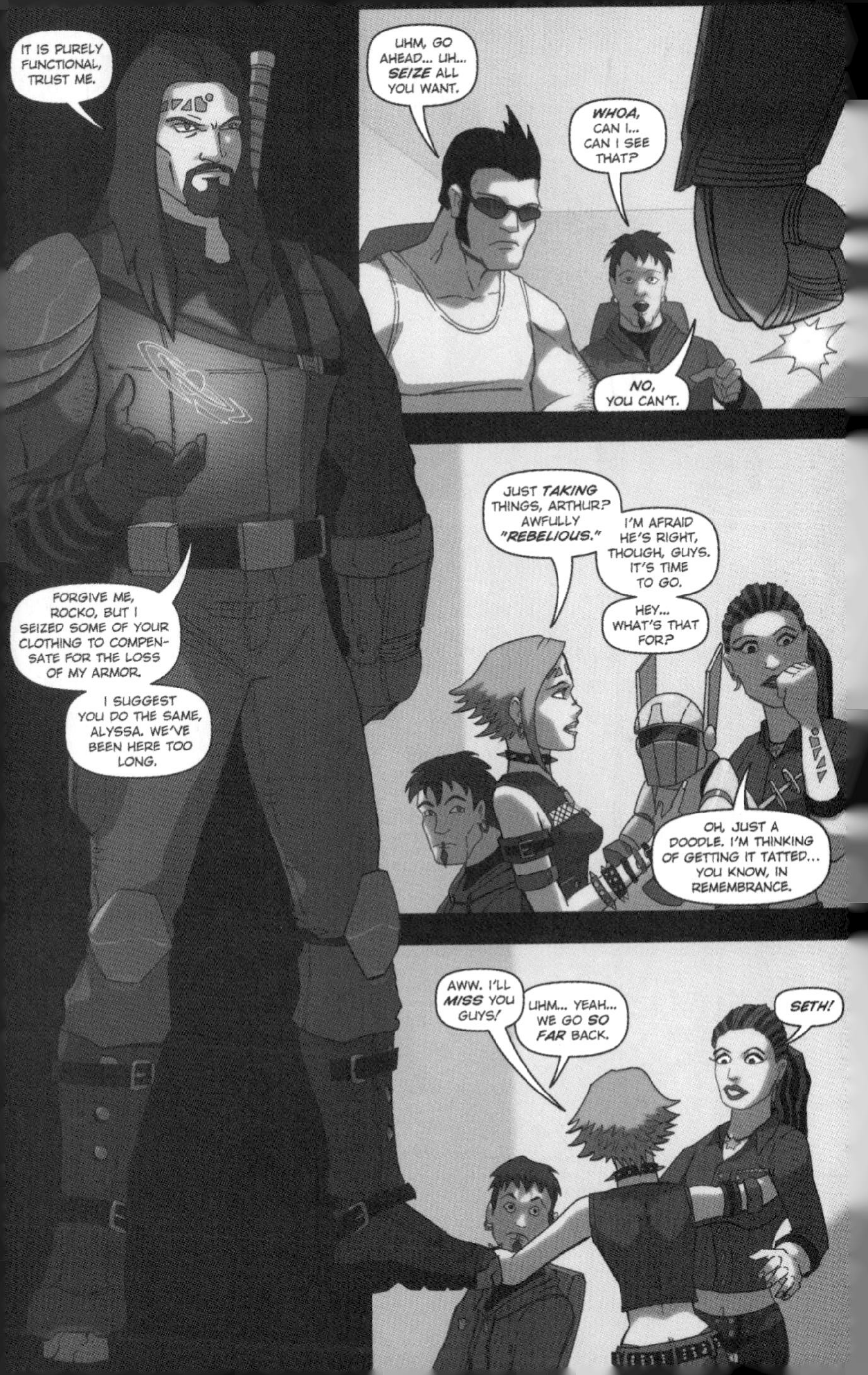
IT IS PURELY FUNCTIONAL, TRUST ME.
FORGIVE ME, ROCKO, BUT I SEIZED SOME OF YOUR CLOTHING TO COMPENSATE FOR THE LOSS OF MY ARMOR.
I SUGGEST YOU DO THE SAME, ALYSSA. WE'VE BEEN HERE TOO LONG.
UHM, GO AHEAD... UH... *SEIZE* ALL YOU WANT.
WHOA, CAN I... CAN I SEE THAT?
NO, YOU CAN'T.
JUST *TAKING* THINGS, ARTHUR? AWFULLY *"REBELIOUS."*
I'M AFRAID HE'S RIGHT, THOUGH, GUYS. IT'S TIME TO GO.
HEY... WHAT'S THAT FOR?
OH, JUST A DOODLE. I'M THINKING OF GETTING IT TATTED... YOU KNOW, IN REMEMBRANCE.
AWW. I'LL *MISS* YOU GUYS!
UHM... YEAH... WE GO *SO FAR* BACK.
SETH!

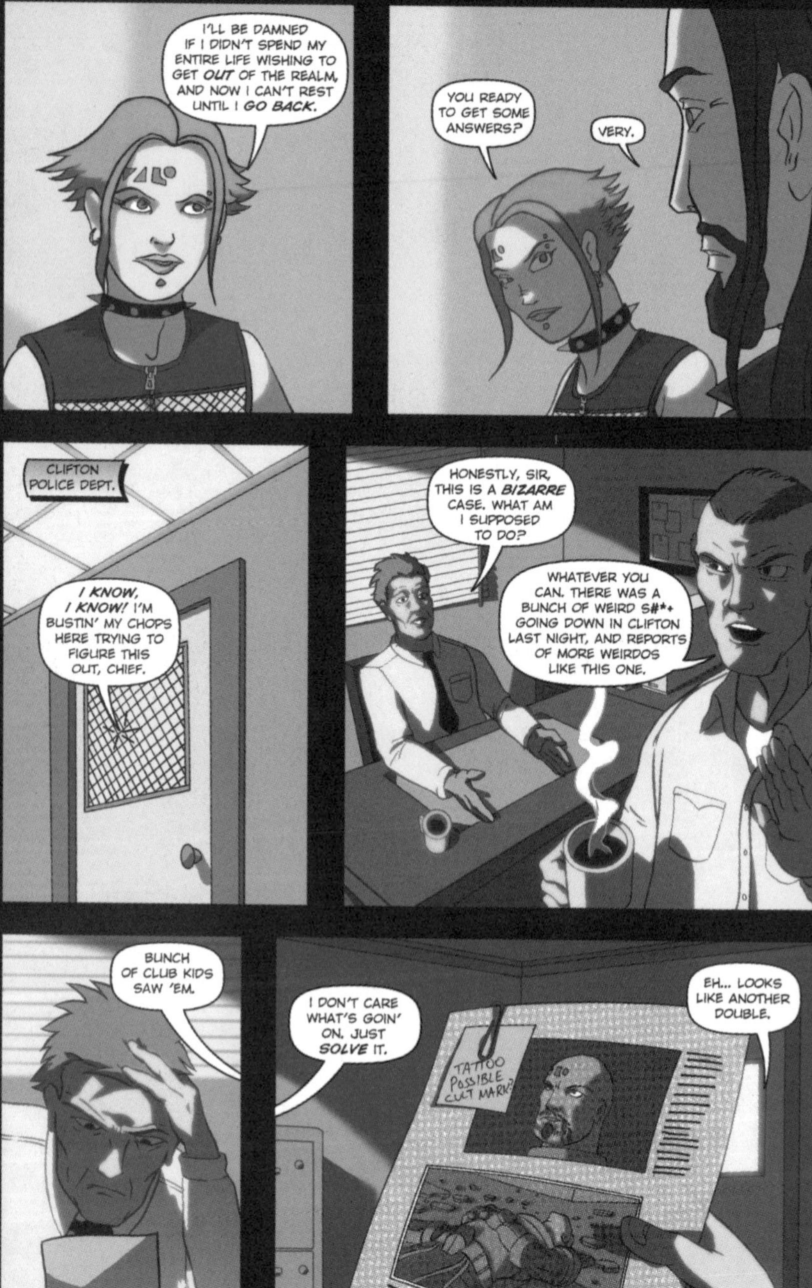
I'LL BE DAMNED IF I DIDN'T SPEND MY ENTIRE LIFE WISHING TO GET *OUT* OF THE REALM, AND NOW I CAN'T REST UNTIL I *GO BACK.*
YOU READY TO GET SOME ANSWERS?
VERY.
CLIFTON POLICE DEPT.
I KNOW, I KNOW! I'M BUSTIN' MY CHOPS HERE TRYING TO FIGURE THIS OUT, CHIEF.
HONESTLY, SIR, THIS IS A *BIZARRE* CASE. WHAT AM I SUPPOSED TO DO?
WHATEVER YOU CAN. THERE WAS A BUNCH OF WEIRD S#*+ GOING DOWN IN CLIFTON LAST NIGHT, AND REPORTS OF MORE WEIRDOS LIKE THIS ONE.
BUNCH OF CLUB KIDS SAW 'EM.
I DON'T CARE WHAT'S GOIN' ON. JUST *SOLVE* IT.
EH... LOOKS LIKE ANOTHER DOUBLE.
TATTOO POSSIBLE CULT MARK?

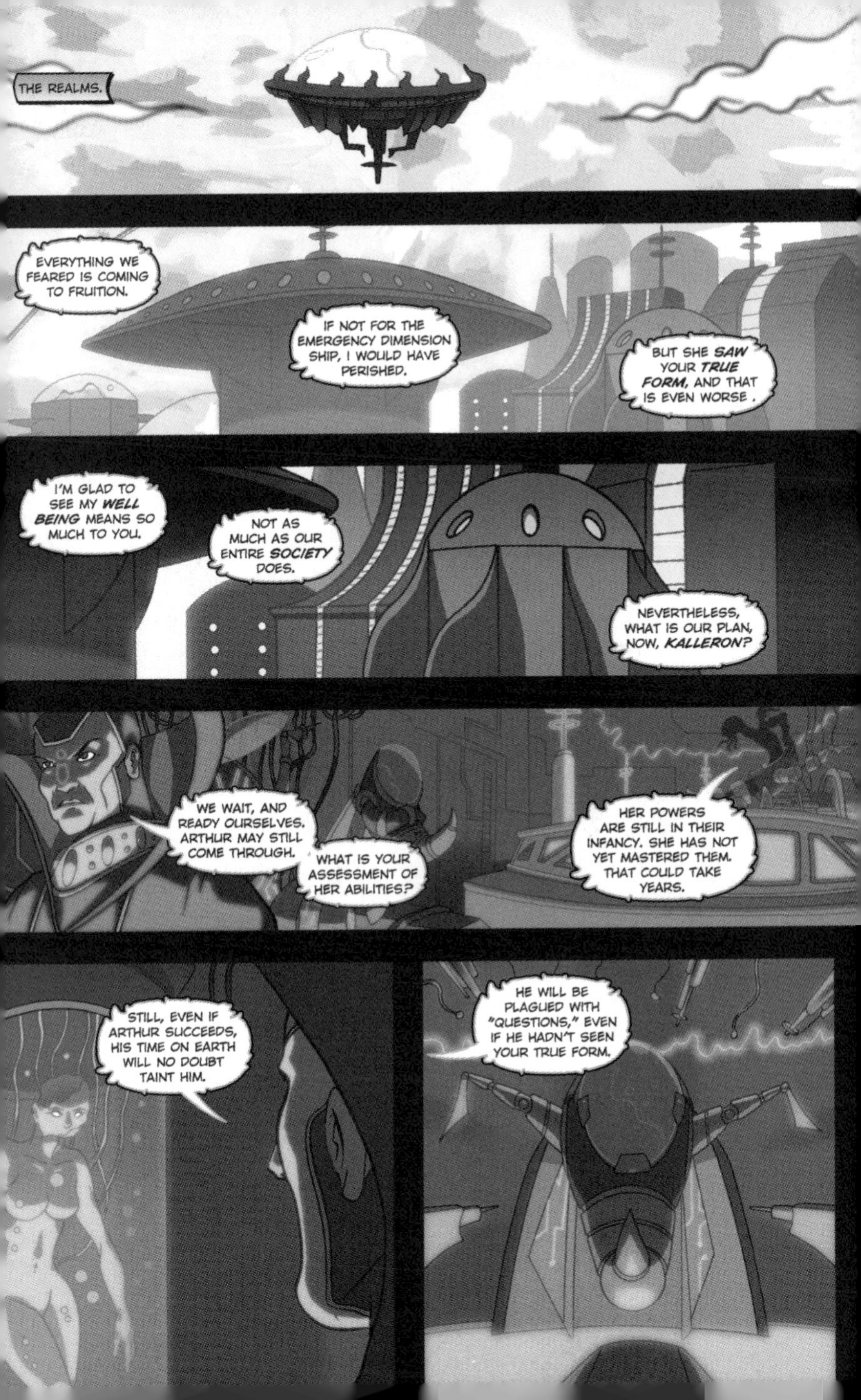
THE REALMS.
EVERYTHING WE FEARED IS COMING TO FRUITION.
IF NOT FOR THE EMERGENCY DIMENSION SHIP, I WOULD HAVE PERISHED.
BUT SHE *SAW* YOUR *TRUE FORM,* AND THAT IS EVEN WORSE.
I'M GLAD TO SEE MY *WELL BEING* MEANS SO MUCH TO YOU.
NOT AS MUCH AS OUR ENTIRE *SOCIETY* DOES.
NEVERTHELESS, WHAT IS OUR PLAN, NOW, *KALLERON?*
WE WAIT, AND READY OURSELVES. ARTHUR MAY STILL COME THROUGH.
WHAT IS YOUR ASSESSMENT OF HER ABILITIES?
HER POWERS ARE STILL IN THEIR INFANCY. SHE HAS NOT YET MASTERED THEM. THAT COULD TAKE YEARS.
STILL, EVEN IF ARTHUR SUCCEEDS, HIS TIME ON EARTH WILL NO DOUBT TAINT HIM.
HE WILL BE PLAGUED WITH "QUESTIONS," EVEN IF HE HADN'T SEEN YOUR TRUE FORM.

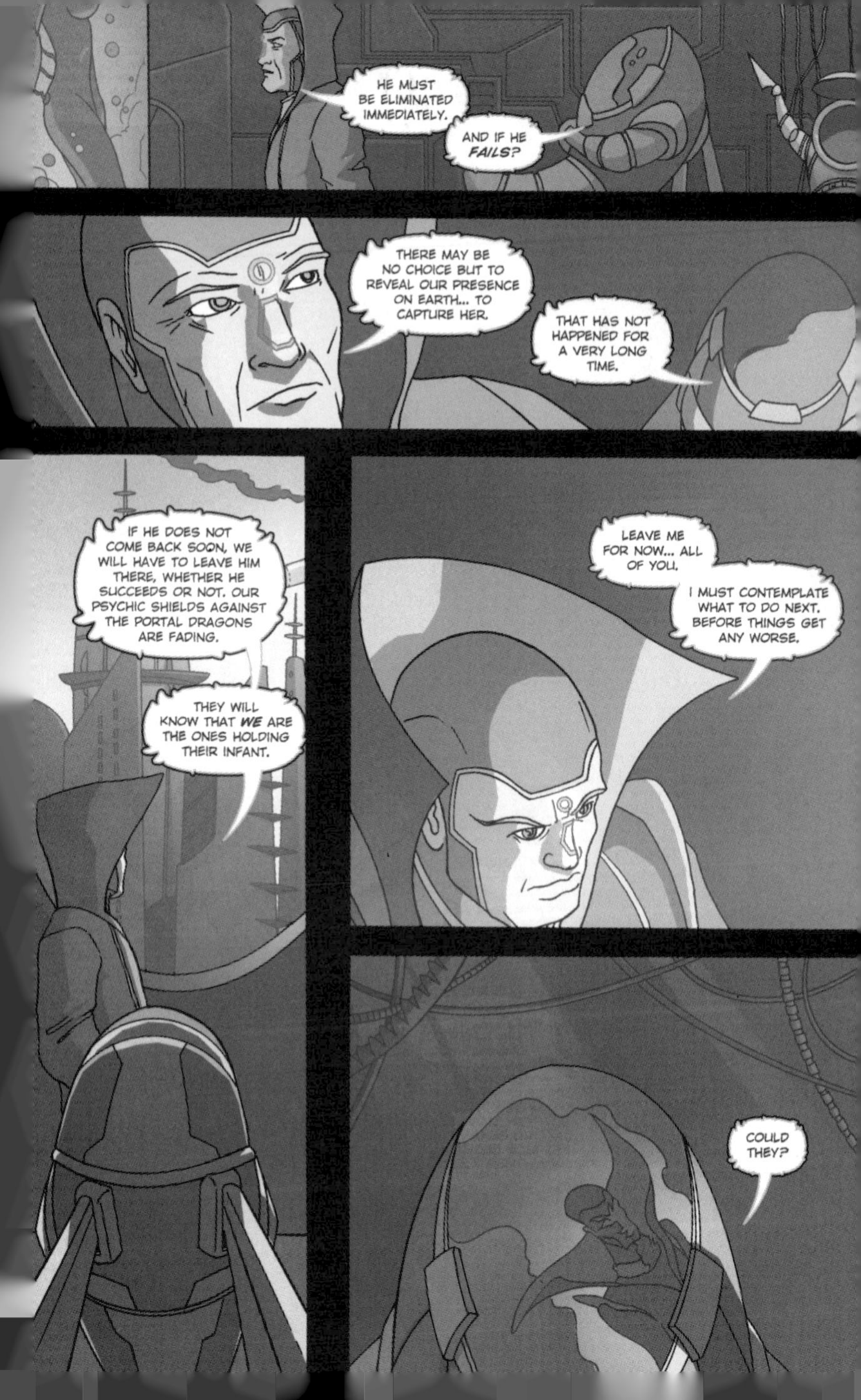
HE MUST BE ELIMINATED IMMEDIATELY.
AND IF HE *FAILS?*
THERE MAY BE NO CHOICE BUT TO REVEAL OUR PRESENCE ON EARTH... TO CAPTURE HER.
THAT HAS NOT HAPPENED FOR A VERY LONG TIME.
IF HE DOES NOT COME BACK SOON, WE WILL HAVE TO LEAVE HIM THERE, WHETHER HE SUCCEEDS OR NOT. OUR PSYCHIC SHIELDS AGAINST THE PORTAL DRAGONS ARE FADING.
THEY WILL KNOW THAT *WE* ARE THE ONES HOLDING THEIR INFANT.
LEAVE ME FOR NOW... ALL OF YOU.
I MUST CONTEMPLATE WHAT TO DO NEXT. BEFORE THINGS GET ANY WORSE.
COULD THEY?

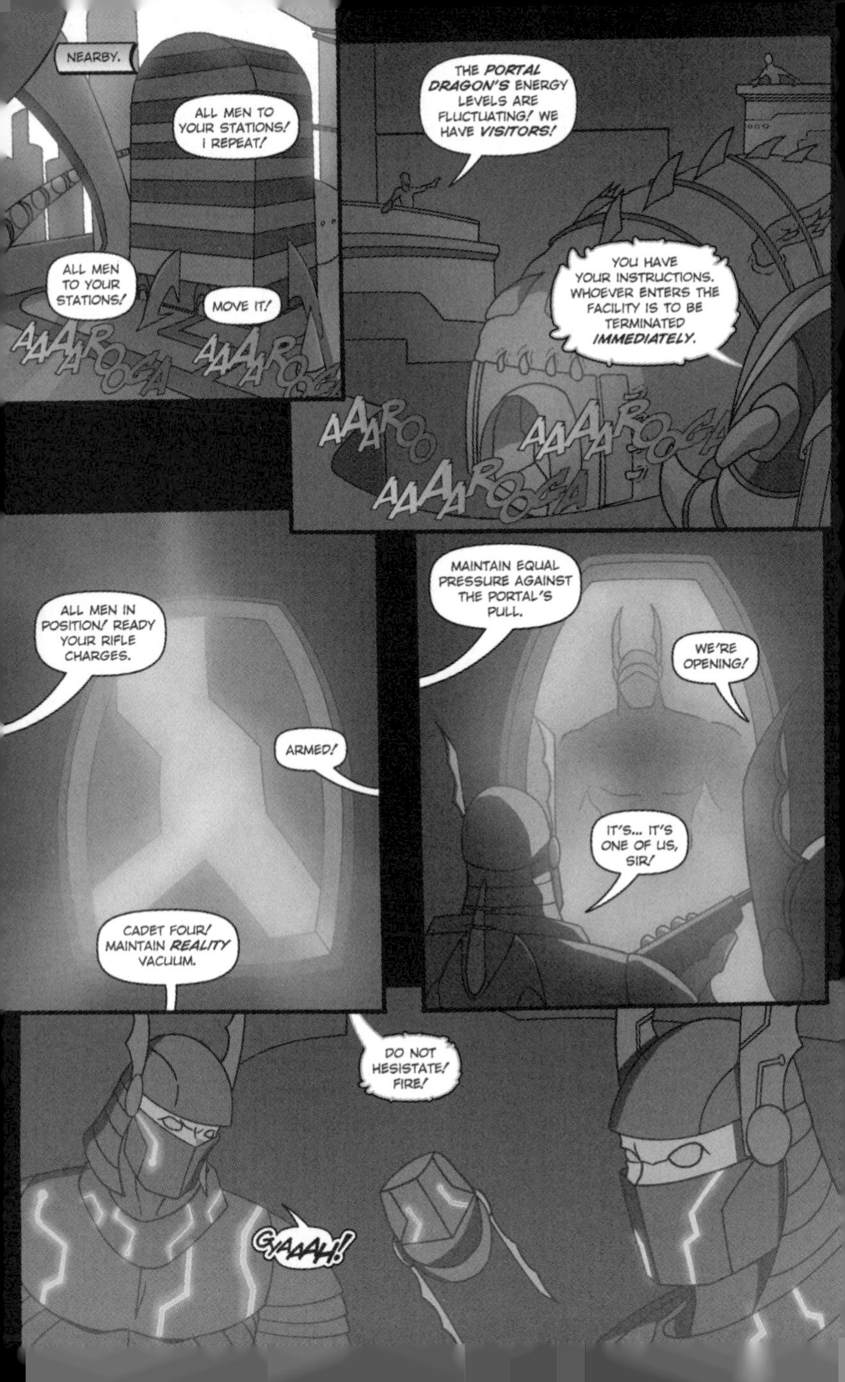
NEARBY.
ALL MEN TO YOUR STATIONS! I REPEAT!
ALL MEN TO YOUR STATIONS!
MOVE IT!
AAAAROOGA
AAAAROOGA
THE PORTAL DRAGON'S ENERGY LEVELS ARE FLUCTUATING! WE HAVE VISITORS!
YOU HAVE YOUR INSTRUCTIONS. WHOEVER ENTERS THE FACILITY IS TO BE TERMINATED IMMEDIATELY.
AAAAROO
AAAAROOGA
AAAAROOGA
ALL MEN IN POSITION! READY YOUR RIFLE CHARGES.
ARMED!
CADET FOUR! MAINTAIN REALITY VACUUM.
MAINTAIN EQUAL PRESSURE AGAINST THE PORTAL'S PULL.
WE'RE OPENING!
IT'S... IT'S ONE OF US, SIR!
DO NOT HESITATE! FIRE!
GYAAAH!

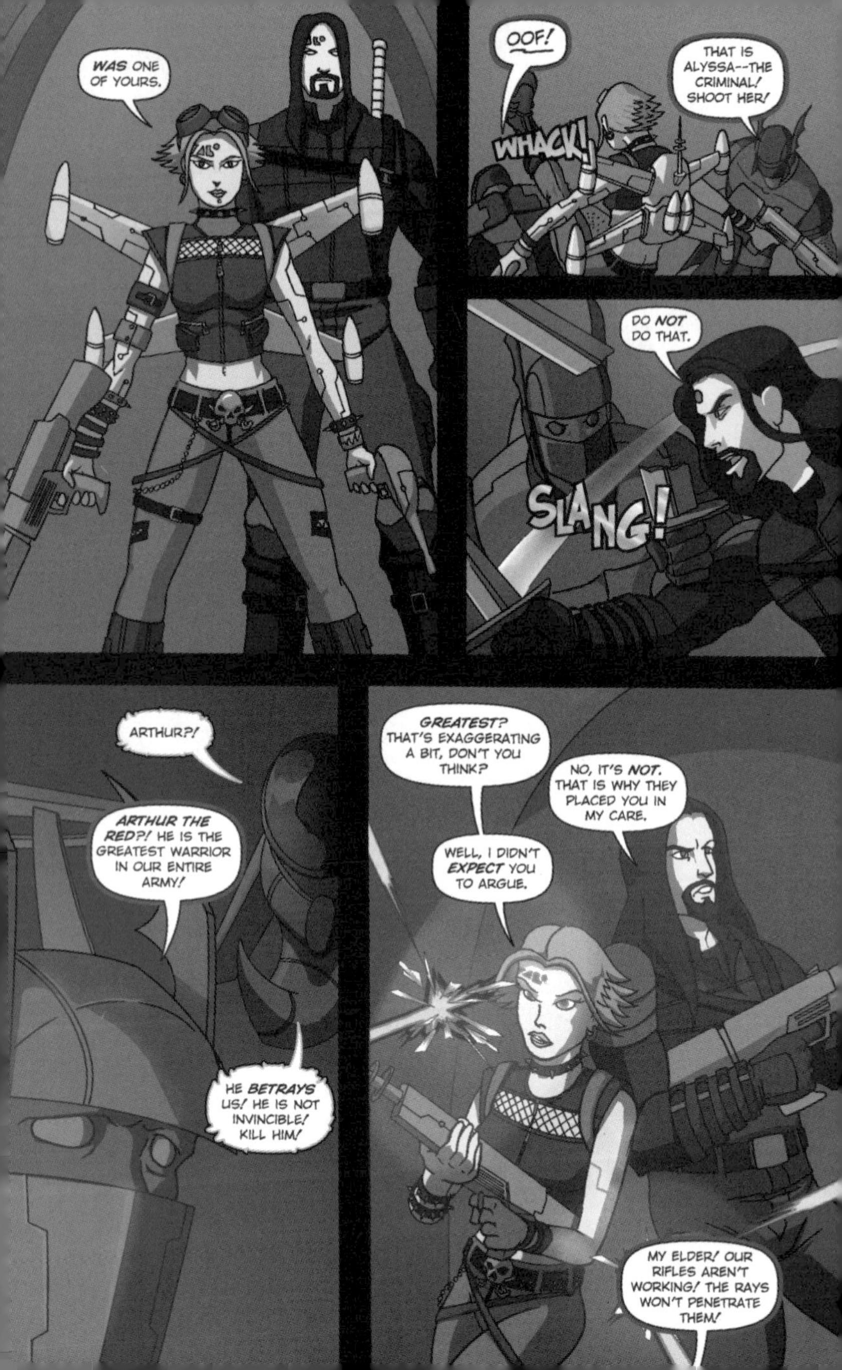
WAS ONE OF YOURS.
OOF!
WHACK!
THAT IS ALYSSA--THE CRIMINAL! SHOOT HER!
DO NOT DO THAT.
SLANG!
ARTHUR?!
ARTHUR THE RED?! HE IS THE GREATEST WARRIOR IN OUR ENTIRE ARMY!
HE BETRAYS US! HE IS NOT INVINCIBLE! KILL HIM!
GREATEST? THAT'S EXAGGERATING A BIT, DON'T YOU THINK?
NO, IT'S NOT. THAT IS WHY THEY PLACED YOU IN MY CARE.
WELL, I DIDN'T EXPECT YOU TO ARGUE.
MY ELDER! OUR RIFLES AREN'T WORKING! THE RAYS WON'T PENETRATE THEM!

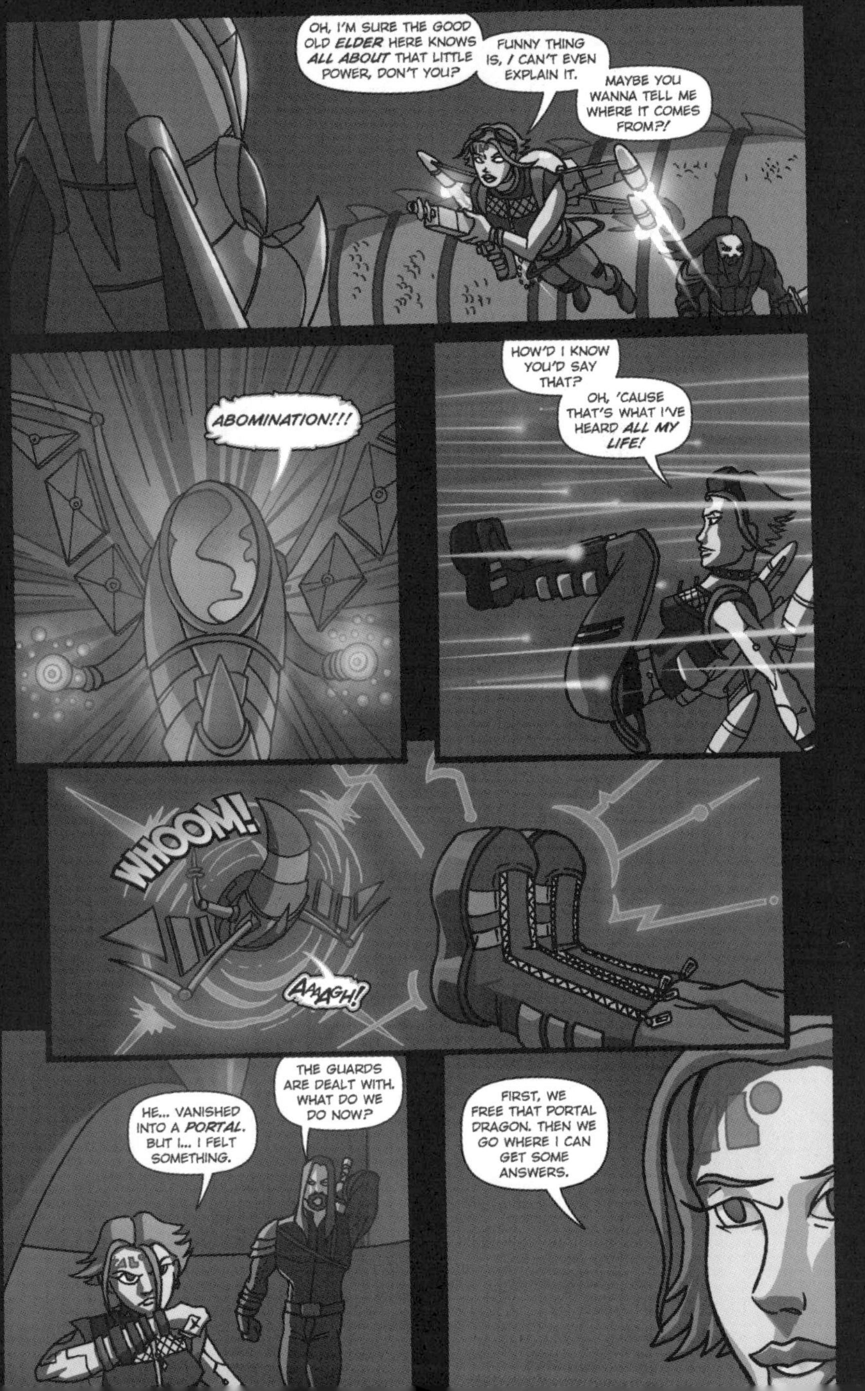
OH, I'M SURE THE GOOD OLD *ELDER* HERE KNOWS *ALL ABOUT* THAT LITTLE POWER, DON'T YOU?
FUNNY THING IS, *I* CAN'T EVEN EXPLAIN IT.
MAYBE YOU WANNA TELL ME WHERE IT COMES FROM?!
ABOMINATION!!!
HOW'D I KNOW YOU'D SAY THAT?
OH, 'CAUSE THAT'S WHAT I'VE HEARD *ALL MY LIFE!*
WHOOM!
AAAAGH!
HE... VANISHED INTO A *PORTAL*. BUT I... I FELT SOMETHING.
THE GUARDS ARE DEALT WITH. WHAT DO WE DO NOW?
FIRST, WE FREE THAT PORTAL DRAGON. THEN WE GO WHERE I CAN GET SOME ANSWERS.

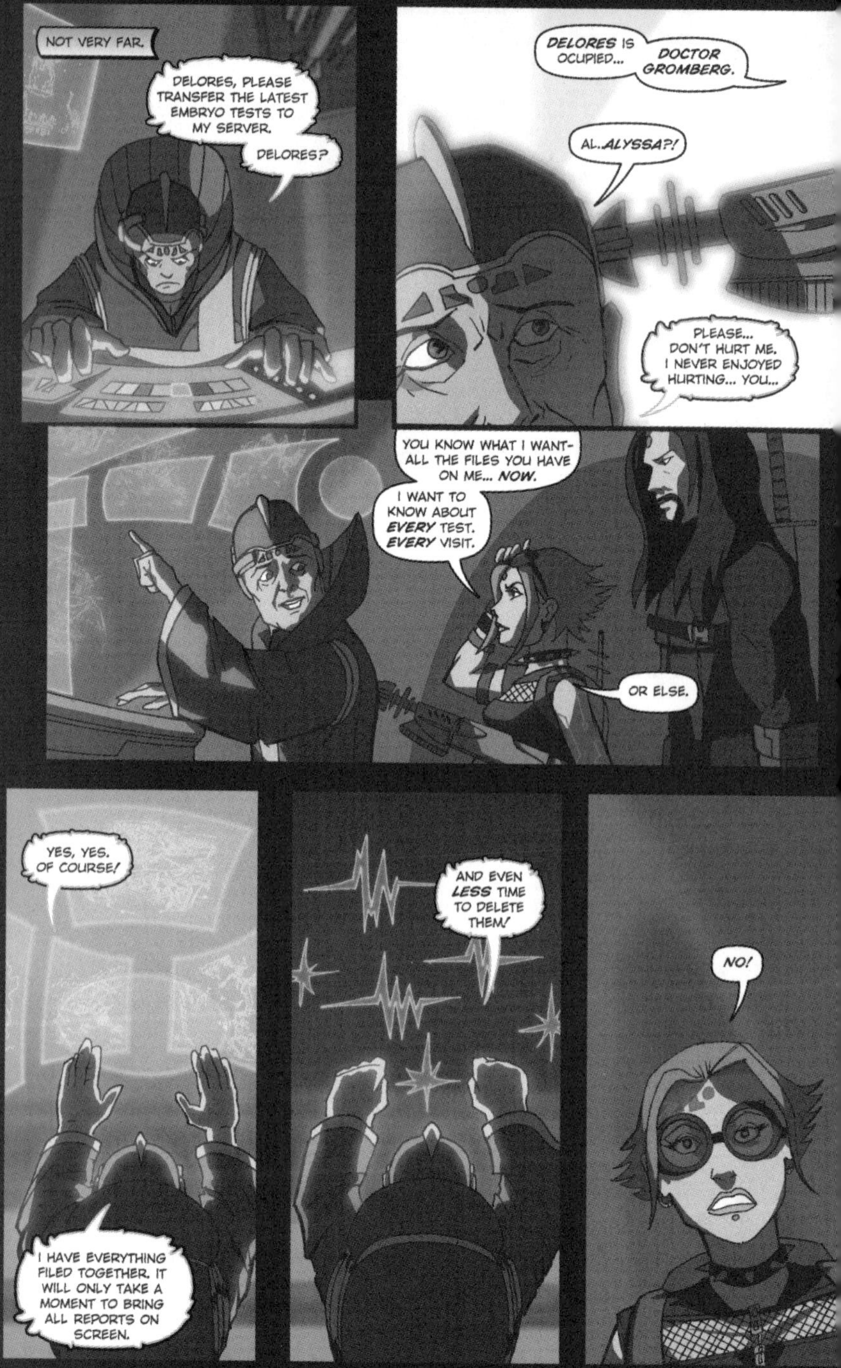
NOT VERY FAR.
DELORES, PLEASE TRANSFER THE LATEST EMBRYO TESTS TO MY SERVER.
DELORES?
DELORES IS OCUPIED... DOCTOR GROMBERG.
AL..ALYSSA?!
PLEASE... DON'T HURT ME. I NEVER ENJOYED HURTING... YOU...
YOU KNOW WHAT I WANT- ALL THE FILES YOU HAVE ON ME... NOW.
I WANT TO KNOW ABOUT EVERY TEST. EVERY VISIT.
OR ELSE.
YES, YES. OF COURSE!
I HAVE EVERYTHING FILED TOGETHER. IT WILL ONLY TAKE A MOMENT TO BRING ALL REPORTS ON SCREEN.
AND EVEN LESS TIME TO DELETE THEM!
NO!

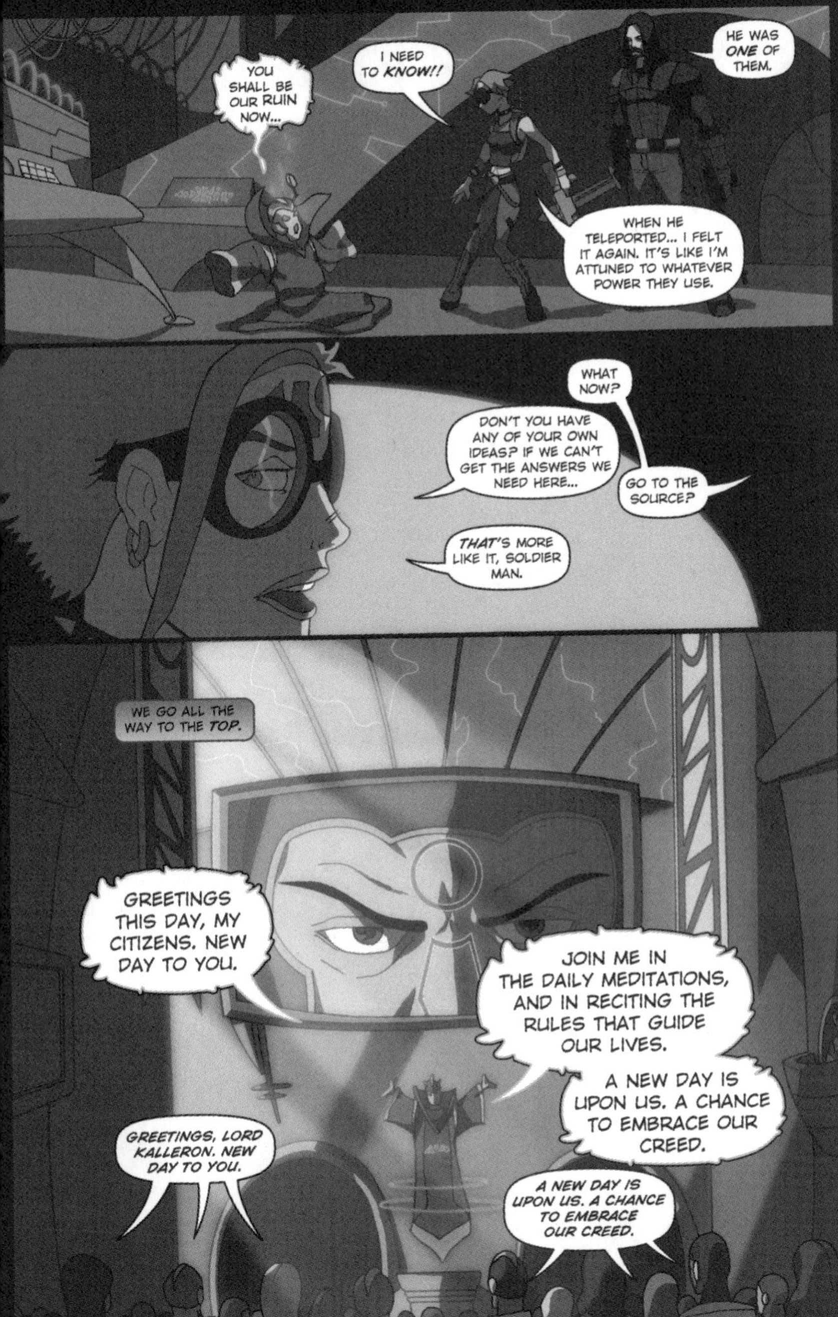
YOU SHALL BE OUR RUIN NOW...
I NEED TO *KNOW!!*
HE WAS *ONE* OF THEM.
WHEN HE TELEPORTED... I FELT IT AGAIN. IT'S LIKE I'M ATTUNED TO WHATEVER POWER THEY USE.
WHAT NOW?
DON'T YOU HAVE ANY OF YOUR OWN IDEAS? IF WE CAN'T GET THE ANSWERS WE NEED HERE...
GO TO THE SOURCE?
THAT'S MORE LIKE IT, SOLDIER MAN.
WE GO ALL THE WAY TO THE *TOP*.
GREETINGS THIS DAY, MY CITIZENS. NEW DAY TO YOU.
JOIN ME IN THE DAILY MEDITATIONS, AND IN RECITING THE RULES THAT GUIDE OUR LIVES.
A NEW DAY IS UPON US. A CHANCE TO EMBRACE OUR CREED.
GREETINGS, LORD KALLERON. NEW DAY TO YOU.
A NEW DAY IS UPON US. A CHANCE TO EMBRACE OUR CREED.

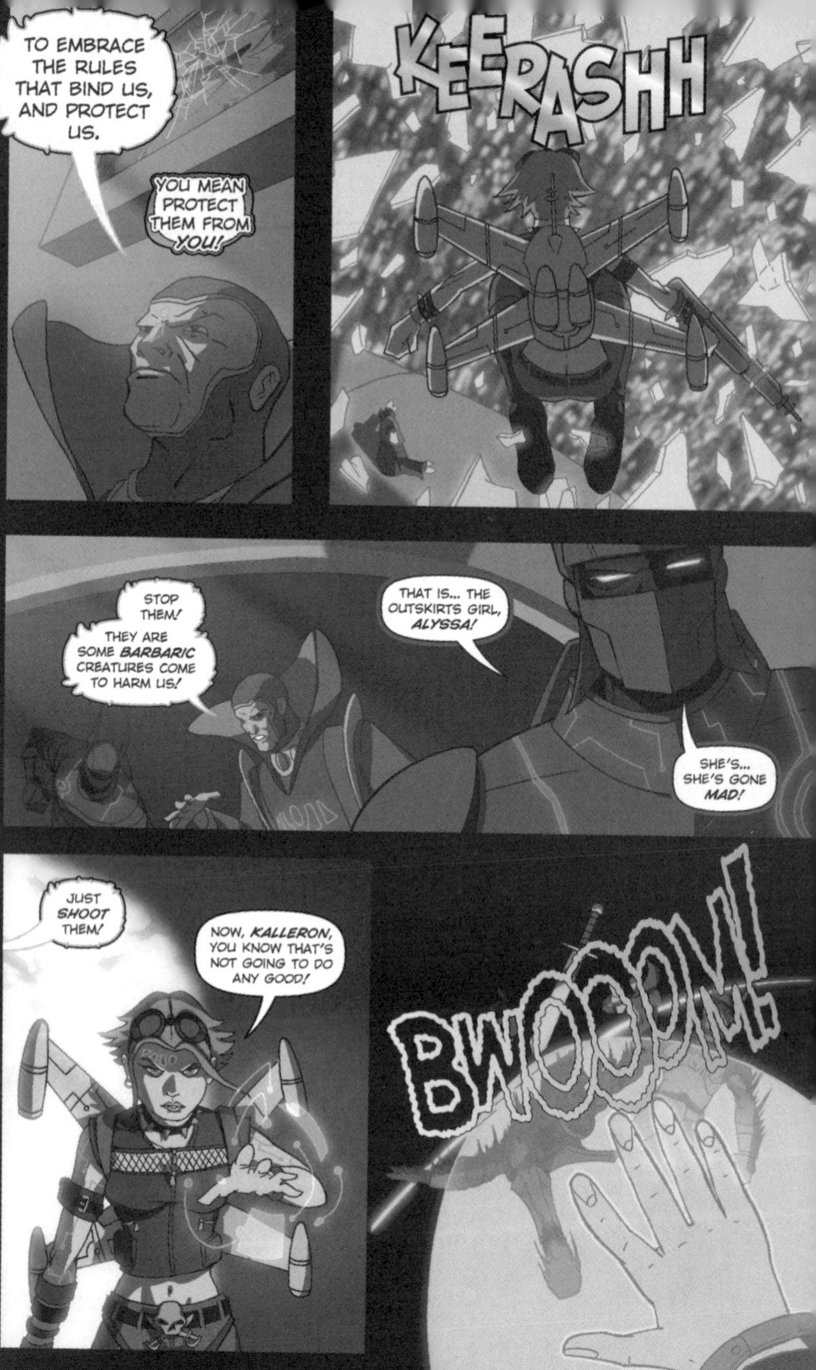
TO EMBRACE THE RULES THAT BIND US, AND PROTECT US.
YOU MEAN PROTECT THEM FROM YOU!
KEERASHH
STOP THEM! THEY ARE SOME BARBARIC CREATURES COME TO HARM US!
THAT IS... THE OUTSKIRTS GIRL, ALYSSA!
SHE'S... SHE'S GONE MAD!
JUST SHOOT THEM!
NOW, KALLERON, YOU KNOW THAT'S NOT GOING TO DO ANY GOOD!
BWOOOM!

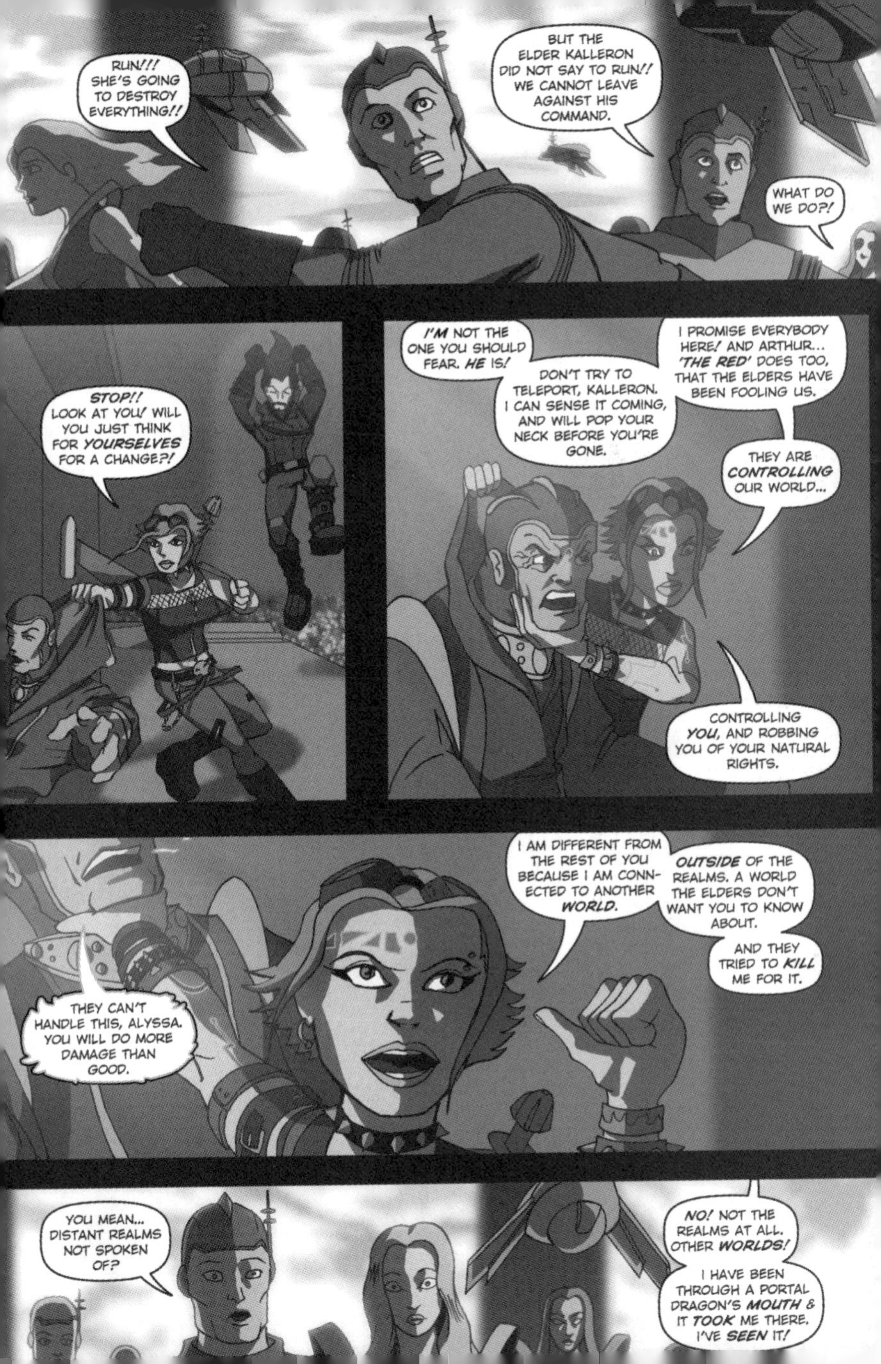
RUN!!! SHE'S GOING TO DESTROY EVERYTHING!!
BUT THE ELDER KALLERON DID NOT SAY TO RUN!! WE CANNOT LEAVE AGAINST HIS COMMAND.
WHAT DO WE DO?!
STOP!! LOOK AT YOU! WILL YOU JUST THINK FOR YOURSELVES FOR A CHANGE?!
I'M NOT THE ONE YOU SHOULD FEAR. HE IS!
DON'T TRY TO TELEPORT, KALLERON. I CAN SENSE IT COMING, AND WILL POP YOUR NECK BEFORE YOU'RE GONE.
I PROMISE EVERYBODY HERE! AND ARTHUR... 'THE RED' DOES TOO, THAT THE ELDERS HAVE BEEN FOOLING US.
THEY ARE CONTROLLING OUR WORLD...
CONTROLLING YOU, AND ROBBING YOU OF YOUR NATURAL RIGHTS.
THEY CAN'T HANDLE THIS, ALYSSA. YOU WILL DO MORE DAMAGE THAN GOOD.
I AM DIFFERENT FROM THE REST OF YOU BECAUSE I AM CONNECTED TO ANOTHER WORLD.
OUTSIDE OF THE REALMS. A WORLD THE ELDERS DON'T WANT YOU TO KNOW ABOUT.
AND THEY TRIED TO KILL ME FOR IT.
YOU MEAN... DISTANT REALMS NOT SPOKEN OF?
NO! NOT THE REALMS AT ALL. OTHER WORLDS!
I HAVE BEEN THROUGH A PORTAL DRAGON'S MOUTH & IT TOOK ME THERE. I'VE SEEN IT!

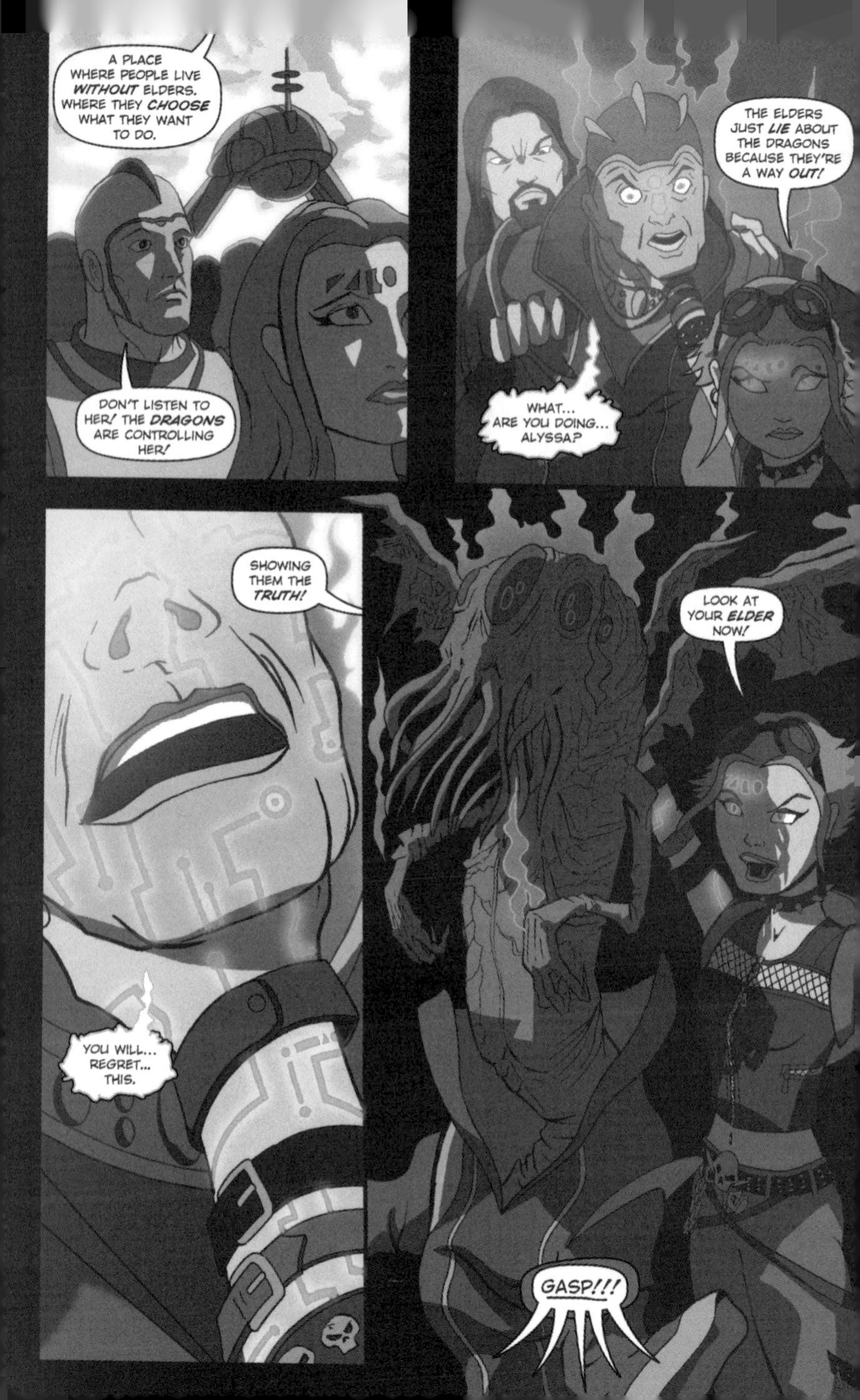
A PLACE WHERE PEOPLE LIVE WITHOUT ELDERS. WHERE THEY CHOOSE WHAT THEY WANT TO DO.
DON'T LISTEN TO HER! THE DRAGONS ARE CONTROLLING HER!
THE ELDERS JUST LIE ABOUT THE DRAGONS BECAUSE THEY'RE A WAY OUT!
WHAT... ARE YOU DOING... ALYSSA?
SHOWING THEM THE TRUTH!
YOU WILL... REGRET... THIS.
LOOK AT YOUR ELDER NOW!
GASP!!!

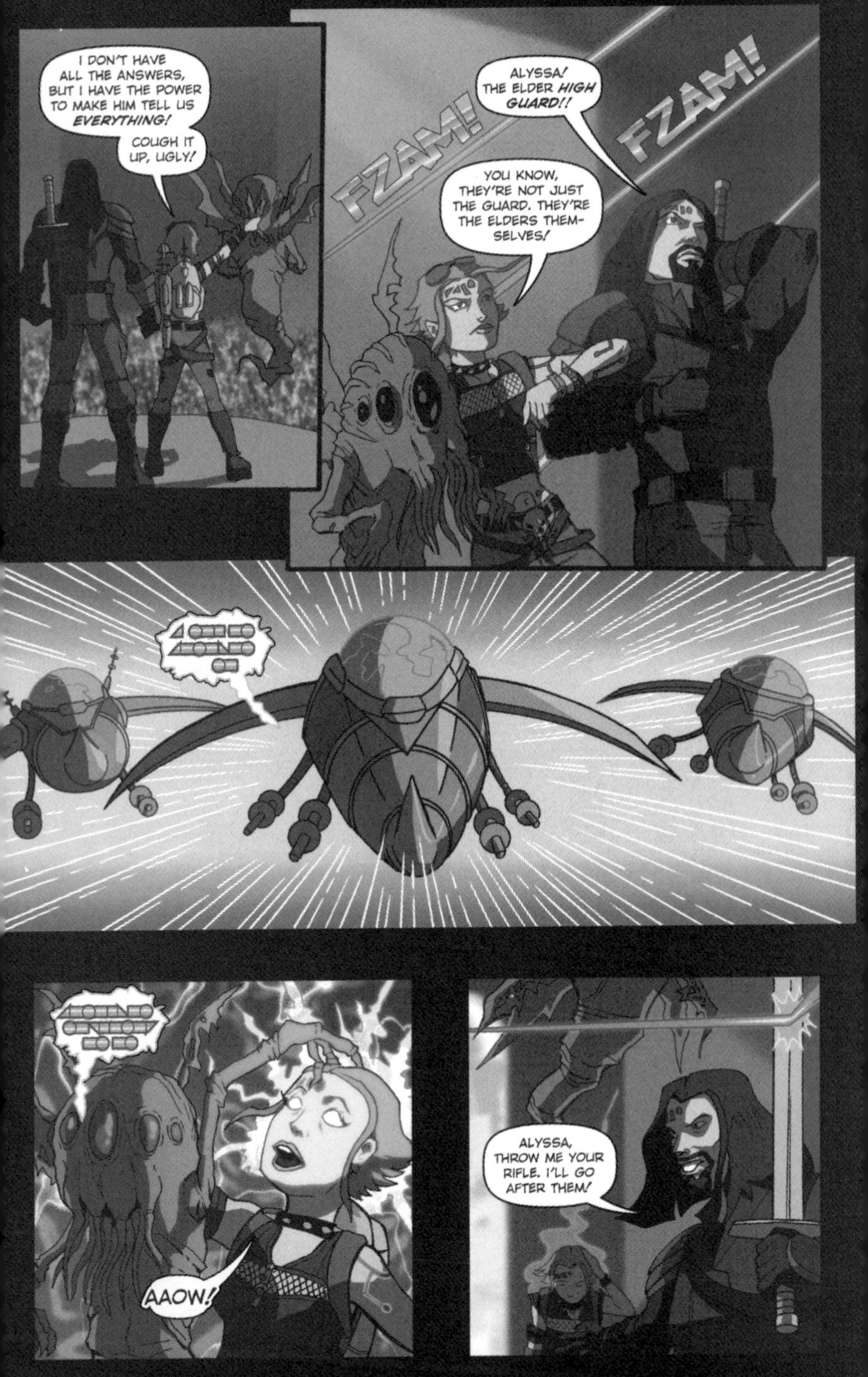

I DON'T HAVE ALL THE ANSWERS, BUT I HAVE THE POWER TO MAKE HIM TELL US *EVERYTHING!*
COUGH IT UP, UGLY!
FZAM!
ALYSSA! THE ELDER *HIGH GUARD!!*
FZAM!
YOU KNOW, THEY'RE NOT JUST THE GUARD. THEY'RE THE ELDERS THEM-SELVES!
AAOW!
ALYSSA, THROW ME YOUR RIFLE. I'LL GO AFTER THEM!

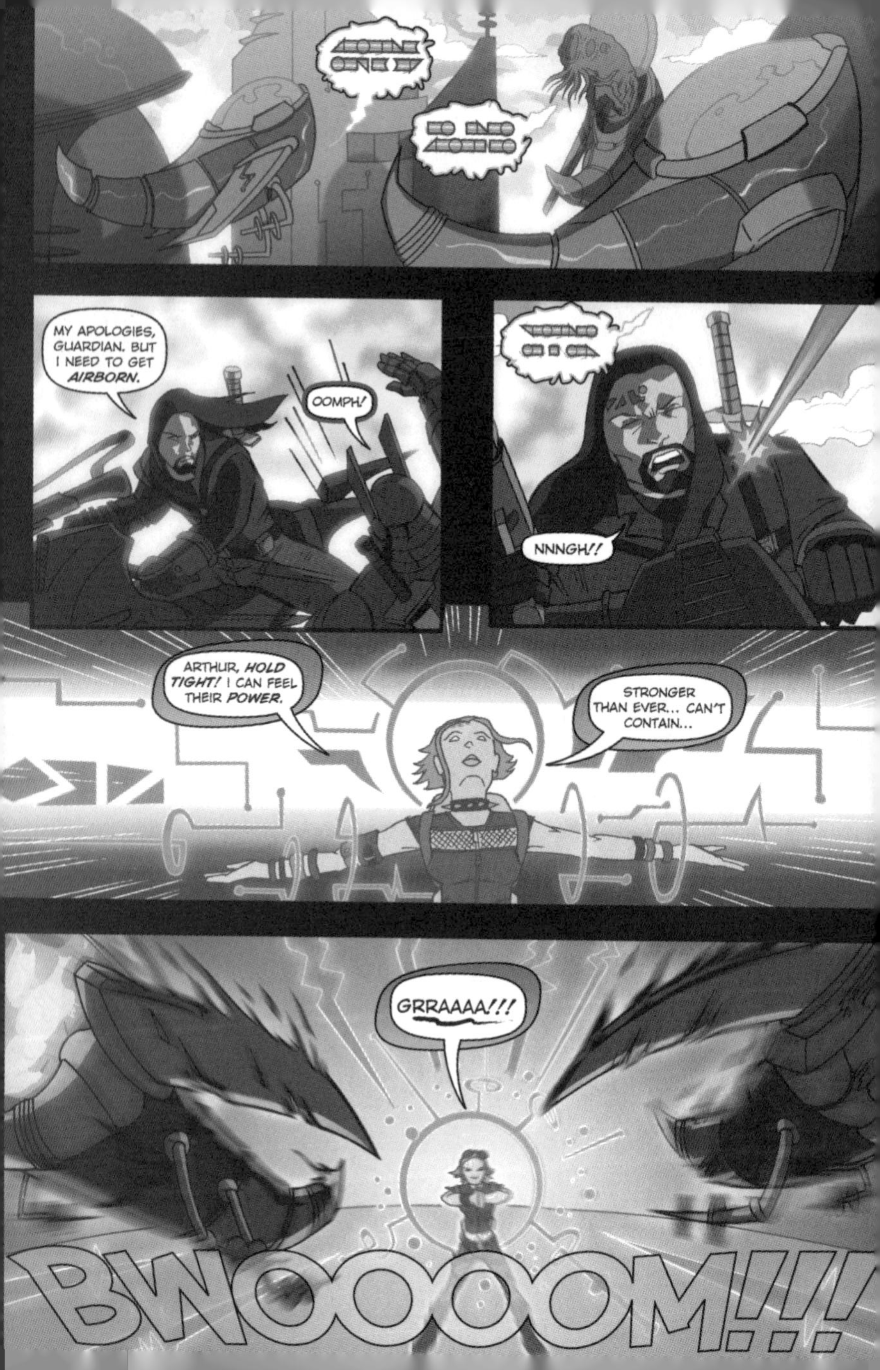
MY APOLOGIES, GUARDIAN. BUT I NEED TO GET *AIRBORN.*
OOMPH!
NNNGH!!
ARTHUR, ***HOLD TIGHT!*** I CAN FEEL THEIR ***POWER.***
STRONGER THAN EVER... CAN'T CONTAIN...
GRRAAAA!!!
BWOOOOM!!!

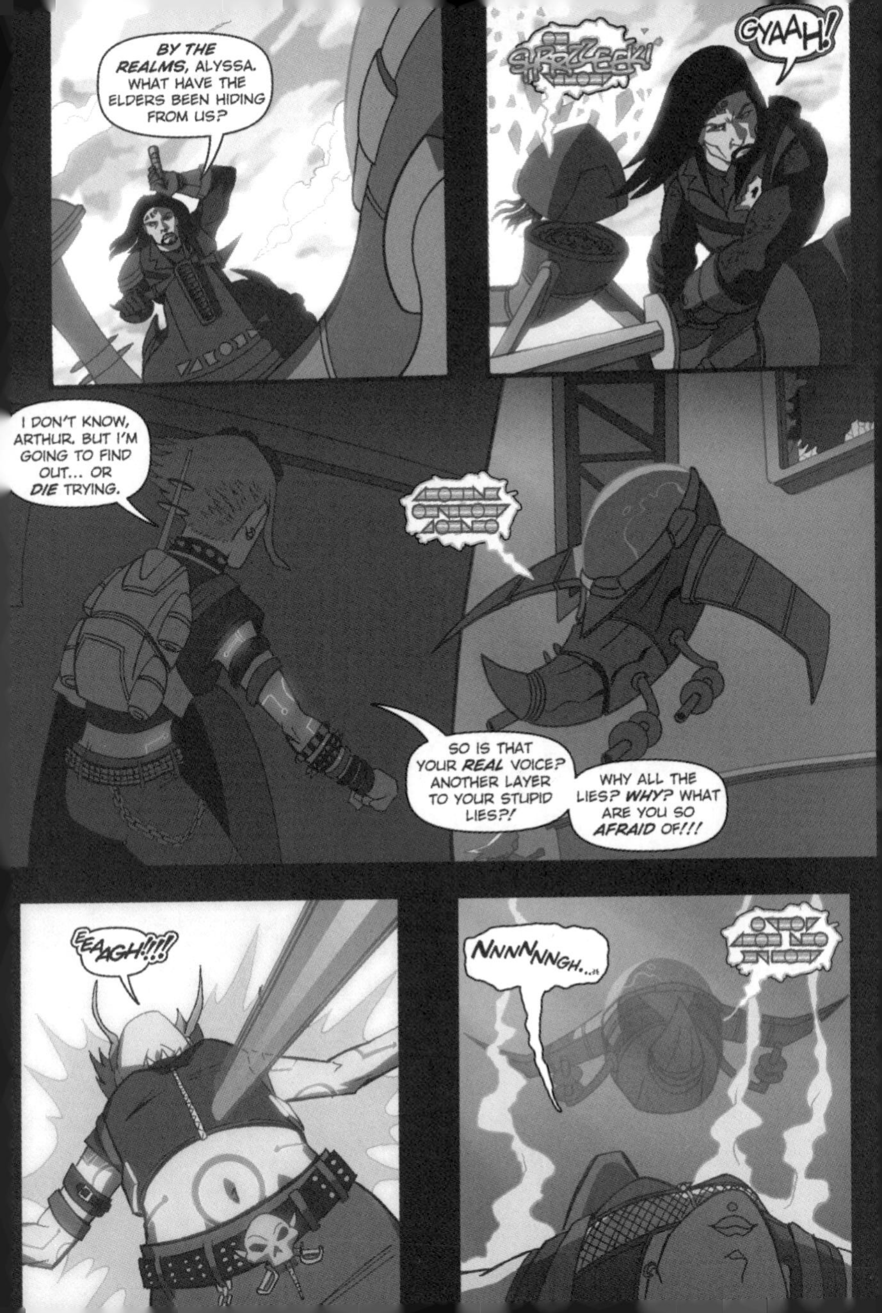
BY THE REALMS, ALYSSA. WHAT HAVE THE ELDERS BEEN HIDING FROM US?
GYAAH!
I DON'T KNOW, ARTHUR. BUT I'M GOING TO FIND OUT... OR DIE TRYING.
SO IS THAT YOUR REAL VOICE? ANOTHER LAYER TO YOUR STUPID LIES?!
WHY ALL THE LIES? WHY? WHAT ARE YOU SO AFRAID OF!!!
EEAAGH!!!!
NNNNNNGH...

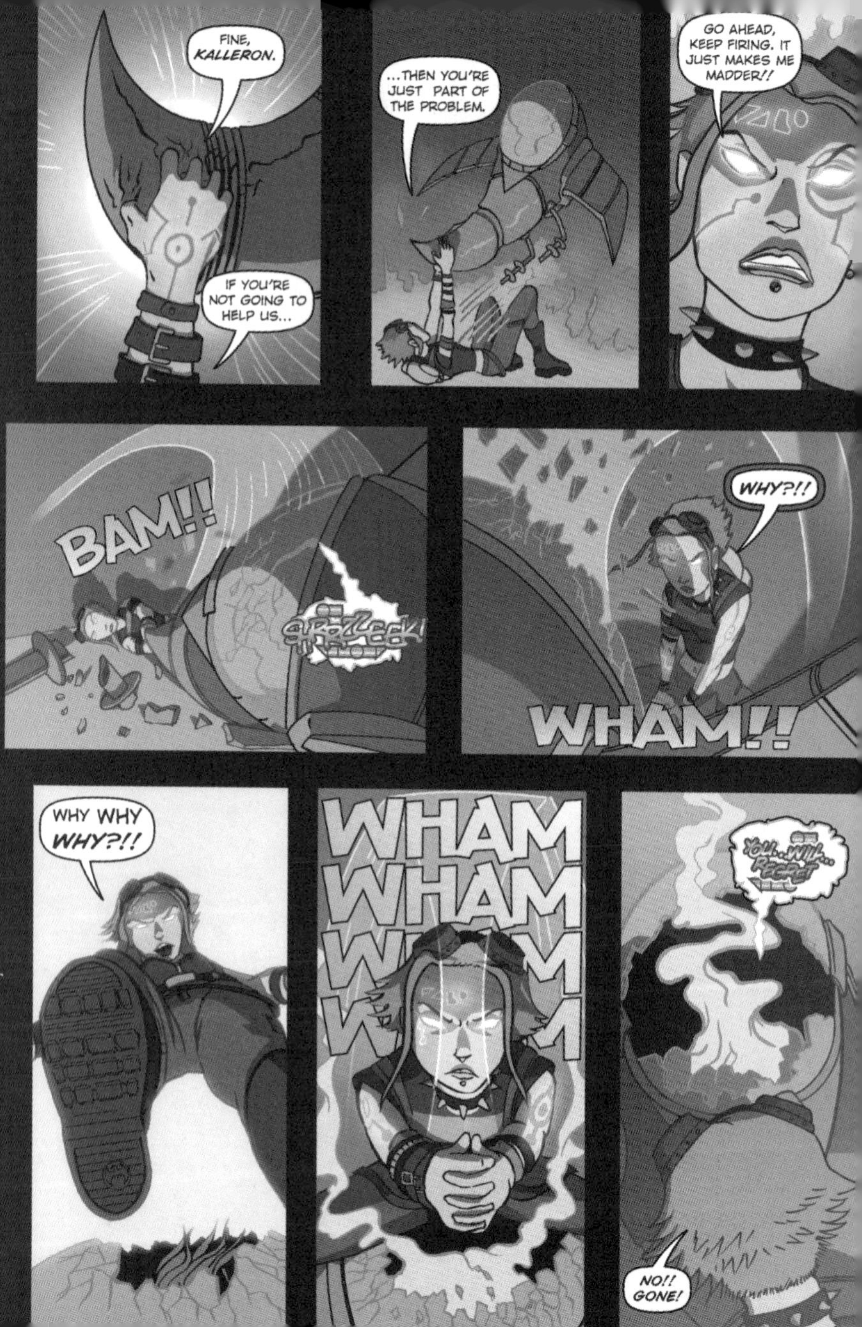
FINE, KALLERON.
IF YOU'RE NOT GOING TO HELP US...
...THEN YOU'RE JUST PART OF THE PROBLEM.
GO AHEAD, KEEP FIRING. IT JUST MAKES ME MADDER!!
BAM!!
WHY?!!
WHAM!!
WHY WHY WHY?!!
WHAM WHAM WHAM WHAM
YOU...WILL... REGRET
NO!! GONE!

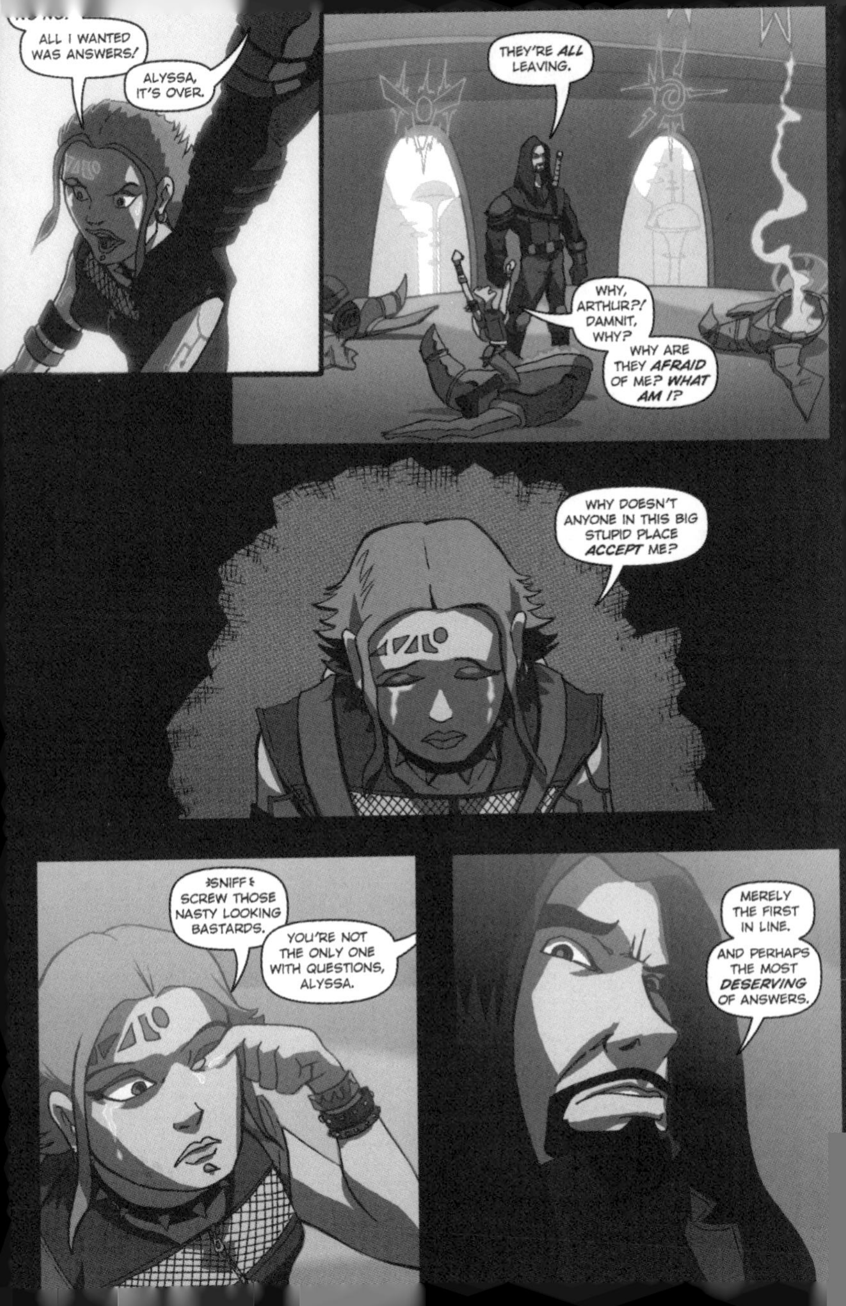
ALL I WANTED WAS ANSWERS!
ALYSSA, IT'S OVER.
THEY'RE *ALL* LEAVING.
WHY, ARTHUR?! DAMNIT, WHY?
WHY ARE THEY *AFRAID* OF ME? *WHAT AM I?*
WHY DOESN'T ANYONE IN THIS BIG STUPID PLACE *ACCEPT* ME?
ƷSNIFFƐ SCREW THOSE NASTY LOOKING BASTARDS.
YOU'RE NOT THE ONLY ONE WITH QUESTIONS, ALYSSA.
MERELY THE FIRST IN LINE.
AND PERHAPS THE MOST *DESERVING* OF ANSWERS.

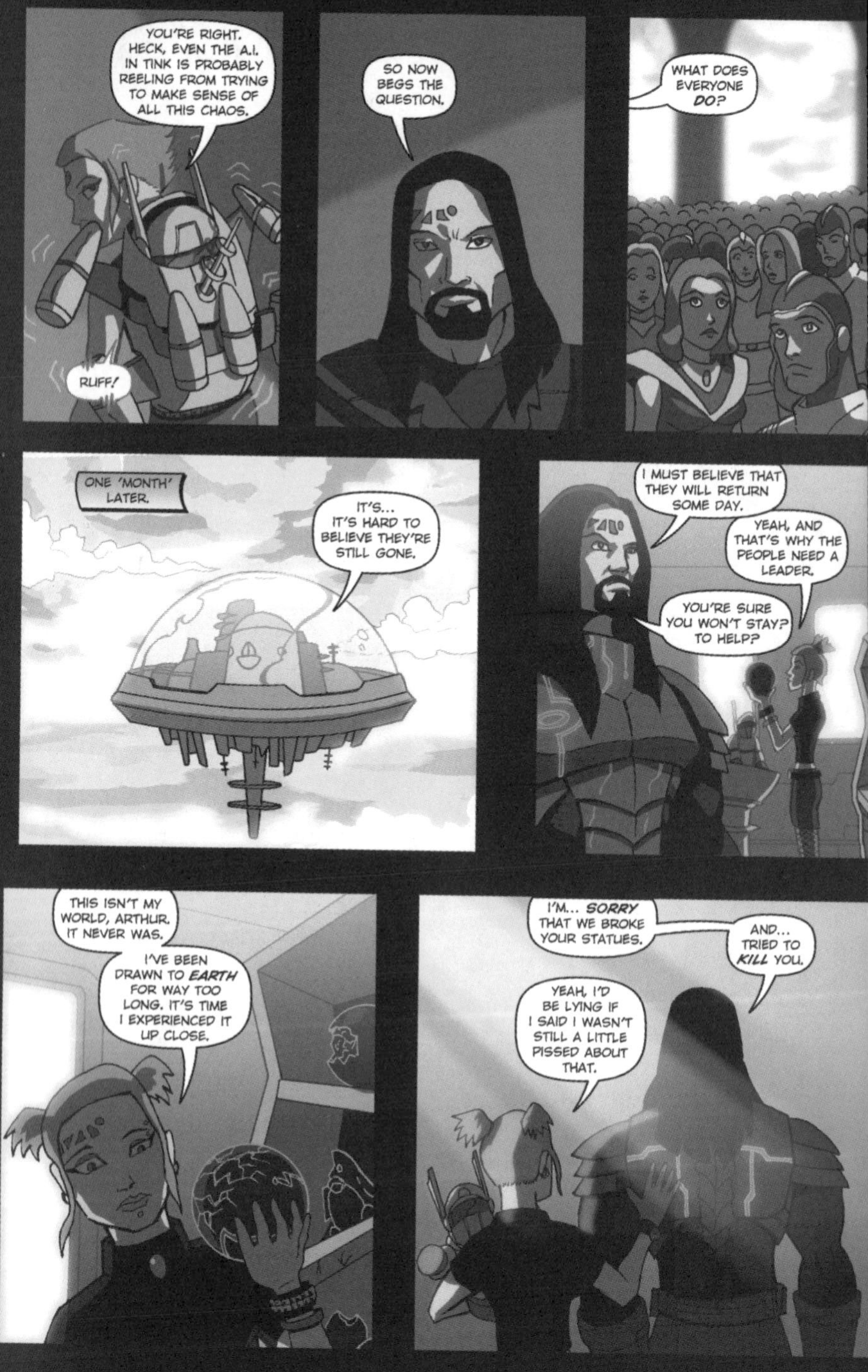
YOU'RE RIGHT. HECK, EVEN THE A.I. IN TINK IS PROBABLY REELING FROM TRYING TO MAKE SENSE OF ALL THIS CHAOS.
RUFF!
SO NOW BEGS THE QUESTION.
WHAT DOES EVERYONE DO?
ONE 'MONTH' LATER.
IT'S... IT'S HARD TO BELIEVE THEY'RE STILL GONE.
I MUST BELIEVE THAT THEY WILL RETURN SOME DAY.
YEAH, AND THAT'S WHY THE PEOPLE NEED A LEADER.
YOU'RE SURE YOU WON'T STAY? TO HELP?
THIS ISN'T MY WORLD, ARTHUR. IT NEVER WAS.
I'VE BEEN DRAWN TO EARTH FOR WAY TOO LONG. IT'S TIME I EXPERIENCED IT UP CLOSE.
I'M... SORRY THAT WE BROKE YOUR STATUES.
AND... TRIED TO KILL YOU.
YEAH, I'D BE LYING IF I SAID I WASN'T STILL A LITTLE PISSED ABOUT THAT.

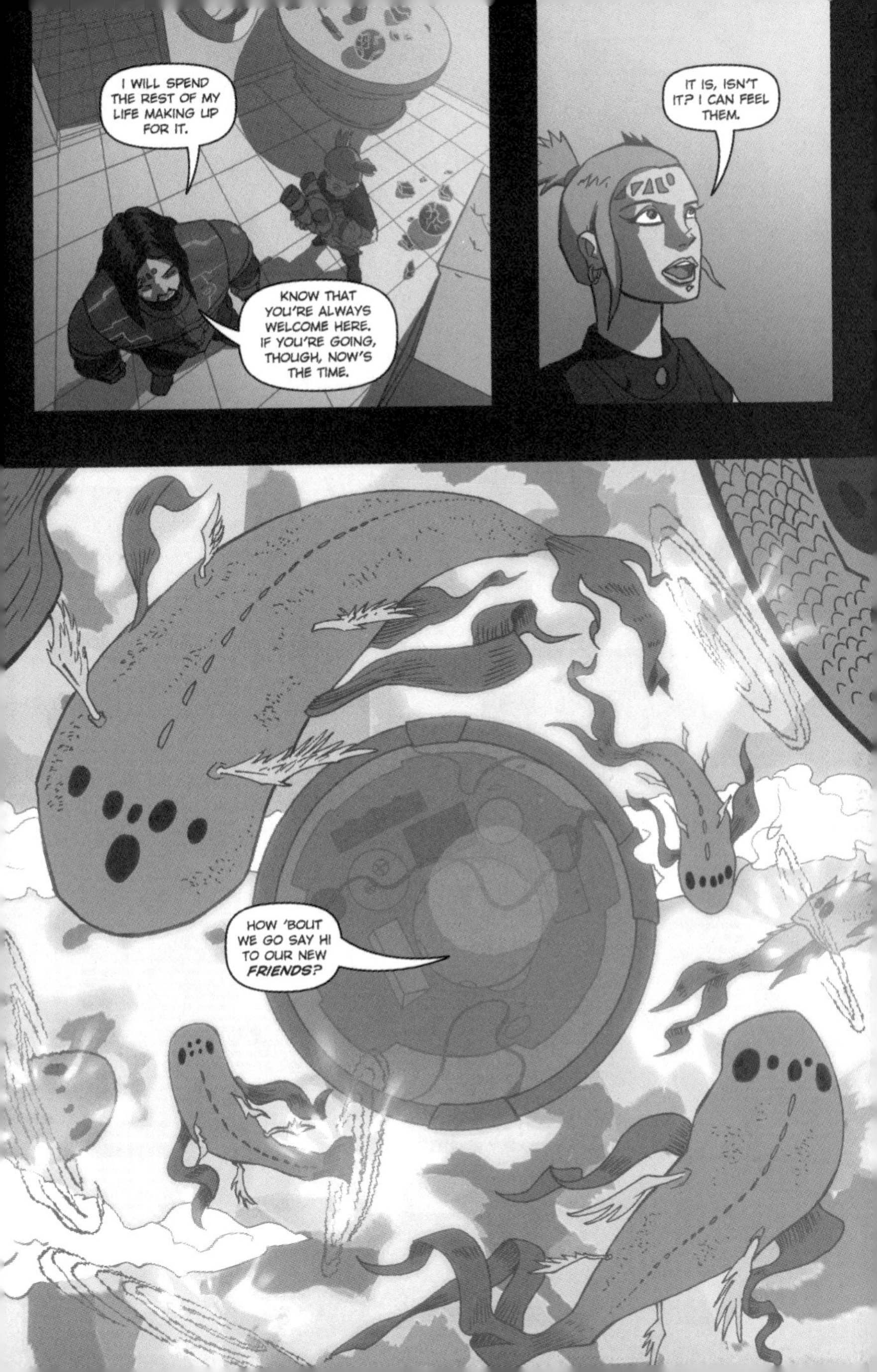
I WILL SPEND THE REST OF MY LIFE MAKING UP FOR IT.
KNOW THAT YOU'RE ALWAYS WELCOME HERE. IF YOU'RE GOING, THOUGH, NOW'S THE TIME.
IT IS, ISN'T IT? I CAN FEEL THEM.
HOW 'BOUT WE GO SAY HI TO OUR NEW *FRIENDS?*

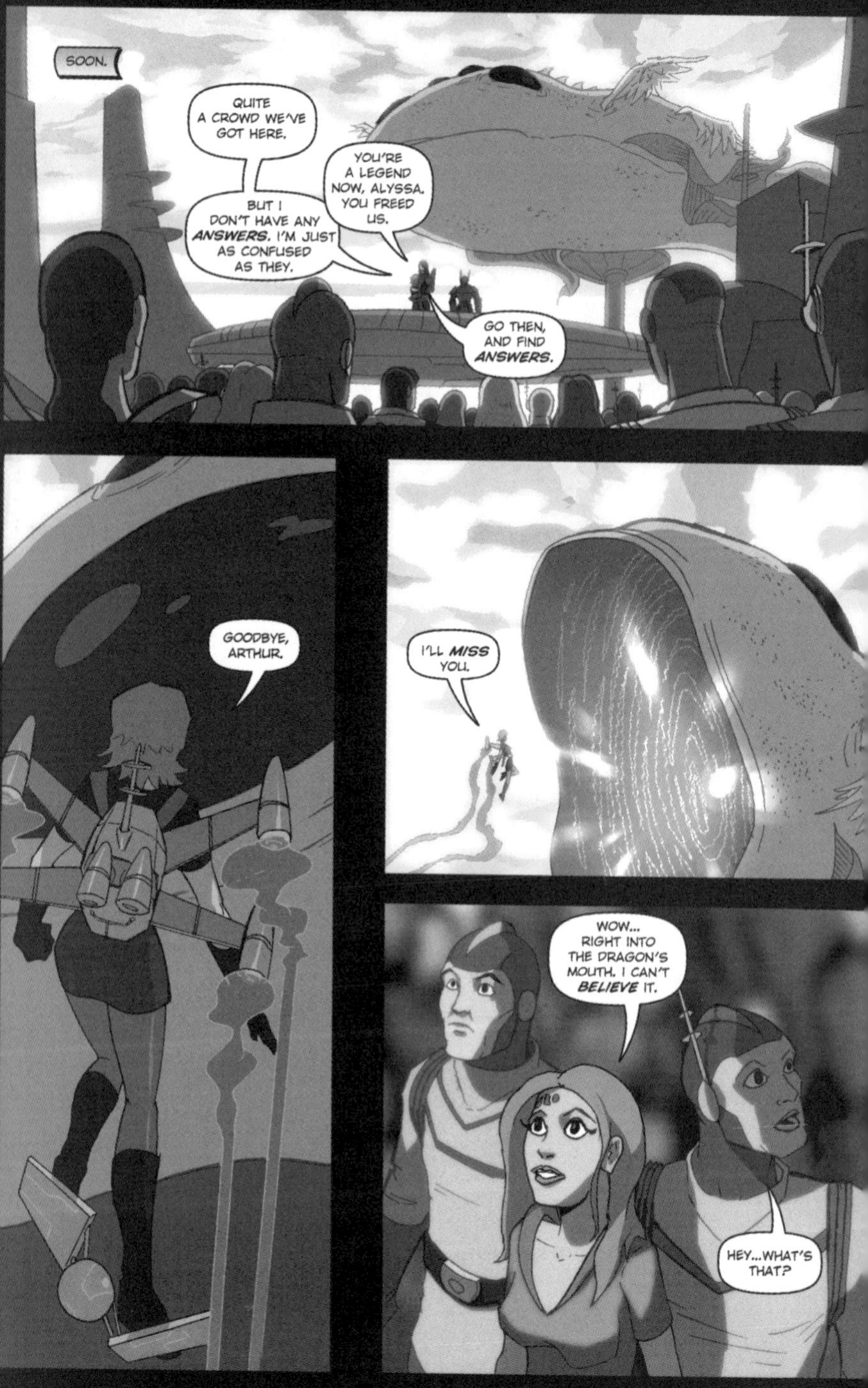
SOON.
QUITE A CROWD WE'VE GOT HERE.
BUT I DON'T HAVE ANY ANSWERS. I'M JUST AS CONFUSED AS THEY.
YOU'RE A LEGEND NOW, ALYSSA. YOU FREED US.
GO THEN, AND FIND ANSWERS.
GOODBYE, ARTHUR.
I'LL MISS YOU.
WOW... RIGHT INTO THE DRAGON'S MOUTH. I CAN'T BELIEVE IT.
HEY...WHAT'S THAT?

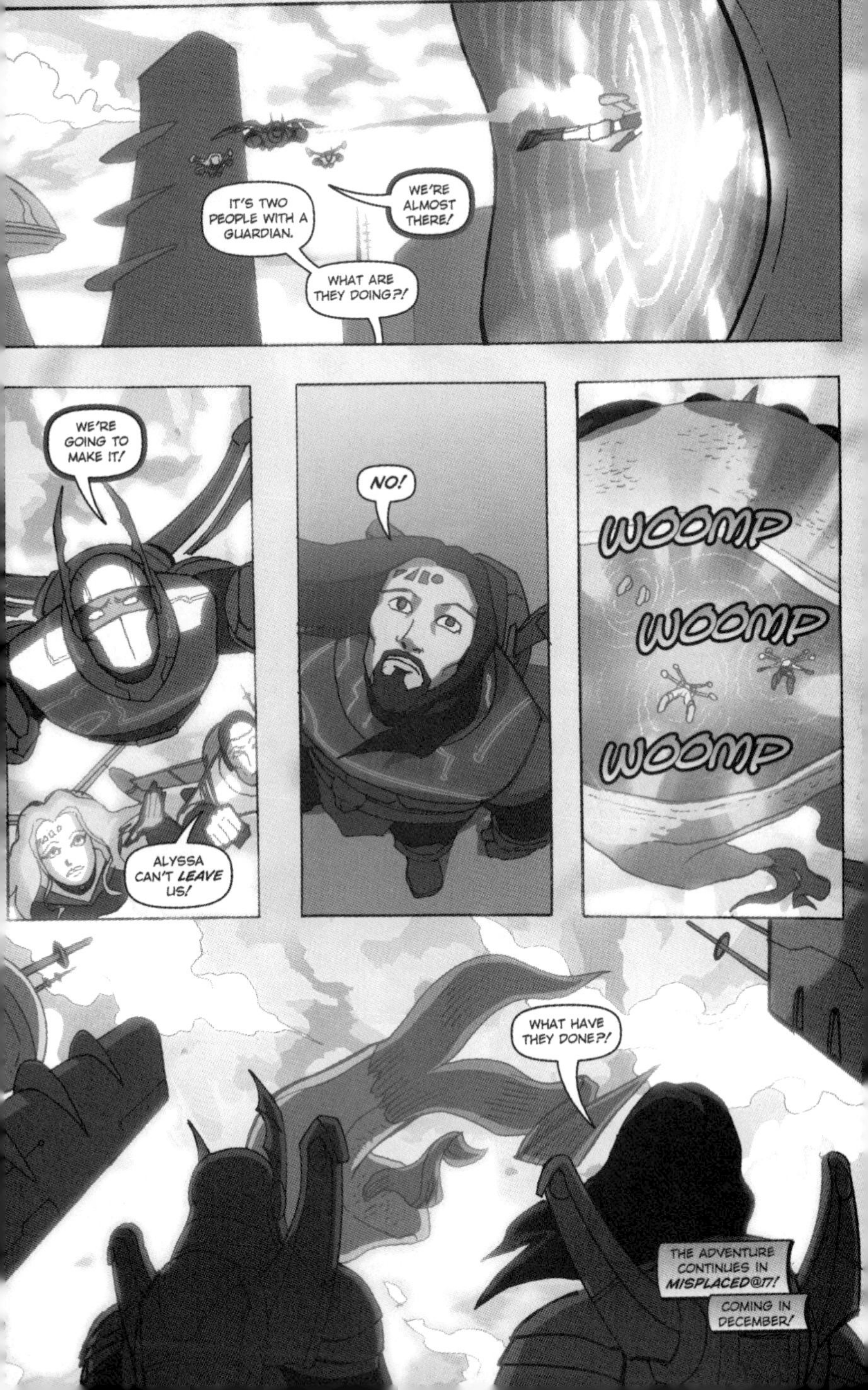
IT'S TWO PEOPLE WITH A GUARDIAN.
WE'RE ALMOST THERE!
WHAT ARE THEY DOING?!
WE'RE GOING TO MAKE IT!
ALYSSA CAN'T LEAVE US!
NO!
WOOMP
WOOMP
WOOMP
WHAT HAVE THEY DONE?!
THE ADVENTURE CONTINUES IN MISPLACED@17!
COMING IN DECEMBER!

Separation of Church and Sanity

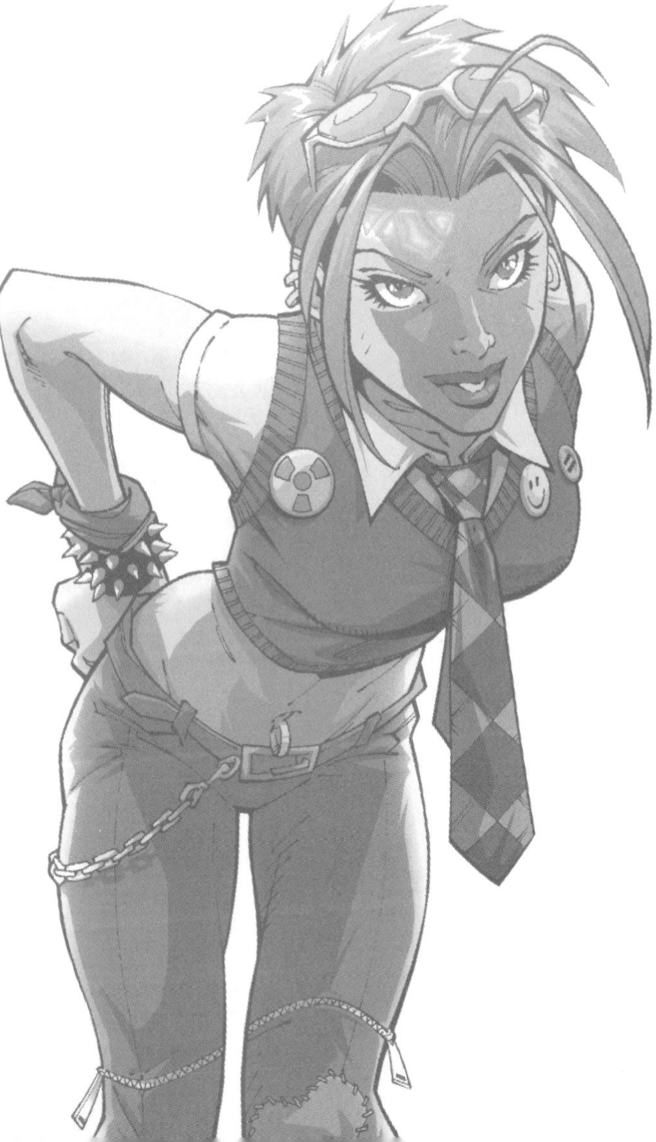

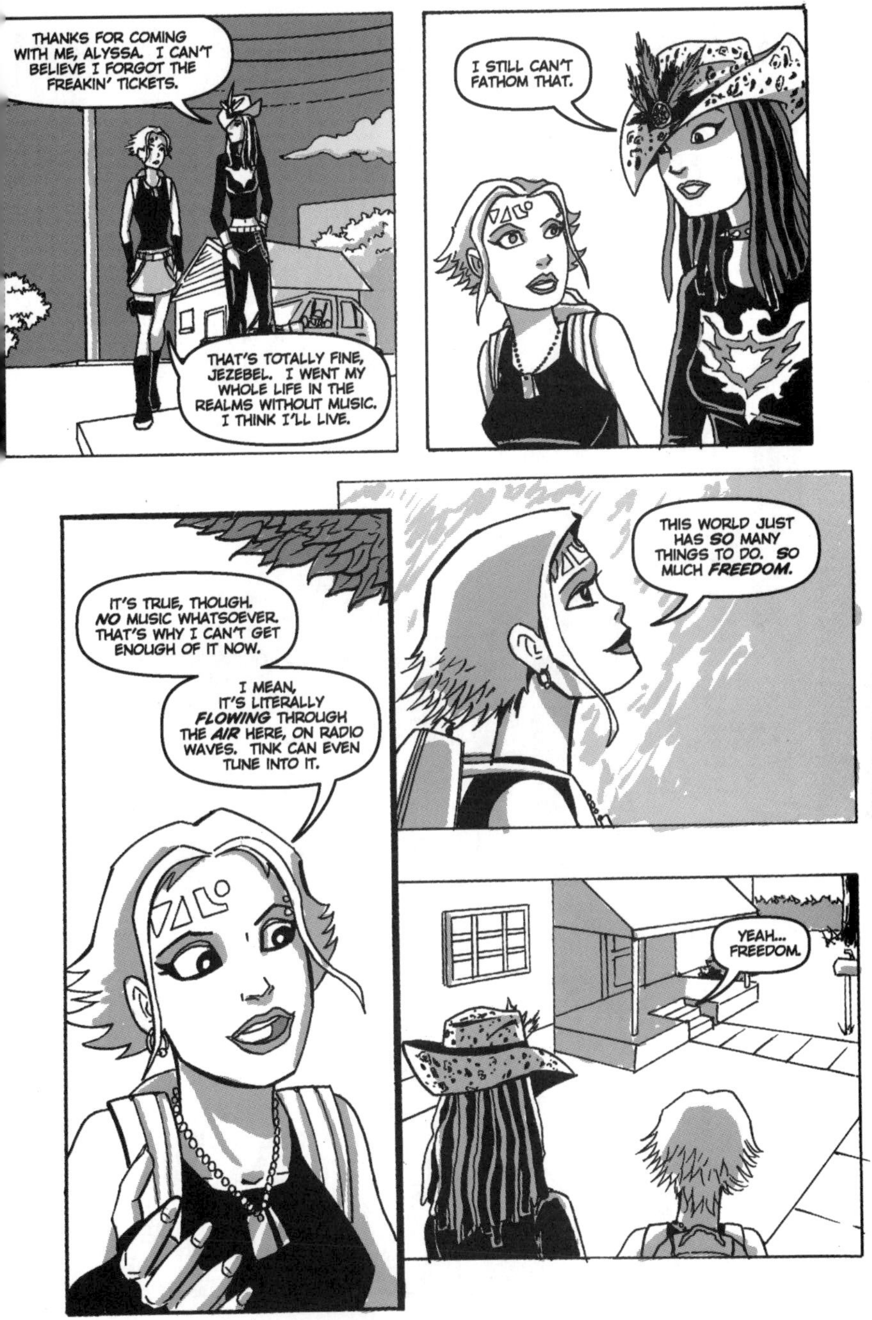
THANKS FOR COMING WITH ME, ALYSSA. I CAN'T BELIEVE I FORGOT THE FREAKIN' TICKETS.
THAT'S TOTALLY FINE, JEZEBEL. I WENT MY WHOLE LIFE IN THE REALMS WITHOUT MUSIC. I THINK I'LL LIVE.
I STILL CAN'T FATHOM THAT.
IT'S TRUE, THOUGH. *NO* MUSIC WHATSOEVER. THAT'S WHY I CAN'T GET ENOUGH OF IT NOW.
I MEAN, IT'S LITERALLY *FLOWING* THROUGH THE *AIR* HERE, ON RADIO WAVES. TINK CAN EVEN TUNE INTO IT.
THIS WORLD JUST HAS *SO* MANY THINGS TO DO. *SO* MUCH *FREEDOM.*
YEAH... FREEDOM.

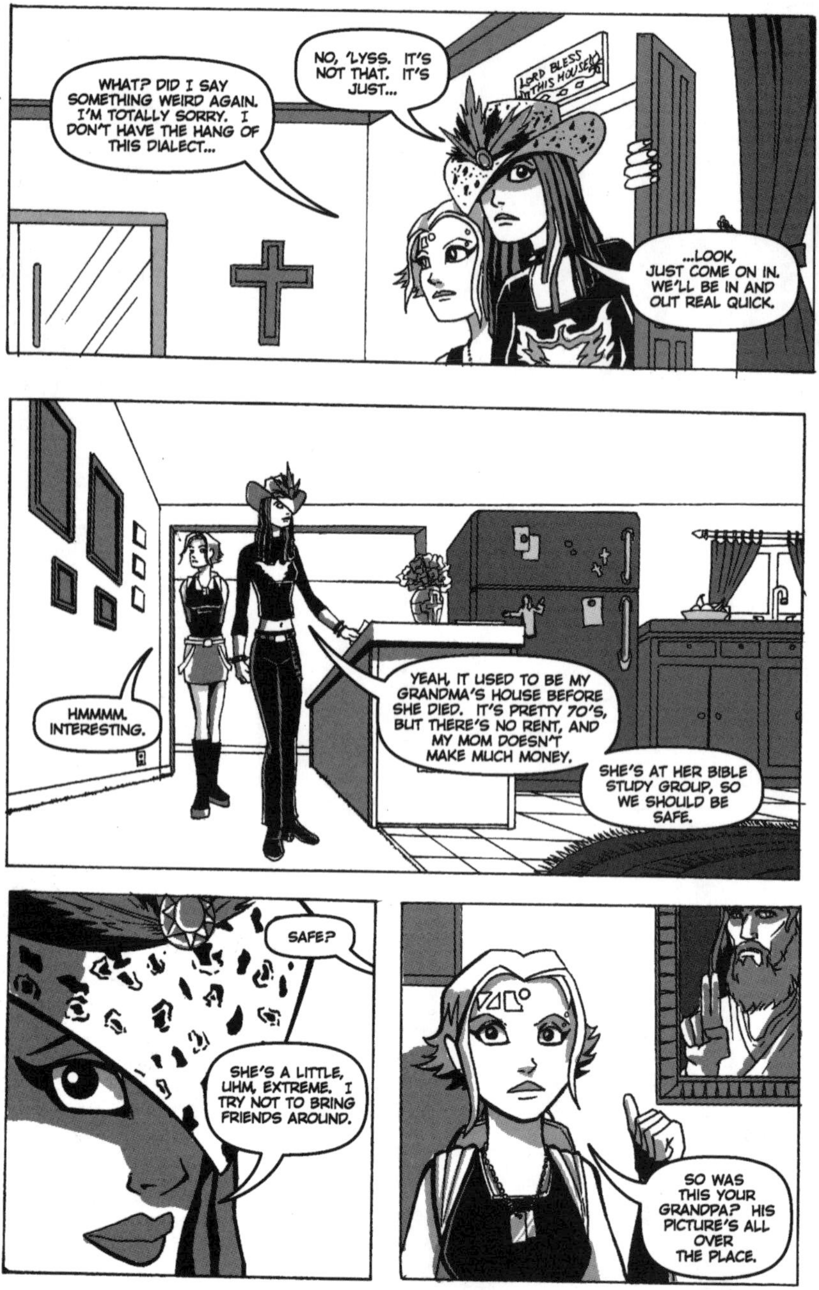
WHAT? DID I SAY SOMETHING WEIRD AGAIN. I'M TOTALLY SORRY. I DON'T HAVE THE HANG OF THIS DIALECT...
NO, 'LYSS. IT'S NOT THAT. IT'S JUST...
LORD BLESS THIS HOUSE
...LOOK, JUST COME ON IN. WE'LL BE IN AND OUT REAL QUICK.
HMMMM. INTERESTING.
YEAH, IT USED TO BE MY GRANDMA'S HOUSE BEFORE SHE DIED. IT'S PRETTY 70'S, BUT THERE'S NO RENT, AND MY MOM DOESN'T MAKE MUCH MONEY.
SHE'S AT HER BIBLE STUDY GROUP, SO WE SHOULD BE SAFE.
SAFE?
SHE'S A LITTLE, UHM, EXTREME. I TRY NOT TO BRING FRIENDS AROUND.
SO WAS THIS YOUR GRANDPA? HIS PICTURE'S ALL OVER THE PLACE.

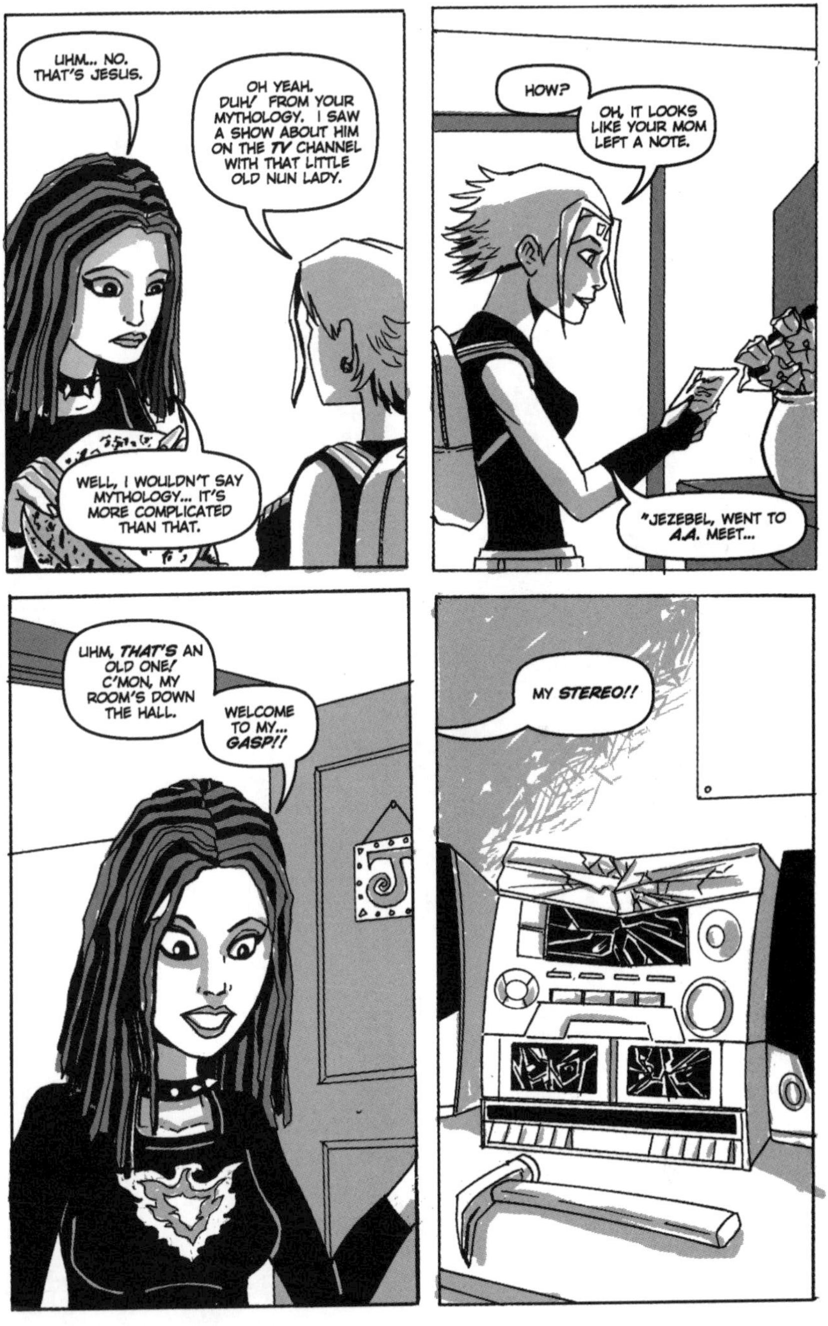
UHM... NO. THAT'S JESUS.
OH YEAH. DUH! FROM YOUR MYTHOLOGY. I SAW A SHOW ABOUT HIM ON THE TV CHANNEL WITH THAT LITTLE OLD NUN LADY.
WELL, I WOULDN'T SAY MYTHOLOGY... IT'S MORE COMPLICATED THAN THAT.
HOW?
OH, IT LOOKS LIKE YOUR MOM LEFT A NOTE.
"JEZEBEL, WENT TO A.A. MEET...
UHM, THAT'S AN OLD ONE! C'MON, MY ROOM'S DOWN THE HALL.
WELCOME TO MY... GASP!!
MY STEREO!!

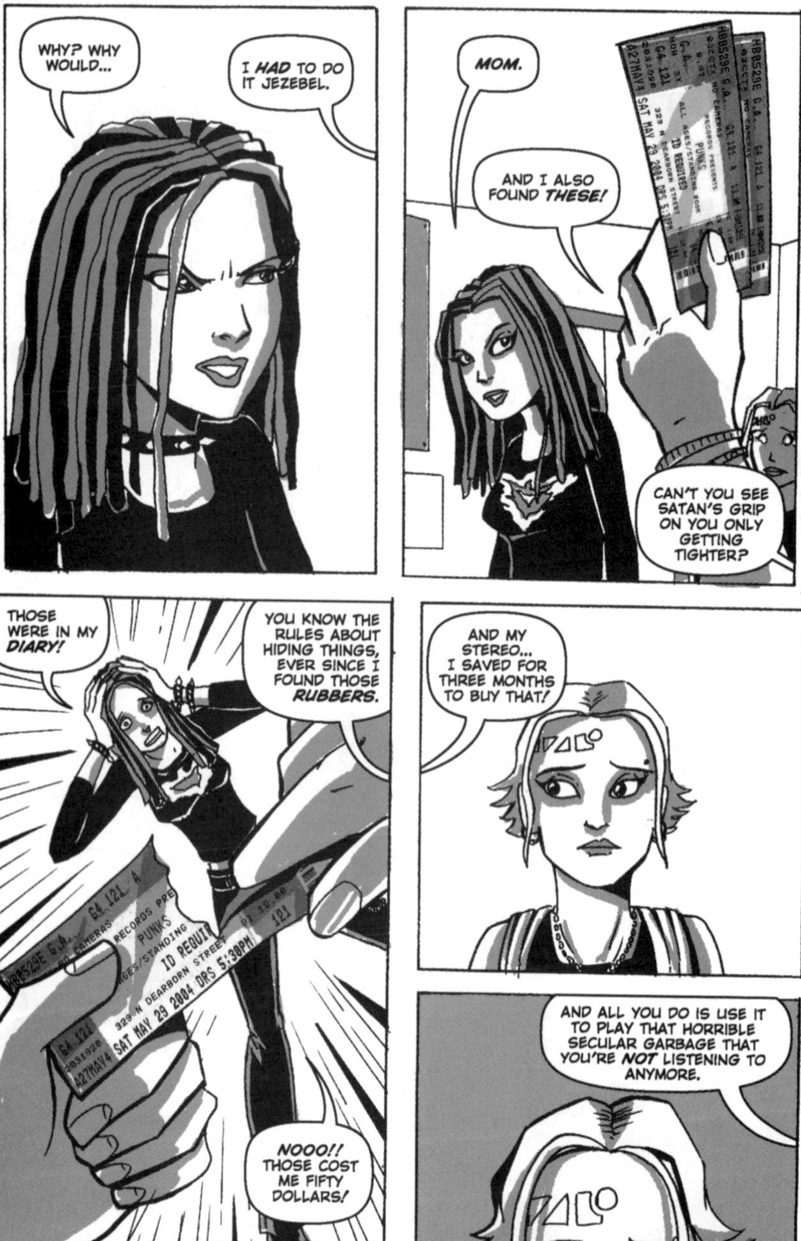
WHY? WHY WOULD...
I **HAD** TO DO IT JEZEBEL.
MOM.
AND I ALSO FOUND **THESE!**
CAN'T YOU SEE SATAN'S GRIP ON YOU ONLY GETTING TIGHTER?
THOSE WERE IN MY **DIARY!**
YOU KNOW THE RULES ABOUT HIDING THINGS, EVER SINCE I FOUND THOSE **RUBBERS.**
NOOO!! THOSE COST ME FIFTY DOLLARS!
AND MY STEREO... I SAVED FOR THREE MONTHS TO BUY THAT!
AND ALL YOU DO IS USE IT TO PLAY THAT HORRIBLE SECULAR GARBAGE THAT YOU'RE **NOT** LISTENING TO ANYMORE.

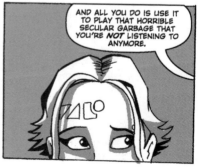

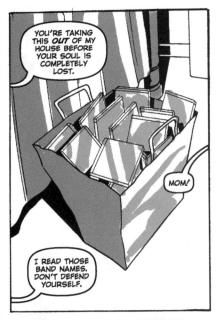

YOU'RE TAKING THIS *OUT* OF MY HOUSE BEFORE YOUR SOUL IS COMPLETELY LOST.

MOM!

I READ THOSE BAND NAMES. DON'T DEFEND YOURSELF.

LIKE THIS ONE, "SUICIDE MACHINES!?" DO YOU THINK THIS IS GLORIFYING THE LORD?

WHY DOES EVERYTHING HAVE TO FRICKING PRAISE GOD?! DID YOU EVEN READ THEIR LYRICS?

I'M SORRY MY MUSIC DOESN'T *BEAT* YOU OVER THE HEAD WITH ITS MESSAGE LIKE YOURS.

YOU KNOW THERE'S MORE TO IT THAN THAT, JEZEBEL.

YOU'RE INSANE, MOM. DO YOU EVEN CARE I HAVE A *FRIEND* HERE?!

GOOD. MAYBE SHE'LL GET OFF OF HER EVIL PATH TOO.

YOU DON'T EVEN *KNOW* HER.

YOU'RE ON THE PATH TO DAMNATION JEZEBEL!

WELL THEN I BETTER GET OUT OF HERE BEFORE I *CHOKE* AND *DIE* ON THE *LOVE* YOU'RE SHOVING DOWN MY THROAT!!

COME ON, ALYSSA.

JEZ, WAIT!

PASTOR? IT'S ME AGAIN.

IT'S... IT'S JEZEBEL. ≡SNIFF≡

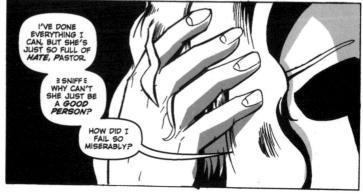

I'VE DONE EVERYTHING I CAN, BUT SHE'S JUST SO FULL OF *HATE*, PASTOR.

≡SNIFF≡ WHY CAN'T SHE JUST BE A *GOOD PERSON?*

HOW DID I FAIL SO MISERABLY?

JEZ!

I JUST WANT TO GO, ALYSSA. I DON'T WANT TO TALK ABOUT IT.

JEZEBEL!

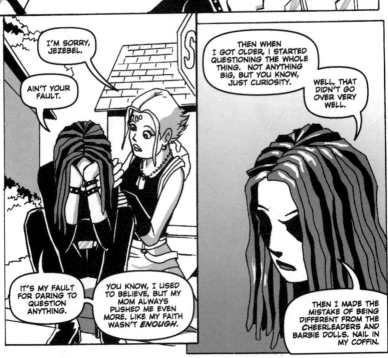

I'M SORRY, JEZEBEL.

AIN'T YOUR FAULT.

IT'S MY FAULT FOR DARING TO QUESTION ANYTHING.

YOU KNOW, I USED TO BELIEVE, BUT MY MOM ALWAYS PUSHED ME EVEN MORE. LIKE MY FAITH WASN'T *ENOUGH*.

THEN WHEN I GOT OLDER, I STARTED QUESTIONING THE WHOLE THING. NOT ANYTHING BIG, BUT YOU KNOW, JUST CURIOSITY.

WELL, THAT DIDN'T GO OVER VERY WELL.

THEN I MADE THE MISTAKE OF BEING DIFFERENT FROM THE CHEERLEADERS AND BARBIE DOLLS. NAIL IN MY COFFIN.

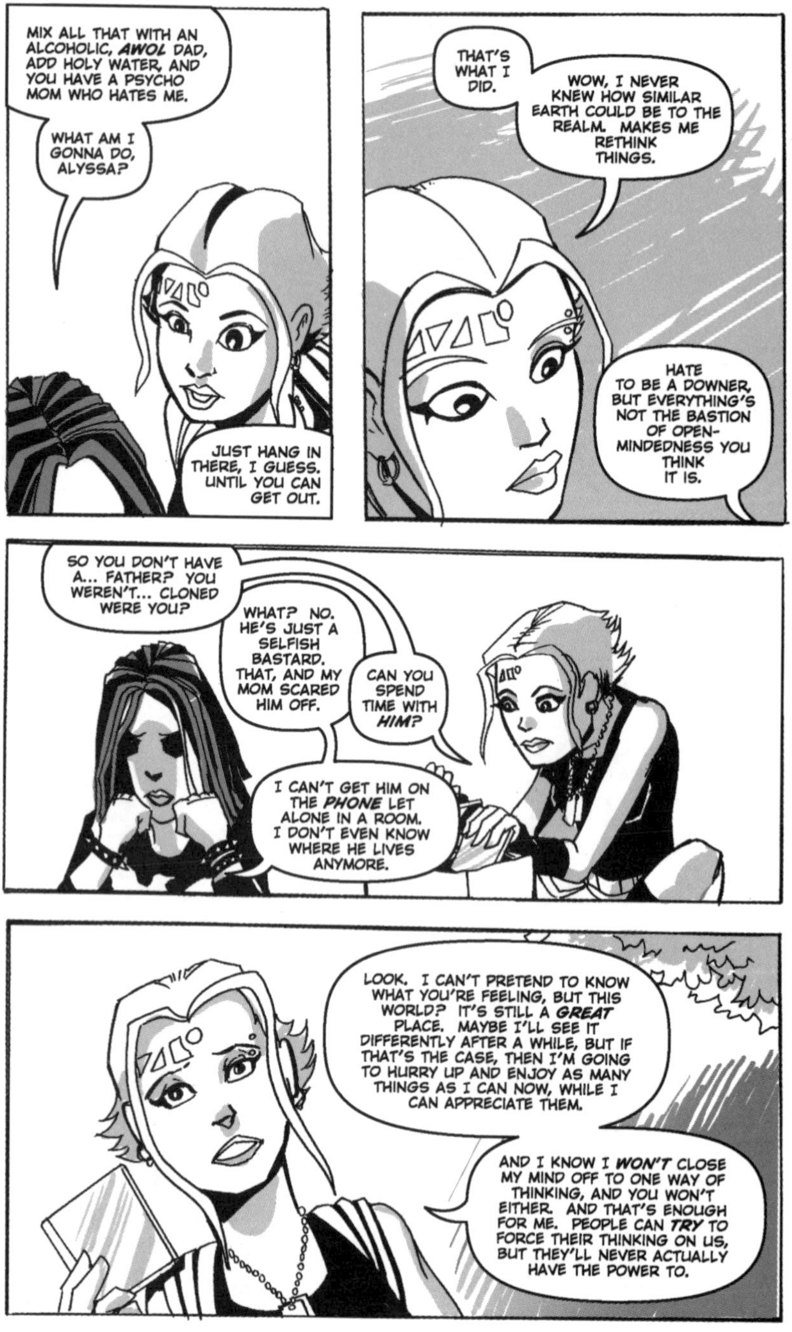
MIX ALL THAT WITH AN ALCOHOLIC, AWOL DAD, ADD HOLY WATER, AND YOU HAVE A PSYCHO MOM WHO HATES ME.
WHAT AM I GONNA DO, ALYSSA?
JUST HANG IN THERE, I GUESS. UNTIL YOU CAN GET OUT.
THAT'S WHAT I DID.
WOW, I NEVER KNEW HOW SIMILAR EARTH COULD BE TO THE REALM. MAKES ME RETHINK THINGS.
HATE TO BE A DOWNER, BUT EVERYTHING'S NOT THE BASTION OF OPEN-MINDEDNESS YOU THINK IT IS.
SO YOU DON'T HAVE A... FATHER? YOU WEREN'T... CLONED WERE YOU?
WHAT? NO. HE'S JUST A SELFISH BASTARD. THAT, AND MY MOM SCARED HIM OFF.
CAN YOU SPEND TIME WITH HIM?
I CAN'T GET HIM ON THE PHONE LET ALONE IN A ROOM. I DON'T EVEN KNOW WHERE HE LIVES ANYMORE.
LOOK. I CAN'T PRETEND TO KNOW WHAT YOU'RE FEELING, BUT THIS WORLD? IT'S STILL A GREAT PLACE. MAYBE I'LL SEE IT DIFFERENTLY AFTER A WHILE, BUT IF THAT'S THE CASE, THEN I'M GOING TO HURRY UP AND ENJOY AS MANY THINGS AS I CAN NOW, WHILE I CAN APPRECIATE THEM.
AND I KNOW I WON'T CLOSE MY MIND OFF TO ONE WAY OF THINKING, AND YOU WON'T EITHER. AND THAT'S ENOUGH FOR ME. PEOPLE CAN TRY TO FORCE THEIR THINKING ON US, BUT THEY'LL NEVER ACTUALLY HAVE THE POWER TO.

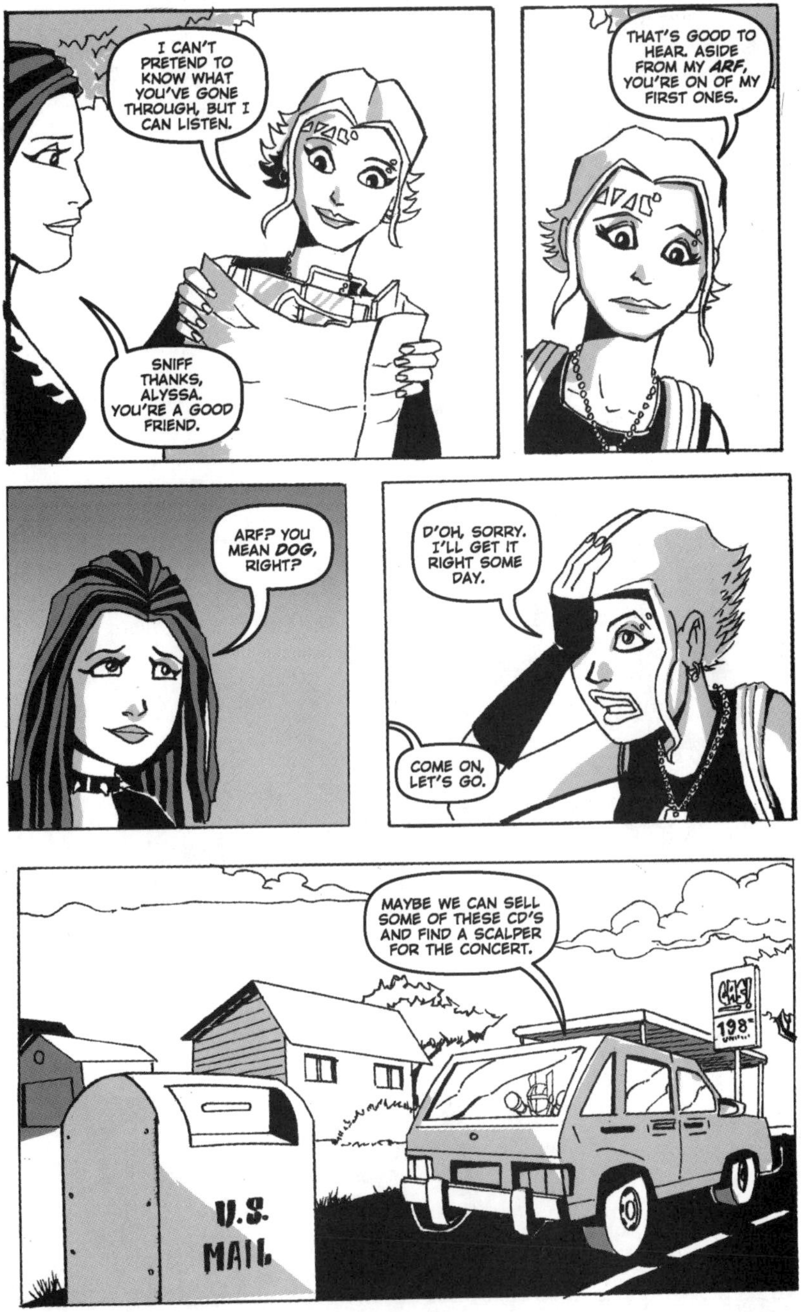
I CAN'T PRETEND TO KNOW WHAT YOU'VE GONE THROUGH, BUT I CAN LISTEN.
SNIFF THANKS, ALYSSA. YOU'RE A GOOD FRIEND.
THAT'S GOOD TO HEAR. ASIDE FROM MY ***ARF***, YOU'RE ON OF MY FIRST ONES.
ARF? YOU MEAN ***DOG***, RIGHT?
D'OH, SORRY. I'LL GET IT RIGHT SOME DAY.
COME ON, LET'S GO.
MAYBE WE CAN SELL SOME OF THESE CD'S AND FIND A SCALPER FOR THE CONCERT.
GAS!
198
U.S. MAIL

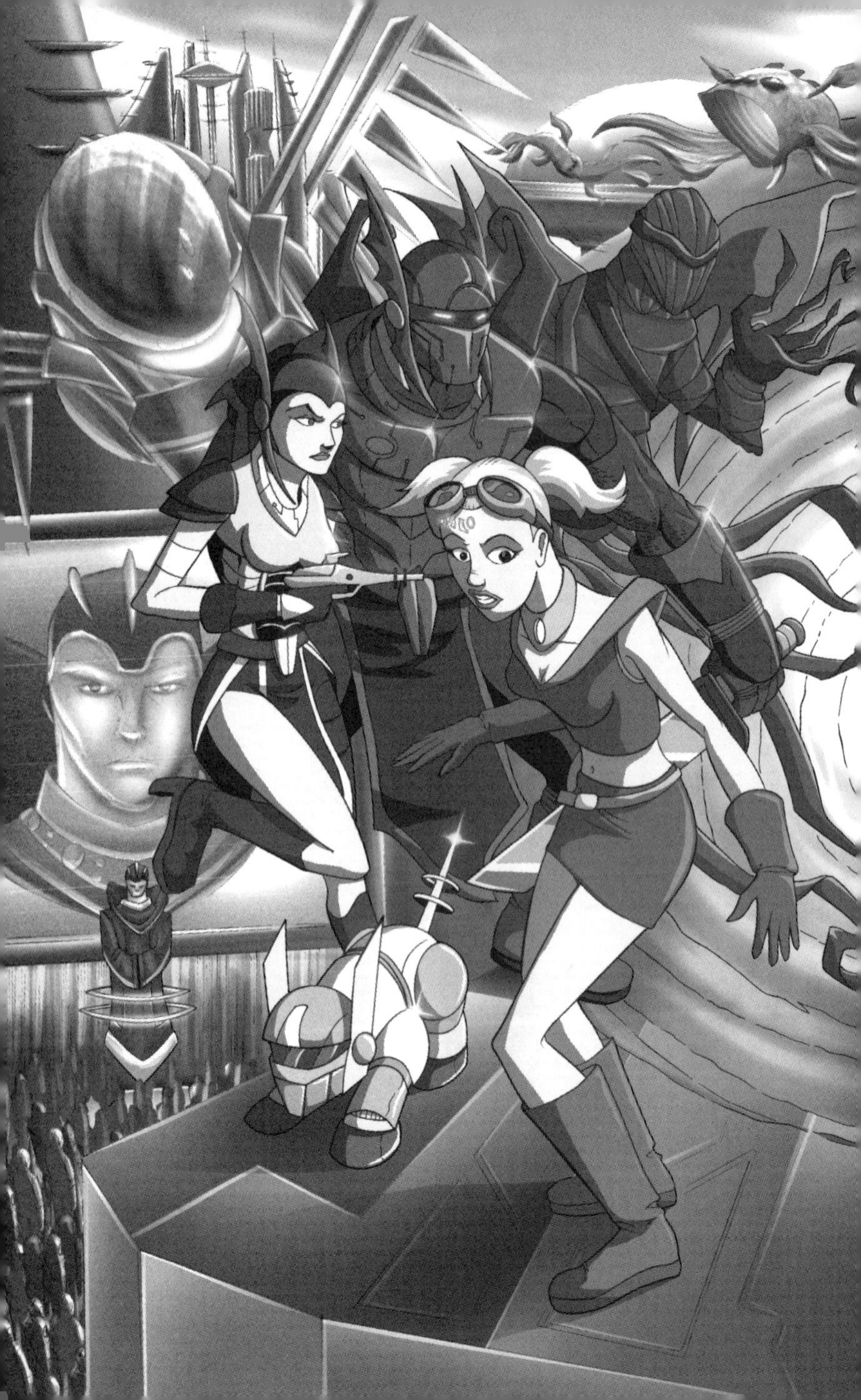

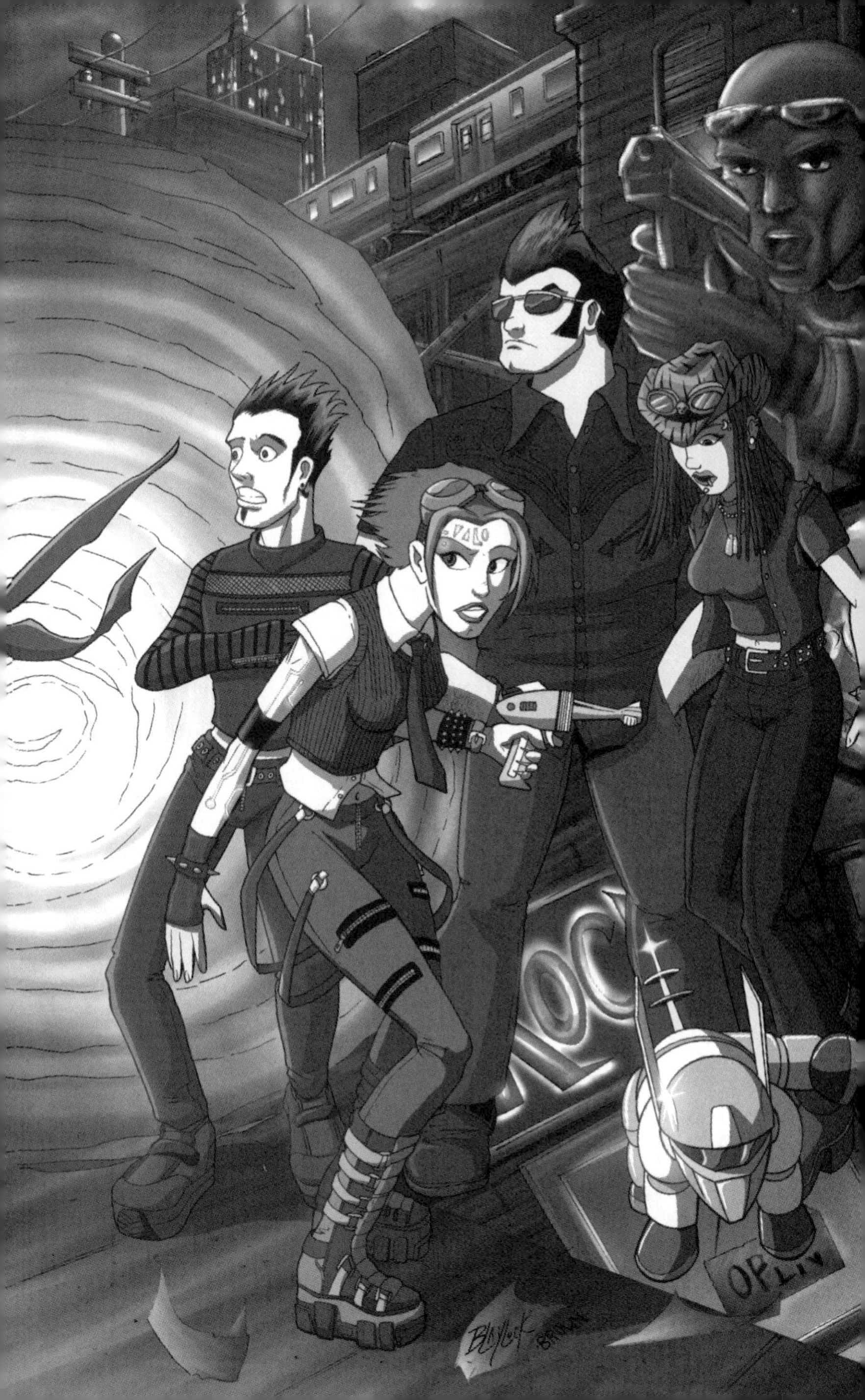

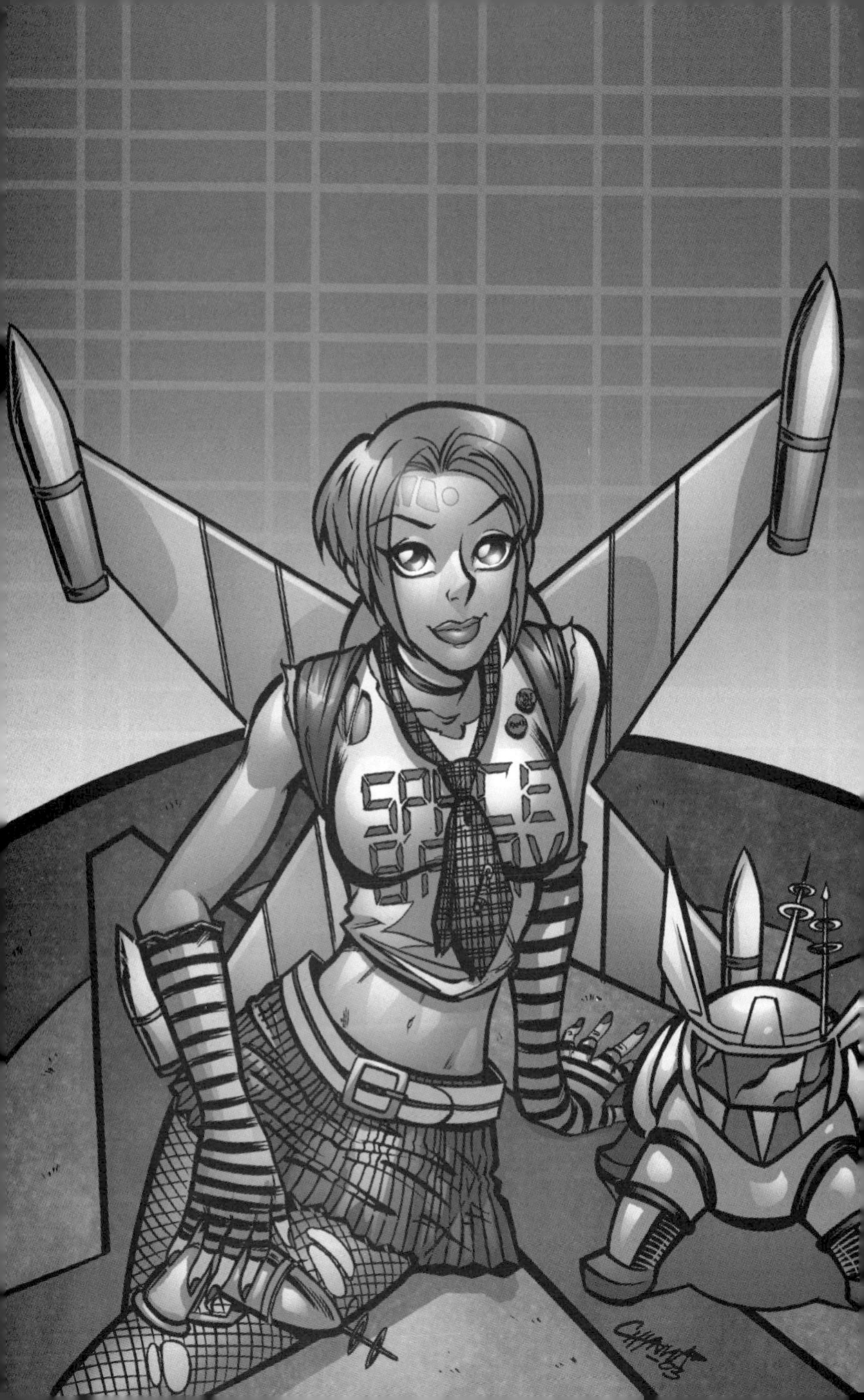

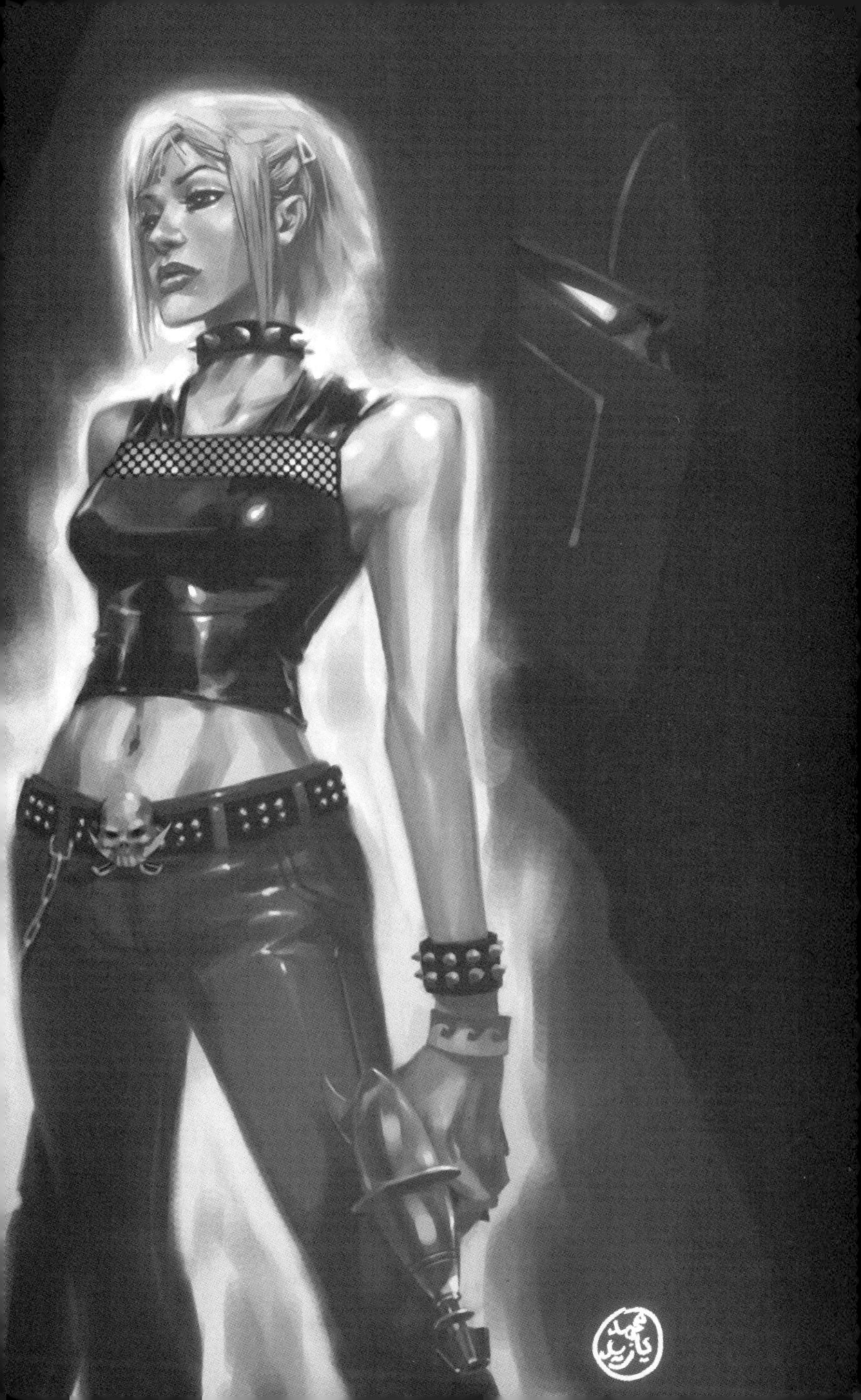

ABOUT THE AUTHOR

Josh Blaylock is the president and founder of Devil's Due Publishing, Inc. and the D3 imprint, but long before that he self-published black and white comic books. Heavily influenced by his music and subculture interests, Misplaced was one of those books. Years later he brought back the title, revamped, and stripped to its essence, without so many obscure references - only one core message: Thinking for Yourself.

Beyond that, Pop Culture is Josh Blaylock's life, whether that's comics, music, movies or toys, and he's thrilled to be able to make a living creating it. After years of running Devil's Due on a corporate side, he hopes to find more time to devote to personal projects, such as this one. Catch him if you can at any number of conventions across the country.

Josh lives in Chicago, Illinois, the best city in the universe.

www.joshblaylock.com